5

BEING HEALTHY

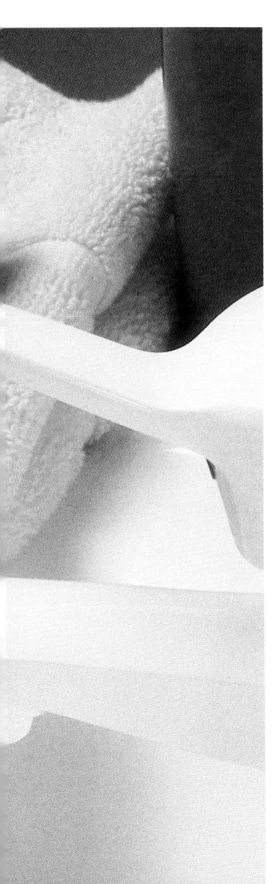

BEING HEALTHY

Larry K. Olsen
Professor and Coordinator of
  Graduate Studies in Health Education
The Pennsylvania State University
University Park, Pennsylvania

Richard W. St. Pierre
Professor and Chair
Department of Health Education
The Pennsylvania State University
University Park, Pennsylvania

Jan M. Ozias
Supervisor of School Nurses
Austin Independent School District
Austin, Texas

SENIOR EDITORIAL ADVISORS

Ernest D. Buck, M.D.
Pediatrician
Corpus Christi, Texas

Barbara A. Galpin
Teacher of Health and Physical Education,
  and Coordinator of Drug Abuse Prevention
Islip Public Schools
Islip, New York

Howard L. Taras, M.D., F.R.C.P.C.
Assistant Professor of Pediatrics
University of California, San Diego
  and District Medical Consultant
San Diego Unified School District
San Diego, California

Harcourt Brace Jovanovich, Publishers
Orlando   San Diego   Chicago   Dallas

ACKNOWLEDGMENTS

CONTENT ADVISORY BOARD

MENTAL HEALTH

Sharon Smith Brady, Ph.D.
School Psychologist
Lawton Public Schools
Lawton, Oklahoma

Charlotte P. Ross
President and Executive Director
Youth Suicide National Center
Burlingame, California

HUMAN GROWTH AND DEVELOPMENT, DISEASES AND DISORDERS, AND PUBLIC HEALTH

Thomas Blevins, M.D.
American Diabetes Association,
 Texas Affiliate, Inc.
Austin, Texas

Ernest D. Buck, M.D.
Pediatrician
Corpus Christi, Texas

Linda A. Fisher, M.D.
Chief Medical Officer
St. Louis County Department
 of Community Health and
 Medical Care
St. Louis, Missouri

Howard L. Taras, M.D., F.R.C.P.C.
Assistant Professor of Pediatrics
University of California, San Diego
and District Medical Consultant
San Diego Unified School District
San Diego, California

CONSUMER HEALTH PRACTICES

Robert C. Arffa, M.D.
Assistant Professor of
 Ophthalmology
School of Medicine
University of Pittsburgh
The Eye and Ear Institute
Pittsburgh, Pennsylvania

Bertram V. Dannheisser, Jr., D.D.S.
Florida Dental Association
Pensacola, Florida

John D. Durrant, Ph.D.
Professor of Otolaryngology
University of Pittsburgh
and Director, Center for Audiology
Eye and Ear Hospital
Pittsburgh, Pennsylvania

NUTRITION

Janet L. Gregoire, M.N.S., R.D.
Instructor in Nutrition
Penn State Nutrition Center
The Pennsylvania State University
University Park, Pennsylvania

Maryfrances L. Marecic, M.S., R.D.
Instructor in Nutrition
Penn State Nutrition Center
The Pennsylvania State University
University Park, Pennsylvania

Linda Fox Simmons, M.S.H.P., R.D./L.D.
Program Specialist
Texas Nutrition Education
 and Training Center
Texas Department of
 Human Services
Austin, Texas

EXERCISE AND FITNESS

Steven N. Blair, P.E.D.
Director, Epidemiology
Institute for Aerobics Research
Dallas, Texas

Donald Haydon
Executive Director
American Health and Fitness
 Foundation
Austin, Texas

Deborah Waters, M.D.
Team Physician
The Pennsylvania State University
University Park, Pennsylvania

MEDICINE

Donna Hubbard McCree, M.P.H., Pharmacist
Professional Affairs Assistant
American Pharmaceutical
 Association
Washington, D.C.

Judith Ann Shinogle, R.Ph.
Executive Resident
American Pharmaceutical
 Association
Washington, D.C.

SUBSTANCE ABUSE

Robert N. Holsaple
Supervisor of Prevention Programs
The School Board of Broward County
Fort Lauderdale, Florida

SAFETY AND FIRST AID

American Red Cross
Washington, D.C.

CONTRIBUTORS AND REVIEWERS

Danny J. Ballard, Ed.D.
Assistant Professor
Health Education
Texas A&M University
College Station, Texas

Linda Barnes
Teacher
Wahl-Coates School
Greenville, North Carolina

**Robert C. Barnes, Ed.D.,
M.P.H.**
Associate Professor and
   Coordinator
Health Education
East Carolina University
Greenville, North Carolina

David L. Bever, Ph.D.
Associate Professor
Health Education
George Mason University
Fairfax, Virginia

James M. Eddy, D.Ed.
Associate Professor and Chair
Health Education
The University of Alabama
Tuscaloosa, Alabama

Sue Ann Eddy
Teacher
Stillman Heights Elementary
Tuscaloosa, Alabama

Ruth C. Engs, Ed.D., R.N.
Associate Professor
Applied Health Science
Indiana University
Bloomington, Indiana

Tina Fields, Ph.D.
Assistant Professor
Health Education
Texas Tech University
Lubbock, Texas

Patricia Barthalow Koch, Ph.D.
Assistant Professor
Health Education
College of Health and Human
   Development
The Pennsylvania State University
University Park, Pennsylvania

**Patricia Langner, P.H.N., B.S.N.,
M.P.H.**
Health Educator and Nurse
San Ramon Valley Unified
   School District
Danville, California

Samuel W. Monismith, D.Ed.
Assistant Professor
Health Education
The Pennsylvania State
   University
Capital College
Middletown, Pennsylvania

Marcia Newey, P.H.N., M.P.H.
Health Educator and Nurse
San Ramon Valley Unified
   School District
San Ramon, California

Brenda North
Chair of Health and Physical
   Education
Lanier Middle School
Houston, Texas

Florence R. Oaks, Ph.D.
Psychologist
San Ramon Valley Unified
   School District
Danville, California

Bea Orr
Past President of the
   American Alliance for
   Health, Physical
   Education, Recreation and
   Dance
Health and Physical Education
   Supervisor
Logan County Public Schools
Logan, West Virginia

Nancy Piña
Teacher
Braeburn Elementary School
Houston, Texas

**Kerry John Redican, Ph.D.,
M.P.H.**
Associate Professor
Health Education
Virginia Polytechnic Institute
   and State University
Blacksburg, Virginia

Roger Rodriguez
Coordinator of Health and
   Physical Education
San Antonio Independent
   School District
San Antonio, Texas

Mildred Solomon
Chair
Mirabeau Lamar
   High School
Houston, Texas

David Sommerfeld
Instructional Supervisor
Elementary Education
Ysleta Independent
   School District
El Paso, Texas

William J. Stone, Ed.D.
Professor
Exercise Physiology
Arizona State University
Tempe, Arizona

Patrick Tow, Ph.D.
Associate Professor
Department of Health,
   Physical Education, and
   Recreation
Old Dominion University
Norfolk, Virginia

Molly S. Wantz, M.S., Ed.S.
Associate Professor
Department of Physiology
   and Health Science
Ball State University
Muncie, Indiana

Donna Winchell, Ph.D.
Assistant Professor
Health Science
James Madison University
Harrisonburg, Virginia

READING/LANGUAGE ADVISOR

Patricia S. Bowers, Ph.D.
Reading and Curriculum
   Specialist
Chapel Hill-Carrboro City
   Schools
Chapel Hill, North Carolina

Contents

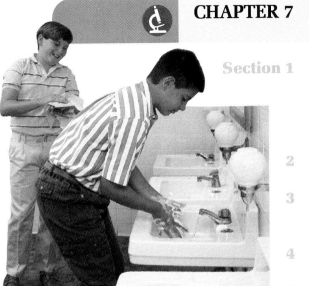

FOR YOUR REFERENCE   **369**

THINKING ABOUT YOUR HEALTH

REAL-LIFE SKILLS

HEALTH CLOSE-UPS

PEOPLE IN HEALTH

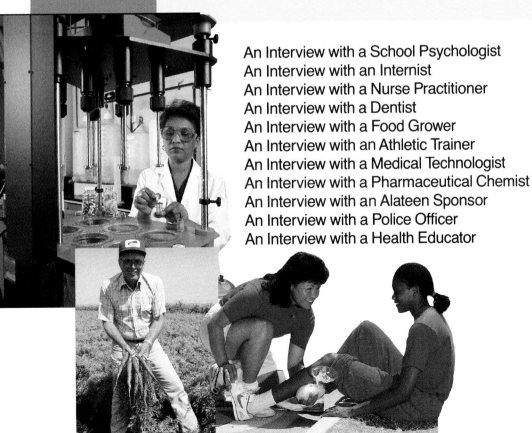

You are at your best when you are healthy. When you feel good, you are able to enjoy life to its fullest. However, staying healthy can be a challenge. To handle this challenge, you will need knowledge—not only about health issues, but about yourself and your environment. With the right information and thoughtful preparation, you will find the challenge of being healthy both exciting and enjoyable.

As you read *Being Healthy,* you will learn about many health habits that can help keep you feeling your best. Some of these habits require special knowledge. With up-to-date health information and good health habits, you can meet the challenge of being healthy. By taking responsibility for your health now, you are preparing for a healthy future.

You probably think that good health requires exercise and a healthful diet. You are right; it does. However, these are not the only things that contribute to good health. To be healthy, you must also satisfy mental, emotional, and social needs. In other words, your mind, feelings, family, friends, and community are also important to your health. Just about everything you do during a day can affect your health.

Practicing good health habits can help you avoid many kinds of diseases. Also, the healthier you become, the better you will feel about yourself. You will increase your self-esteem. When you refuse to use dangerous drugs, you will increase your self-esteem even more. In refusing harmful substances, you are protecting not only your own health, but also the health of others in your community.

Being healthy does not just happen. You must choose to live in a healthful way. You must take responsibility for your well-being and develop habits that will help keep you healthy. This responsibility will require you to make some important and sometimes difficult decisions. By reading *Being Healthy* you will help yourself prepare for these decisions. You will then be ready to make the wise choices for being safe and being healthy.

FIRST
PLACE
WINNER

CHAPTER 1

YOUR FEELINGS AND ACTIONS

What do you need to feel happy? Do you always know? Some needs are easy to understand. When you are hungry, you probably know you need food. But some needs are more puzzling. There may be times when you feel sad or worried without knowing why. Maybe you want to feel better but do not know what to do.

Your feelings are an important part of your health. Understanding your needs can help you understand your feelings. Understanding your feelings can help you make choices that will help you feel good about yourself.

GETTING READY TO LEARN

Key Questions

- Why is it important to learn about yourself?
- Why is it important to understand how you feel and act?
- How can you learn to make healthful choices about handling your feelings?
- What can you do to help yourself feel good about yourself?
- How can you take more responsibility for the ways you act and feel?

Main Chapter Sections

1 Identifying Your Needs
2 Your Needs Affect Your Feelings and Actions
3 Choosing Healthful Ways to Handle Your Feelings
4 Other People Affect Your Feelings and Actions

1 Identifying Your Needs

People of all ages have basic needs. **Basic needs** are what you must meet or satisfy to live, stay healthy, and feel good about yourself. Everybody has the same basic physical, intellectual, emotional, and social needs. You have to understand your needs before you can begin to understand how you feel and act. How you satisfy your basic needs helps determine your self-concept. **Self-concept** is the way you think about yourself.

What Are People's Basic Needs?

Jeremy is writing a story about a journey in space. In the story, a lonely space traveler crashes his ship on a planet far away from Earth. The space traveler is alone and must be rescued. Jeremy is trying to think of all the basic needs the space traveler would have to meet in this adventure.

Jeremy knows that the space traveler would need water, air, food, and shelter. Those are basic physical needs of people. Meeting basic *physical needs* keeps the body alive.

In his story, Jeremy meets some of the traveler's basic physical needs by giving him plenty of water and food. Jeremy also remembers that the planet might not have air. So he gives the space traveler air tanks. Jeremy gives the space traveler clothing. He also gives the space traveler materials to make a warm, dry shelter.

Jeremy sees that as the author of the story, he must also meet the space traveler's basic intellectual needs. Trying to learn about the new planet meets his *intellectual needs*.

Jeremy's story tells how the basic emotional and social needs of the traveler are met. *Emotional needs* have to do with a person's feelings. *Social needs* have to do with getting along with other people.

The emotional need to feel safe is a feeling all people have. Jeremy's space traveler tries to meet this need in many different ways. He checks his supplies of water, air, and food. He makes sure his shelter will hold up.

KEY WORDS

basic needs
self-concept
priority
resources
wellness
self-esteem
strength
weakness

basic needs, what you must meet or satisfy to live, stay healthy, and feel good about yourself.

self-concept (sehlf KAHN sehpt), the way you think about yourself.

■ Jeremy is writing about the needs of a space traveler lost and alone in space.

The lonely traveler has a basic social need to be with other people. At one point in the story, the traveler thinks of a way to signal another spaceship that has come from Earth. The ship eventually arrives and saves him. When he is saved, his basic social need is met. At the end of the story, all of the traveler's basic needs have been met.

To meet the social needs of the space traveler in his story, Jeremy has the traveler signal another spaceship.

Why Do Some Needs Come Before Others?

All your basic needs are important. Some, however, are more important than others. The most important needs must be met first. Those needs are priorities. A **priority** is something that should get attention before other things.

Groups of needs can be shown as a pyramid. In this way, different priorities can be described. The base of the pyramid shows your most important physical needs. Physical needs are the most basic because you need water, air, food, and shelter to stay alive. When those needs are not met, you cannot think much about your other needs.

priority (pry AWR uh tee), something that should get attention before other things.

3

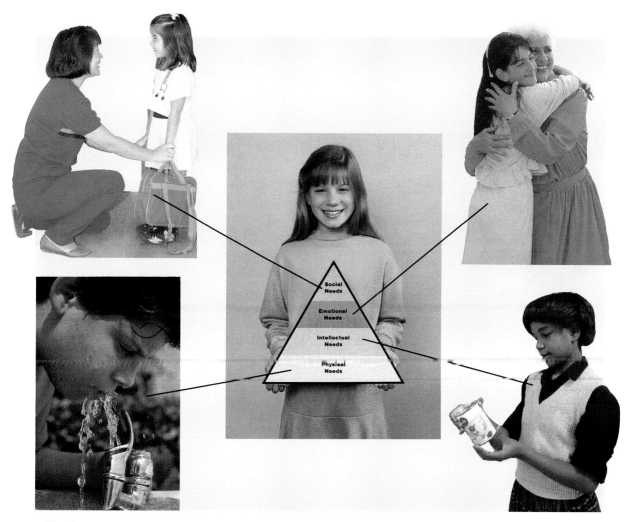

Social Needs

Emotional Needs

Intellectual Needs

Physical Needs

■ *Physical needs must be met before intellectual, emotional, and social needs can be satisfied.*

resources (REE sohr suhz), things you can use to meet your needs.

Suppose you were very hungry. You would most likely think about getting food to eat. You would not think much about doing other things. The same would be true if you were very thirsty or very cold. The basic physical needs must be met first.

Your intellectual needs may be a second priority. You need to know how to use resources to meet your physical needs. **Resources** are things you can use to meet certain needs. You need knowledge and skills to be able to use the resources in the best way possible.

Your need for safety may be your next most important need. If you could not meet the need to feel safe, you would be worried and frightened most of the time. You would not be able to concentrate on meeting other needs. One way this need is met is by having family members and friends to trust.

When your basic physical and intellectual needs and your need for safety have been met, you can then try to satisfy your needs for love and a sense of belonging. Love and belonging are basic social needs. Everyone needs to feel loved. Being loved is being cared about just for yourself, not for what you do or how you look. You may feel loved when a family member smiles at you or does something nice for you. Everyday acts of friendship are also ways in which this need is met.

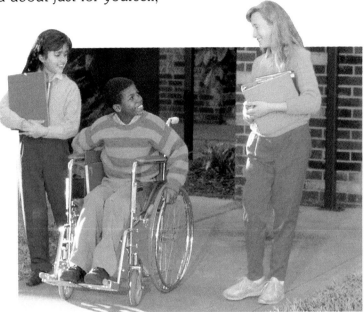

■ *Being a friend and having friends help meet your social needs.*

People also need to feel that they belong somewhere. They need to feel that they are part of a group. Your greatest feeling of belonging may be with your family. One kind of belonging is feeling at home in a certain place. You may feel that you belong in your school, neighborhood, or town. You may think that you would not be comfortable living anywhere else. Another kind of belonging is feeling that you have friends you can trust or that you can get along well with people.

When your basic needs have been met, you can work to meet other important needs. Meeting your needs can help make you feel healthy and happy.

What Does It Mean to Be Healthy?

Each time you meet one of the needs in the pyramid, your health is affected. It is possible for you to meet a basic need and yet harm your health. For example, eating foods that are not nutritious may satisfy hunger but will not help build a healthy body.

REAL-LIFE
SKILL

Making Friends

Remember that making friends takes effort. Ask someone you would like for a friend to do something with you, such as go bicycle riding.

wellness, a high level of health.

self-esteem (sehl fuh STEEM), a feeling of liking and respecting yourself.

strength, something you can do well.

weakness (WEEK nuhs), something you do not do well.

People balance weaknesses and strengths to meet their needs.

Think of your health as a mobile with these important parts: physical, intellectual, emotional, and social. Meeting these needs wisely helps keep your health in balance.

Balanced health is wellness. **Wellness** is a high level of health. It means that all your health needs are being met. As you grow older and change in many ways, you will still have needs to be met. Your wellness will come from the new ways you learn to meet those needs.

But wellness involves more than meeting basic needs. Wellness includes self-esteem. Having **self-esteem** means liking and respecting yourself. Once you feel good about yourself, you can believe in yourself even when you are not well or when things go wrong. When you feel good about yourself, you feel more in control of your life.

Self-esteem is built on good feelings about your strengths. A **strength** is something you can do well. One of your strengths might be your ability to make friends. Strengths make it easier for you to climb the pyramid to wellness. Self-esteem also means accepting and understanding a **weakness,** something you do not do well. All people have both strengths and weaknesses. If you try to improve your weaknesses and use your strengths to the best of your ability, you can meet your needs. Meeting those needs can help you stay a healthy person.

 **REVIEW**
SECTION 1

REMEMBER?

1. What needs must you satisfy to stay healthy and feel good about yourself?
2. Being thirsty is an example of what kind of basic need?
3. What are some groups to which people belong?

THINK!

4. What do you think it means to be "healthy"?
5. Why is self-esteem important for reaching wellness?

6

2 Your Needs Affect Your Feelings and Actions

When you have a need, you try to meet it. When a need is not being met, you feel a certain way. When you need food, you feel hungry. When you need to know something, you may feel puzzled. When you need safety, you feel frightened. When you need to feel loved and to feel that you belong, you feel sad and lonely. When you lack good self-esteem, you do not feel sure about yourself. All these feelings lead you to respond in ways that will meet your needs.

KEY WORDS

behavior
personality

Why Do Your Feelings Come from Your Needs?

Everyone has the same basic needs. But at any one time, your needs are most likely different from anyone else's needs. You may have different feelings than other people do, even in the same situation.

Julie and Carlos are visiting a zoo with their class. They are both trying to learn more about the zoo, but they have different feelings.

■ *Although everyone's basic needs are the same, not everyone feels the same way in the same situation.*

Julie did not eat breakfast this morning. Now she is so hungry that she cannot pay attention to what her teacher is saying. Her physical need for food has not been met.

Carlos ate a healthful breakfast this morning. Now he is thinking about what the teacher is saying. He feels that he is learning many things. Carlos feels good about himself. He has already met a basic physical need. By listening to his teacher he can help meet his needs for knowledge and self-esteem.

Why Do Your Actions Come from Your Feelings?

People respond to their feelings by acting in certain ways. Their actions come from their feelings. What they do may then change how they feel. When Karen feels lonely, she looks for one of her friends. Then her needs for love and belonging are met. When you feel frightened, you try to do something to make yourself safe. You act because of your feelings. Such action helps you meet your needs.

People may act in different ways even when they are trying to meet the same needs. Sid and Sharon both feel lonely. Sid and Sharon act in different ways to meet their need for belonging. The way you act is your **behavior.**

Sid wants to feel that he belongs. He tries to make friends by making fun of other people. He thinks people will like him if he puts on a show. Putting on a show is not a positive behavior.

Sharon also wants to feel that she belongs. She feels lonely, too. She wants to become Kerri's friend. She asks Kerri about her schoolwork. Sharon takes an interest in what Kerri is doing.

Sid's and Sharon's behaviors are different partly because they have different personalities. Your **personality** is the way you think, feel, and act. Your way of responding to your needs depends a lot on your personality. The way you feel about your needs also depends a lot on your personality.

■ *Sharing interests shows that you feel close to other people.*

behavior (bih HAY vyuhr), the way you act.

personality (puhrs uhn AL uht ee), the way you think, act, and feel.

8

How Do Your Feelings Show?

Wayne has moved to a new neighborhood and goes to a new school. He is homesick. He feels sad and lonely because he misses his friends. Everything about him shows how he feels. His face looks unhappy. His body slumps a little. When he talks, his voice is low and quiet.

Priscilla has done well on her spelling test. She is proud of her work. Her face has a broad smile on it. She is eagerly talking to her friend. Her voice is higher than usual.

People can show their feelings in many ways. Your face often shows best how you feel. When you are happy or proud or excited, you most likely smile. When you are puzzled or sad, you may frown. Your face often shows whether you are angry, afraid, surprised, or worried.

Your voice also shows how you feel. When you are sad, your voice probably sounds low and quiet. You may talk faster and in a higher and louder voice when you are excited or angry.

Sometimes your whole body shows the way you feel. The way your body shows your feelings is sometimes called *body language.* For example, you may hold your head down when you are sad. When you are interested in something, you may hold your head up.

■ Body language can show how people feel. What does body language say about each of these people's feelings?

REMEMBER?

1. Why do you respond to your feelings?
2. Why do people with the same needs sometimes have different feelings and act in different ways?
3. Name three ways in which people may show their feelings.

THINK!

4. How might understanding your feelings and actions help your self-esteem?
5. How might you help a friend understand his or her feelings and actions?

Thinking About Your Health

Can You Put Feelings into Words?

Three situations are described below. Each one has to do with a need. Read about each situation. How does each one make you feel? Think of a word or phrase to describe your feeling. Being able to put your feelings into words is a way to help you understand yourself. When you understand yourself better, you can build your self-esteem. Expressing yourself in words can also help you share your feelings with others. It can help them understand the needs you have.

- One of Peggy's parents was just laid off from work. Now her parents are not sure how they can pay their bills.

- Marsha was chosen as the class representative to help plan school activities. Her classmates chose her.

- A new student in class wears a cap all the time. He and the school nurse have explained to the class that his treatment for cancer has caused him to lose his hair for a while. He knows he looks different from others.

10

3 Choosing Healthful Ways to Handle Your Feelings

Barry tried to meet his need for self-esteem by drawing a good picture. Barry's picture did not turn out as well as he wanted. His need was not met. He became angry. Barry showed his anger by tearing up his picture.

At times everyone has needs that are not satisfied. Having to wait for a need to be satisfied can make you feel angry, sad, or upset. Your actions often show those feelings. You may cry when you are sad or yell when you are angry.

Crying or yelling are not the only ways to act when you have feelings that come from a need that has not been met. You can also choose to act in ways that will make others respect you more. Responsible people usually find a way to satisfy the need later.

KEY WORD

consequences

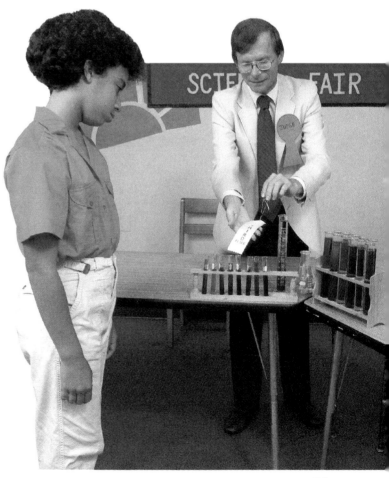

■ Susan felt disappointed about placing third in the school science fair, but she chose to act in a healthful way.

How Can You Choose to Act in a Healthful Way?

Susan worked hard on a project for the school science fair. She was sure it was a good project. She expected to win first prize.

When the prizes were awarded, Susan was given a third-place ribbon. She felt disappointed. She really wanted to win. Susan could not help the way she felt. She could, however, choose the way she would act.

Susan could have chosen to show anger to the judges or to the students who won better prizes. She could have chosen to yell at people or to kick something. Or she might have decided to stop trying so hard in school.

SCIENCE FAIR

Susan chose not to be angry. She congratulated Bill on winning first place.

Susan did not choose to act in any of those ways. She knew that those ways of acting would probably make her feel worse instead of better. Also, other people might think of her as a poor loser. Susan chose instead to congratulate the students who had won first and second prizes. And she decided to feel proud of herself for winning a prize, even though it was not first prize. She remembered that there were many students who did not win any prize. She would try even harder next year.

Susan followed some steps for choosing a healthful way to act:

1. She saw there were several choices about how to act.
2. She identified her possible choices. She could choose to act in ways that showed her feelings without helping her feel better. Or she could act in ways that made her feel better.

consequences (KAHN suh kwehn suhz), results.

3. She thought about the **consequences,** or results, of her possible choices. She knew she would have to take responsibility for the consequences of her choice. Susan realized acting angry would make her feel worse. Choosing to be a good loser might help her meet her need for self-esteem.
4. She made what she thought was the best choice for herself. Susan decided to feel proud of herself for winning a prize.
5. She acted in a way that she thought would make her feel better. She congratulated the students who had won first and second prizes.

6. She noticed the consequences of her choice. Susan saw that the first and second prize winners felt good at hearing her congratulations. She saw that it is important to react in ways that make her feel better.

Having steps to follow can help you make healthful choices. You will be making many choices during your life. Some choices will involve your needs, feelings, or actions. Many of your choices will have an effect on your self-esteem and can help you reach wellness. You will want your choices to be reasonable. You will have to take much responsibility for the results.

Why Is It Good to Talk About Your Feelings?

Choosing the best way to respond to your feelings is not always easy. You have to know what needs have caused your feelings. Talking with someone, perhaps a parent or a teacher, may help you to know what those needs are.

Laura had to give a report to her class. The day before the report, she had her notes ready, but she was still feeling a little scared. She could not change the feeling by herself, so she talked with her father about how she felt. She learned that her father sometimes felt worried when he had to talk in front of a group of people.

Talking with her father helped Laura handle her feelings. She found out that someone understood how she felt. She also discovered that she was not the only person to feel scared sometimes. That made her feel better.

■ Laura was afraid to give a speech in school. Talking with her father about her fear made Laura feel better.

One way to respond to unhappy or worried feelings is to talk about them. When you are sad or angry, talking with someone can help you feel better. Sometimes, talking about a problem helps you realize that the actual problem is not so great. It may only seem so great because your feelings about it are so strong. Understanding your needs and your feelings can help you choose to act in ways that will help keep you happy and healthy.

STOP REVIEW
SECTION 3

REMEMBER?

1. What are two different ways someone can choose to act when he or she feels sad or angry?
2. What is one healthful way to respond to unhappy or worried feelings?

THINK!

3. Why might it be a good health choice to have older family members or other adults help you with difficult decisions?
4. Why is it not realistic to think all your needs can be met instantly?

Making Wellness Choices

Kelly and Katie are sisters. Kelly is in seventh grade. Katie is in fifth. Kelly is a good softball player. Katie tries very hard, but she always seems to make mistakes when she plays softball. At a neighborhood picnic, teams are being chosen for softball. No one wants to choose Katie.

? How might both Kelly and Katie act in this situation? Identify the possible choices they could make. Think about the consequences of their choices. Choose a way for each girl to act so that both of them will feel good about themselves. Explain your wellness choices.

14

Reacting to Stress

You respond to different situations many times each day. You respond to needs that are not met. You also respond to needs that are met. Because life has so many changes, you may often feel stress. *Stress* is any strain that makes you feel uncomfortable. Stress can come from within you or from the people, places, and things around you. Both pleasant and unpleasant situations can cause stress. Seeing parents separate, enjoying a holiday, winning a prize, and taking a test are all situations that can be stressful.

Stress can change your health because it puts extra demands on your body. Stress can make your muscles tighten. It can make your stomach feel as if it is tied in a knot. It can also change the rate, or speed, at which your heart beats. If those changes go on for a long time, you can become ill.

Your mind also reacts to stress. Stress can make a small worry grow until it seems very big. Suddenly you may feel very sad and lonely.

One healthful way to handle stress is to try to find out what has caused the increased level of stress. Then you can try to change what is causing it. Another good way is to talk about your feelings with someone you trust, such as a parent or a teacher. Letting someone know how you feel helps keep small worries small. Exercising and working on a hobby are other healthful activities that can help you handle stress. When you are busy

■ *Exercising and having fun are good ways of handling stress.*

doing things you enjoy, you feel better. When your body is working hard, you release some of the extra energy that stress can cause to build up.

Thinking Beyond

1. Howie shares a bedroom with his little brother, Josh. Josh needs a night-light to feel safe, but the only place to plug it in is next to Howie's bed. The light hits Howie's eyes and keeps him awake. How can Howie change this stressful situation?
2. JoAnn's parents argue sometimes. Their arguing makes JoAnn feel nervous and scared. Sometimes her stomach feels upset. How can JoAnn handle this stress?

15

Other People Affect Your Feelings and Actions

relationships (rih LAY shuhn shihps), contacts with family members and other people.

■ Your first relationships are with family members.

Your first and most important **relationships,** or contacts, are with members of your family. In a family, people learn skills and behaviors for the first time. They learn the meaning of special feelings such as love, caring, and trust. Your family affects many of your feelings and actions.

Part of growing up is meeting people outside your family. You form relationships with neighbors, other relatives, and classmates. Relationships with other people help you meet your social and emotional needs. Some of your relationships may become friendships. Friends and other people can cause you to change how you feel and act.

What Makes a Good Friend?

The students in Mrs. Santos's class are studying why friends are important. "What makes a good friend?" asks Mrs. Santos.

Sonya says that a friend should be fun. William agrees. He adds, "A friend should care about me."

Some people seem to make friends easily. Such people act in ways that others like. They may be what Sonya calls "fun" or what William might call "caring." Friends are interested in you. They make you feel important. They keep their word. Friends never push you to do something that could hurt you or others. Friends do not push you to go against family rules. They try to understand you.

When you and your friends talk about your thoughts and your feelings, you are able to learn more about each other.

■ *Having common interests and doing things together help people become friends.*

17

Friends can be physically very different in age, size, or race and still share the same interests and activities. You may think of friends as people about your age. However, a brother, a sister, or a grandparent also may be a close friend as well as a family member.

Who Are Your Peers?

Another set of relationships you have is peer relationships. A **peer** is someone who is about your same age or is in your class. Because of these similarities, you and your peers might share many of the same needs, likes, or dislikes.

Peers can help one another meet social and emotional needs. You need other people, such as peers, to talk with about feelings that you might share. You might talk about feeling proud and happy. You might also talk about feeling afraid, sad, and angry. Peers can sometimes help you understand your feelings. They can help you understand that other people feel the same way you do.

peer (PIHR), someone about your age or in your class.

■ *Andrew's decision not to skateboard without the proper safety equipment may influence his friends to stay safe while playing.*

18

The influence of peers may help Aaron decide to join the Scouts. This decision may help Aaron satisfy a need for belonging.

Because you spend a lot of time with your peers, they have an effect on the ways you feel and act. They can influence you, just as your friends and family do.

Several of Aaron's classmates have joined a Scout troop. One classmate told Aaron that he should ask his parents if he could join, too. Aaron had never thought about the Scouts before. But he likes doing the same things his classmates do. He wants to be like his peers. Peers have an effect on the way Aaron feels about joining the Scouts. They have an influence on him.

Sometimes peers push you to feel or act the way they do. A few weeks ago, some of Lydia's classmates told her that she needed a certain kind of jacket. Several of the classmates had started wearing that kind of jacket to school. One of Lydia's classmates told her she should be like them. If she was not, her classmates might not be friendly to her. But Lydia knows that her parents might not approve.

Peer pressure happens when peers try to influence your feelings or behavior. Sometimes, they do so by teasing you, daring you, or saying something to hurt your feelings. Deciding not to give in to peer pressure is a choice you can make.

peer pressure (PIHR • PREHSH uhr), the influence on a person by a group of people about the same age.

19

Lydia faces a common problem from peer pressure. She wants to be like her friends, but she does not want to cause trouble at home.

Being in control of your own feelings and behavior is your responsibility to yourself. It can help you stay well. It also shows you are becoming an independent and responsible person.

How Can You Turn Down Peer Pressure?

Peers can influence you in many positive ways. A classmate might help you find a new interest or activity. At times, however, peers may dare you to do something you know is not safe. They may want you to steal, cheat, or break school rules, things that you know are wrong. You can feel good about yourself when you resist peer pressure.

Remember Lydia and her problem? Lydia was not sure what to do when classmates tried to persuade her to get a new kind of jacket. They wanted Lydia to be like them.

Lydia knew that she wanted her classmates to be friendly toward her. She also knew that asking her parents for a new jacket might cause trouble at home. Her parents had bought her a new jacket at the beginning of the school year. For Lydia the choice was between trouble at home and trouble with her classmates. Not all choices are easy ones, she thought.

Lydia's relationship with her family was very important to her. And her peer relationships were important, too. Though both were important, Lydia's family needs and relationship came first. They were a priority for her. Knowing what comes first in your life can help you choose to refuse peer pressure. Lydia told her friends why she would not ask her parents for the jacket. She told them she thought they could be friends even though she did not have a jacket.

At some other time, peers might push Lydia to do something that is not good for her health. They might push her to use drugs or tobacco. If they do, Lydia will need to know that her health, safety, and self-esteem are priorities for her. By resisting peer pressure to do something that could harm her health, Lydia is becoming a responsible person. She is adding to her self-esteem.

Good mental health is having friends, getting along with family members, feeling good about yourself, and being able to talk about your feelings and your problems.

REVIEW
SECTION 4

REMEMBER?

1. What are four qualities of a friend?
2. What are two kinds of needs that can be met through relationships?
3. Why do peers share many of the same needs?

THINK!

4. What are some things you can do to form long-lasting relationships?
5. How can you act responsibly when faced with peer pressure that could harm you?

People in Health

An Interview with a School Psychologist

Sharon Smith Brady helps young people feel good about themselves. She is a school psychologist in Lawton, Oklahoma.

What does a school psychologist do?

A school psychologist helps students solve their problems. Some students have trouble learning. Others have trouble getting along with teachers and classmates. Some students act sad or angry. The school psychologist is someone they can talk with to figure out the reasons for their problems.

What makes some students act unhappy or angry?

Many students do not think much of themselves. They lack self-esteem. Often their behavior in class indicates that something else is wrong in their lives. For example, some students may be having a tough time adjusting to a family problem, such as a divorce. Acting really sad or angry is one way some people show the pain they feel. Finding the cause of some students' problems requires a lot of talking among the student, the teacher, and me.

How do you help students who are having problems?

Sometimes students are scared or unwilling to talk about a problem. Maybe something that is happening at school or at home really bothers them, and they want to keep it a secret. Some are afraid that if they say what is wrong, they will be "telling." I say that whatever they have to tell me is just between them and me. Students learn to trust me. They know that I am there to help them.

■ *School psychologists try to help students with their problems.*

What are the worst problems you have had to help students solve?

There are many bad problems. One problem that upsets students very much is the death of a classmate. Many students feel unhappy and insecure when this happens. Of course, the way students feel also affects their school-work. Another serious problem is child abuse. Students who are abused need a lot of help but may be afraid to tell anyone about their problem.

What would you tell students who are suffering from child abuse but have not said anything to anyone?

I would say that they should know they can be helped. But they must talk to someone as soon as possible. If they would only go to their teachers and say what is wrong or that they need help! It is not the same as telling on someone at all. There are people waiting to help them. They should tell a teacher, counselor, or even an older brother or sister that they need help. If they do not know where to turn, they can even call the National Child-Abuse Hot Line. That number is 1-800-422-4453.

What education does a person need to become a school psychologist?

To become a school psychologist, a person needs six to eight years of schooling past high school. A school psychologist must understand how children learn, as well as how to help

■ Dr. Brady likes to see good changes in students.

them solve their problems. A school psychologist must have some of the same training that a teacher has.

What has been your happiest time as a school psychologist?

It always makes me feel good when I work with students and see good changes in them. But what is most special is seeing students who once had difficult problems finish school. When I see them and they are happy and well, I am pleased.

Learn more about people who work as school psychologists and what they do. Interview a school psychologist. Or write for information to the National Association of School Psychologists, 655 Fifteenth Street, N.W., Washington, DC 20005.

23

Main Ideas

- Learning about people's basic needs can help you understand your own and others' feelings and actions.
- Many of the choices you will make throughout your life will involve your needs, feelings, and actions.
- You are responsible for making wise choices and acting in ways that will help you meet your needs.
- Relationships with people help you meet your social and emotional needs.
- Peers can help one another meet needs, and peers can affect the ways you feel and act.

Key Words

Write the numbers 1 to 14 in your health notebook or on a separate sheet of paper. After each number, copy the sentence and fill in the missing term. Page numbers in ( ) tell you where to look in the chapter if you need help.

basic needs (2)	weakness (6)
self-concept (2)	behavior (8)
priority (3)	personality (8)
resources (4)	consequences (12)
wellness (6)	relationships (16)
self-esteem (6)	peer (18)
strength (6)	peer pressure (19)

1. A high level of health you can enjoy is ___?___ .

2. You must meet or satisfy your ___?___ in order to live, stay healthy, and feel good about yourself.

3. The ways you think, act, and feel make up your ___?___ .

4. The most important need, which comes before others, is a ___?___ .

5. Your ___?___ are things you can use to meet needs.

6. When you like and respect yourself, you have ___?___ .

7. The way you act is your ___?___ .

8. Contacts with other people are called ___?___ .

9. A ___?___ is someone about your age or in your class.

10. As you decide how to act, you need to consider the ___?___ , or results, of your actions.

11. When peers try to control your feelings or behavior, they are using ___?___ .

12. Something you do well is a ___?___ .

13. When you cannot do something well, you are said to have a ___?___ .

14. The way you think about yourself is your ___?___ .

Remembering What You Learned

Page numbers in ( ) tell you where to look in the chapter if you need help.

1. What are four physical needs that a person must satisfy in order to stay alive and healthy? (2)

2. What are a person's needs in order from most to least important for health and happiness? (3–5)

3. How can you know if you have an unmet basic need? (4)

4. How might a friend feel if you do something nice for him or her? (5)

5. What needs are satisfied when you feel at home in a place and feel that you have friends? (5)

6. How can feeling good about yourself help you when something goes wrong? (6)

7. How do people respond to their feelings? (8)

8. What can happen if a person has to wait for a need to be satisfied? (11)

9. How should a person react to feelings that make him or her unhappy? (11–14)

10. What can talking with a family member or friend do for a person who is feeling sad? (13–14)

Thinking About What You Learned

1. How might not eating a nutritious breakfast affect a person's intellectual needs?

2. Suppose you just moved to a new neighborhood. What are some actions you might take to meet your need for belonging in the new neighborhood?

3. How might being a poor listener have an effect on a person's self-esteem?

4. How is personality important in the different ways people respond to the same situation?

5. Think of a feeling and of two different ways that a person might respond to it. Then describe the feelings that the person might have after each of the two possible responses.

Writing About What You Learned

1. Look at this list of feelings:
   - fear
   - anger
   - excitement

   For each feeling, name one healthful action you might take if you had the feeling. Write a paragraph explaining how the action would be helpful.

2. Stuart is at summer camp for the first time. He feels lonely. List the unmet needs that could have made Stuart feel this way. Write three or more paragraphs about what Stuart can do to help himself feel better while he is at camp. Write about three different actions he can take to meet all of his needs.

Applying What You Learned

ART

In a way, each part of your health is like a part of a mobile. Your physical, intellectual, emotional, and social health should be in balance. Build a mobile with straws, string, and cardboard. Include shapes with labels that describe good health habits. Use the mobile to show how wellness is maintained and health stays in balance.

Modified True or False

Write the numbers 1 to 15 in your health notebook or on a separate sheet of paper. After each number, write *true* or *false* to describe the sentence. If the sentence is false, also write a term that replaces the underlined term and makes the sentence true.

1. If you like and respect yourself, then you have high <u>self-esteem</u>.
2. <u>Peers</u> can affect the way you think.
3. The need for shelter is an example of one <u>intellectual</u> need.
4. The basic physical needs are a <u>priority</u>.
5. The ways you think, act, and feel are part of your <u>behavior</u>.
6. Smiling broadly and moving quickly are examples of <u>body language</u>.
7. People learn skills and behaviors for the first time from their <u>peers</u>.
8. The results of your actions are called <u>resources</u>.
9. Having friends meets a <u>social</u> need.
10. <u>Peer pressure</u> is not always bad.
11. <u>Consequences</u> are things you can use to meet certain needs.
12. A strength is something you <u>do not</u> do well.
13. Wellness is a high level of <u>health</u> you can achieve.
14. Keeping worried feelings a secret is <u>healthy</u>.
15. Your first <u>relationships</u> are with members of your family.

Short Answer

Write the numbers 16 to 23 on your paper. Write a complete sentence to answer each question.

16. How are your physical needs different from all your other basic needs?
17. What need is involved when people respond to peer pressure? Explain your answer.
18. Why is it important to understand what your needs are?
19. How can peer pressure affect your self-esteem?
20. How does body language tell people how you feel?
21. Why is it important to think about the consequences of your actions?
22. What needs do friends meet?
23. How can your behavior affect your self-esteem?

Essay

Write the numbers 24 and 25 on your paper. Write paragraphs with complete sentences to answer each question.

24. Sue and Antonia are friends. Antonia had a birthday party but did not invite Sue. Describe how Sue must have felt and tell how she could handle her feelings and act in a healthful manner toward Antonia.
25. Describe how meeting your basic needs can also help you to meet many other needs.

ACTIVITIES FOR HOME OR SCHOOL

Projects to Do

1. With your teacher and classmates, plan an activity that all of you can do together. It could be a class picnic or a field trip. It could be a play or a talent show. Plan the activity so that everyone in class can take part in it. Be sure each person has a job that contributes to the activity. Doing such a job will help each person develop a feeling of belonging to the group.

■ *Planning group activities can be fun.*

2. Choose a feeling, such as happiness or fear. Then make or do something that shows what having that feeling is like. You may want to write a song, a poem, or a short story. You may also want to use body language. Have a partner guess what feeling you are trying to show.

Information to Find

1. Suppose a person were alone in a desert. What needs would be difficult for that person to meet? How could he or she try to meet those needs? Look in the library for books about people who have survived alone in a desert. Find out what they did to stay alive.

2. Find out about homeless people in your community. You can do this by reading the newspaper or calling the local office of the Salvation Army. How do homeless adults try to meet their needs? How do communities help homeless people meet their needs?

3. Mimes are actors who show actions, ideas, and feelings by gestures alone. Mimes use no spoken words. Find out about the words *imitate* and *mimic*. How are they related to the word *mime*? How is mime related to the way we show feelings?

Books to Read

Here are some books you can look for in your school library or the public library to find more information about the ways you feel and act.

Daniels, Kim. *Your Changing Emotions.* Pinnacle.

Hickman, Marthe W. *Good Manners for Girls and Boys.* Crown.

Swenson, Judy Harris, and Roxane Kunz. *No One Like Me.* Dillon Press.

CHAPTER 2

HOW YOUR BODY WORKS

Each part of your body works with all the other parts. All your body parts working together keep your whole body working as it should. They let you work and play and do all the things you need to do to be healthy.

Keeping the parts of your body working together and healthy requires attention. This attention must come from you. It means following good health habits. When your daily health habits are good for your whole body, you are helping yourself enjoy wellness.

GETTING READY TO LEARN

Key Questions
- What are the parts of your body, and what do they do?
- Why is it important to learn how your body works?
- How does knowing about body systems help you understand the ways to take care of them?

Main Chapter Sections

29

1 About Your Body

KEY WORDS

cells
tissues
organs
body system

Jane sees the tennis ball coming. She runs toward it, keeping her eyes on the ball. At just the right moment, she swings her racket. Whap! The strings hit the ball, and it flies back across the net for a winning shot.

Jane has clear eyesight and strong muscles. Her eyes and muscles work very well together. Jane can play tennis because the parts of her body that are needed to play the game work well together.

Different parts of your body must work together every time you do something. When you run, you know your legs are moving. But have you noticed that your arms must work at the same time?

Many different parts of your body work together to allow you to walk.

30

By swinging them back and forth, you help keep your body in balance. Even when you seem to be doing nothing, many parts of your body are working together. Your heart is always beating. Your lungs are always working. Your brain is always doing its many jobs.

What Are Your Cells?

You are made up of millions of tiny cells. **Cells** are the smallest living parts of your body. They are the building blocks of your body. A single cell is too small to be seen without a microscope. Hundreds of cells would fit inside this letter o.

You have many different kinds of cells in your body. Your bones are made up of bone cells. Your skin is made up of skin cells. Your muscles are made up of muscle cells. Bone, skin, and muscle cells all have different shapes. Cells are different from each other because they do different jobs. Your body can work best only if all the different kinds of cells are healthy.

cells (SEHLZ), the smallest living parts of your body.

What Are Your Tissues?

Cells work together in groups called **tissues.** Each kind of tissue does a certain job. For example, skin cells fit together like pieces of a jigsaw puzzle. They make up flat, thin sheets of skin tissue. These sheets of tissue help cover and protect your body.

Your body has many kinds of tissues. Groups of bone cells make up bone tissue. Groups of muscle cells make up muscle tissue. Each kind of tissue is special. It does something that no other kind of tissue does.

tissues (TIHSH OOZ), groups of cells of the same kind that work together to do the same job.

■ Each kind of body tissue has its own job to do.

Fat Tissue

Muscle Tissue

Skin Tissue

What Are Your Organs?

Groups of tissues working together to do a job form body parts called **organs.** The many organs of your body all do different jobs. For example, your ears are sense organs. They are made up of several different kinds of tissues. Your ears have the jobs of helping you hear sounds and helping with balance. Your heart, brain, and kidneys are also organs. They have their own jobs to do.

organs (AWR guhnz), body parts formed by different tissues that work together.

■ Groups of specialized cells form tissues. Different tissues form organs. Organs work together in body systems.

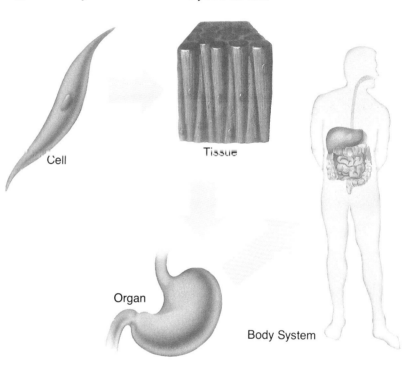

Cell

Tissue

Organ

Body System

What Are Your Body Systems?

Like cells and tissues, groups of organs also work together. Several organs working together to do one job make up a **body system.** The organs in a body system do not look the same. They may not work in the same way, either. But they all help accomplish a certain job. That job is what makes them parts of the same system.

body system (BAHD ee • SIHS tuhm), several organs that work together to do one job.

For example, your tongue and stomach are organs of one system. This system breaks down your food into pieces that your cells can use. Your tongue helps you chew and swallow. Your stomach mixes the swallowed food with chemicals. Each organ does a different part of the job. But they work together to do one job.

All the parts of your body, from the smallest cell to the largest organ, must work together. Each part has an effect on other parts. If cells are not healthy, the tissues cannot do their jobs. If tissues are not healthy, the organs cannot work as well as they might. Organs must work well together in order for your body systems to work smoothly. When all your body systems are working well together, they help make your whole body healthy.

REVIEW
SECTION 1

REMEMBER?

1. Why are cells called "the building blocks of the body"?
2. What is the name for a group of different tissues working together?
3. What is the difference between an organ and a system?

THINK!

4. For the whole body to be healthy, why must all parts of the body work as they should?
5. Do you think one body system could be more important than another body system? Explain your answer.

Making Wellness Choices

George sometimes likes to try stunts that are dangerous. Often he wants to get other students to try the stunts with him. During recess one day, George wanted Ellen and William to try to walk backward down the front steps at school with their hands behind their backs.

Ellen noticed that the steps were very steep. George told them it was easy.

? After reading about how your body parts work together, what could you tell George? Explain your wellness choice.

2 Your Skeletal System

Inside your body, you have 206 bones that are connected to form a framework called your skeletal system, or **skeleton.** Your skeleton is the same height as you are. It helps hold up your body and gives you your general size and shape.

What Are the Parts of the Skeleton?

Suppose that you had no bones in your hand. Your hand would be limp, like a bean bag. Your whole body would be shapeless without bones. Your skeleton gives your body shape. It lets you stand up and move. Some parts of your skeleton also surround and protect your organs, such as your brain and your lungs.

Most bones are connected to other bones. The place where two bones connect, or join, is called a **joint.** Strong bands of tissue called **ligaments** hold the bones together at a joint. Ligaments are strong, but they can let your bones move.

You have two kinds of joints in your body: movable and immovable. *Movable joints* let your skeleton bend in many places. You have two important kinds of movable joints. *Ball-and-socket joints* let bones move around in a circle.

Your shoulders and your hips are ball-and-socket joints. Another movable joint is a hinge joint. *Hinge joints* only let bones fold open and shut, like the covers of a book. Your elbows and your knees are hinge joints.

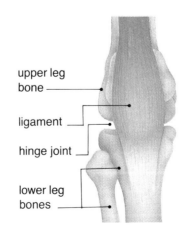

upper leg bone

ligament

hinge joint

lower leg bones

■ *The knee is a kind of movable joint.*

KEY WORDS

skeleton
joint
ligaments
cartilage
vertebrae
pelvis
marrow

skeleton (SKEHL uht uhn), the body's framework made up of bones.

joint (JOYNT), a place where two bones connect, or join.

ligaments (LIHG uh muhnts), tough bands of tissue that hold bones together at a joint.

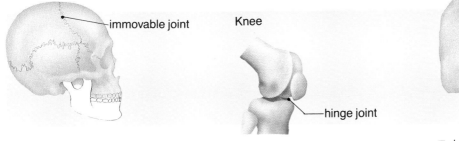

Skull

immovable joint

Knee

hinge joint

Shoulder

ball-and-socket joint

Movable joints have a slippery liquid between the bones. The liquid acts like oil. Your bones would grind together painfully if they were dry. Most joints also have a tough tissue called **cartilage** between the bones. Cartilage also helps protect bone ends from damaging each other. Cartilage acts like a shock absorber.

Some bones in your body fit together too tightly to move. The places where these bones join are *immovable joints*. Your skull is really made up of many bones. Most of these bones have locked together in immovable joints by the time the brain is full size. Your skull always keeps the same shape. This helps it protect your brain.

What Kinds of Bones Do You Have?

Your skull is the set of bones in your head. The three chief parts of the skull are the cranium, the face bones, and the jawbone. Your brain fits inside eight bones that form the *cranium.* Your eyes fit in the eye sockets. Your jawbone, or *mandible,* is the only bone in your skull that moves. It is connected to the face by a hinge joint.

Your spine holds up the top part of your body. It is made up of 33 **vertebrae,** or backbones. Pads, or discs, of cartilage are between most of the vertebrae. They cushion the bones and let your spine bend. The nerves in your spine that make up the spinal cord pass through holes in the vertebrae. The way you hold your body is called your *posture.* Posture depends on how you hold the muscles around your spine.

You have 12 pairs of ribs. They all connect to your spine, in the back. Seven of these rib pairs connect in the front.

■ *Joints in the skull do not move. Joints in the knees and shoulders help you move.*

cartilage (KAHRT uhl ihj), the tough tissue between the bones at most movable joints.

vertebrae (VURT uh bray), bones that make up the spine.

THE SKELETAL SYSTEM

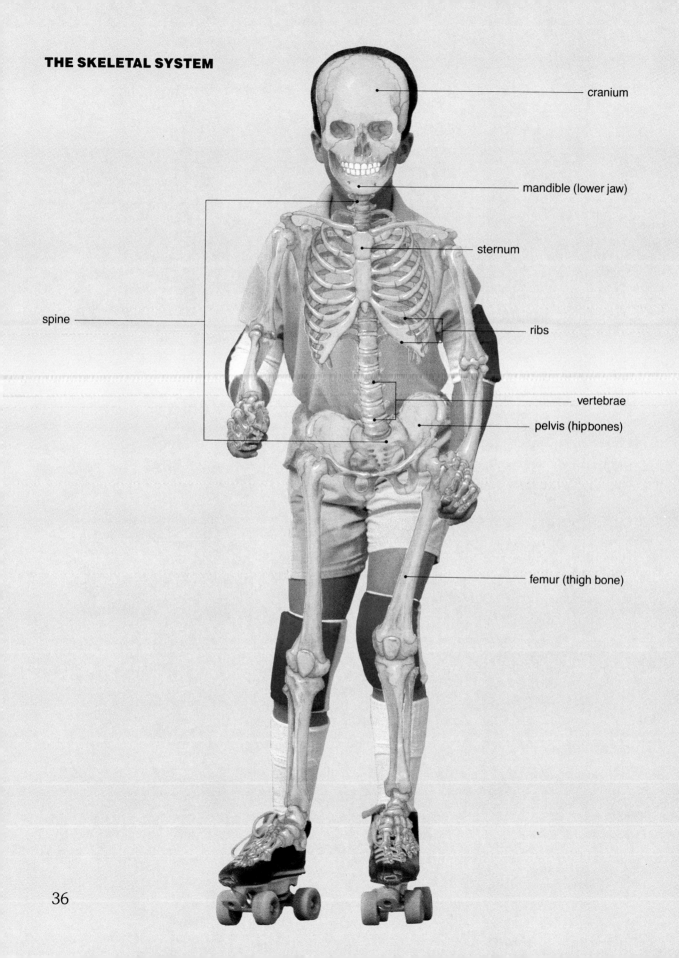

cranium

mandible (lower jaw)

sternum

spine

ribs

vertebrae

pelvis (hipbones)

femur (thigh bone)

They connect to your *sternum,* or breastbone. Your ribs form a kind of cage that protects your heart and lungs. The bones of your chest are sometimes called your rib cage.

The bones in your hips support your upper body when you sit. They join as one piece, called the **pelvis.** Your pelvis holds and protects some of your lower body organs. Your spine is connected to the back part of the pelvis.

The long bones in your arms and legs help you make big motions such as walking, throwing, and jumping. The bone in your thigh, or upper leg, is thick and strong. When you stand, your thigh bone helps hold up your upper body.

Your feet also have many connected bones. These joints, however, do not bend very much. Your foot bones make a surface on which you can balance. The bones in your toes help you keep your balance when you walk. The arch of the bones in the middle of your foot acts like a spring. It puts some bounce in your walk. The bones in your feet work with the bones in your legs to help you stand.

Your hands are made up of many small bones. Together, the bones form many joints. These joints allow you to move your hands in many ways.

What Are the Parts of Each Bone?

Your bones are so hard that they may seem like stones. But your bones are alive and growing. Each bone has many different parts. Look at the picture of a long bone from the thigh.

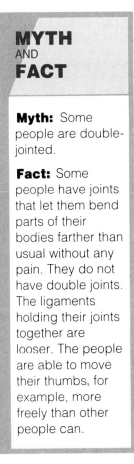

pelvis (PEHL vuhs), formed by the hipbones; helps support your body when you sit.

MYTH AND **FACT**

Myth: Some people are double-jointed.

Fact: Some people have joints that let them bend parts of their bodies farther than usual without any pain. They do not have double joints. The ligaments holding their joints together are looser. The people are able to move their thumbs, for example, more freely than other people can.

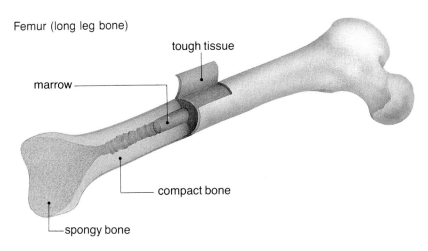

Femur (long leg bone)

tough tissue

marrow

compact bone

spongy bone

A tough membrane covers the hard layer of a bone. Inside many bones is marrow.

A tough tissue goes around the bone and protects bone cells. Under this tissue is the hard layer of bone called *compact bone.* The ends of the bone are filled with *spongy bone.* This kind of bone gets its name because it has many holes, like a sponge. It is made up of many hard, crisscrossing tubes. All the holes help make the bone light without making it weak.

The main part of a long bone is called the *shaft.* Long bones are light and very strong because their shafts are hollow. The hollow space inside holds marrow. **Marrow** is a soft tissue that supplies the body with blood cells.

marrow (MAIR oh), soft tissue in the shaft of bones; supplies the body with blood cells.

REVIEW

SECTION 2

REMEMBER?

1. What are two things your skeleton does for your body?
2. What is the difference between a ball-and-socket joint and a hinge joint?
3. What are four kinds of bones?

THINK!

4. Why are bones considered to be alive?
5. Which other body systems are important to the health of the skeletal system? Explain your answer.

3 Your Muscular System

Most of your muscles are connected to your bones. Muscles cover your skeleton and fill out the shape of your body and make you firm. They also help you keep your posture. You have muscles in many organs. All your muscles together make up your muscular system.

Muscles mostly work to move your body. But they also help hold your body together and protect certain organs inside it. Feel the front of your body where your stomach is. You have no bones there. Instead, a wall of muscle helps protect the organs inside.

KEY WORDS

voluntary
  muscles
involuntary
  muscles
tendons

What Different Kinds of Muscles Do You Have?

Your body has more than 600 muscles. More than 400 are *skeletal muscles.* They are connected to your bones. They move parts such as your arms, legs, and fingers. You can use these muscles to make movements whenever you want. Skeletal muscles that you can control are called **voluntary muscles.**

voluntary muscles
(VAHL uhn tehr ee • MUHS uhlz), muscles that you can control whenever you want.

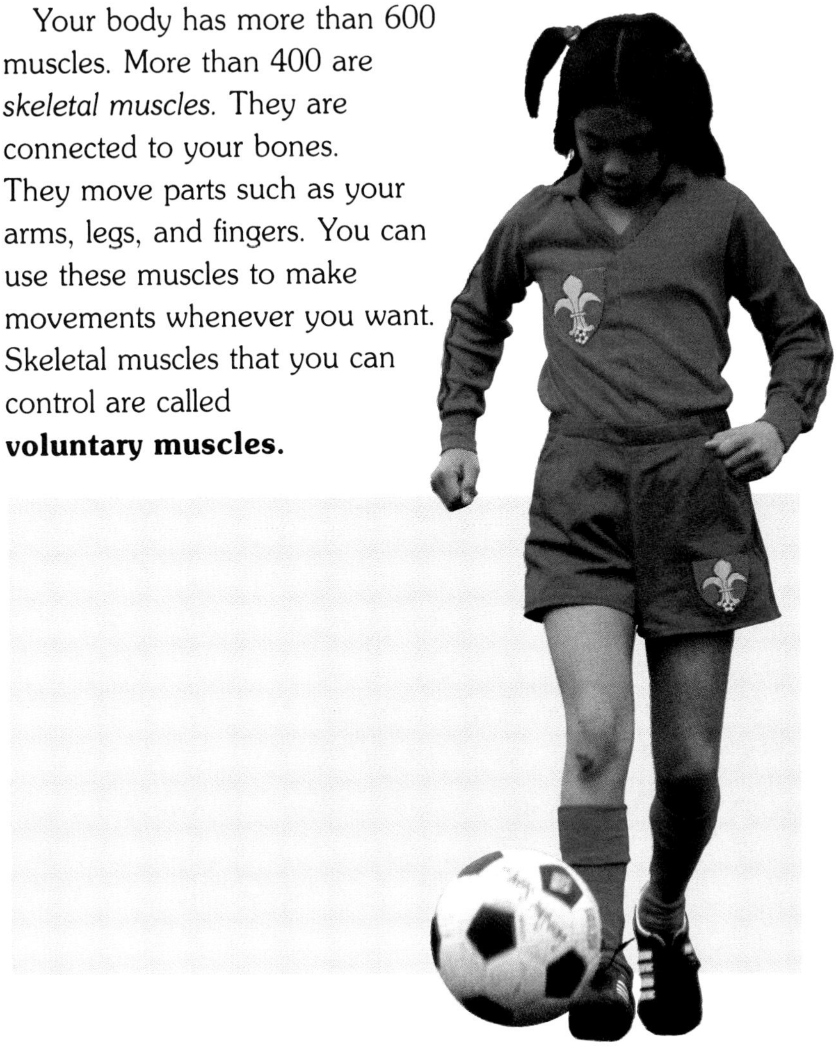

■ *The muscles that allow this girl to kick the ball are voluntary muscles.*

39

Another kind of muscle makes many of your organs work. Muscles of this kind are **involuntary muscles.** You cannot use involuntary muscles whenever you want. Your digestive system is lined with involuntary muscles. Chewing and swallowing food start these muscles working. You do not have to think about digesting food. You cannot easily change how an involuntary muscle works. Your heart is an involuntary muscle.

Both voluntary and involuntary muscles are made up of hundreds of tiny threads, or fibers, fastened together. Each fiber is a long bundle of muscle cells. There are three kinds of fibers. Each kind makes up a different kind of muscle tissue.

Striated Muscle. All your voluntary skeletal muscles are made of striated muscle tissue. This kind of muscle tissue is made up of striped fibers. You can see the stripes through a microscope. Striated muscle can move quickly. It is also very powerful, but it tires easily. Striated muscles can be very tiny, such as the muscles that cause each eye to move. Striated muscles also can be large, such as the muscle in the front of your thigh.

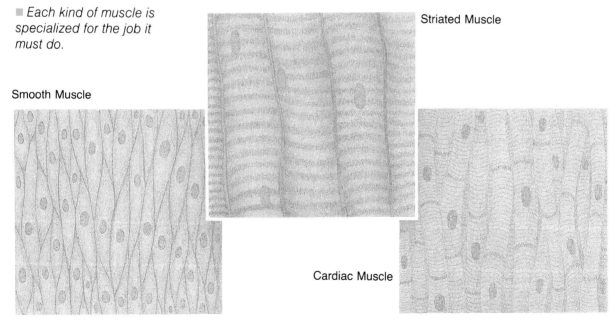

■ Each kind of muscle is specialized for the job it must do.

Smooth Muscle

Striated Muscle

Cardiac Muscle

40

Smooth Muscle. Most involuntary muscles have smooth fibers. That is why the tissue in your involuntary muscles is called smooth muscle. Smooth muscles are slower and weaker than striated ones. But they can work for a long time without tiring. Most smooth muscles protect the organs of the digestive, respiratory, and circulatory systems. These kinds of muscles control the size of blood-vessel openings.

Cardiac Muscle. Only your heart is made of cardiac muscle. It has stripes, like striated muscle tissue. It also has the speed and power of striated muscle. Yet the cells in cardiac muscle tissue look more like the cells in smooth muscle tissue. Like smooth muscle, cardiac muscle can work for a long time without tiring. That is why your heart can keep working day and night, all your life. It rests only between heartbeats. Like all muscle, cardiac muscle can be strengthened through regular exercise.

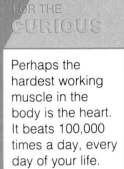

FOR THE CURIOUS

Perhaps the hardest working muscle in the body is the heart. It beats 100,000 times a day, every day of your life.

How Do Your Muscles Work?

All your muscles work in the same way. They tighten up, and then they relax. When muscles tighten up, they contract, or become shorter. Contracting a muscle makes it work. When a muscle relaxes, it stretches back out again. Muscles in the walls of your stomach pull together by contracting. When the muscles relax, your stomach stretches out. This action, repeated again and again, helps digest the food in your stomach.

Your skeletal muscles are connected to your bones. They move the parts of your body by pulling on your bones. The muscles pull the bones by contracting. Muscles can only pull. They cannot push.

To move the parts of your body, muscles almost always work in pairs. For example, when you open and close your hand, two different sets of muscles work together. One set of muscles pulls the fingers of your hand closed to make a fist. Another set of muscles pulls the same bones in the other direction to make your fingers straighten.

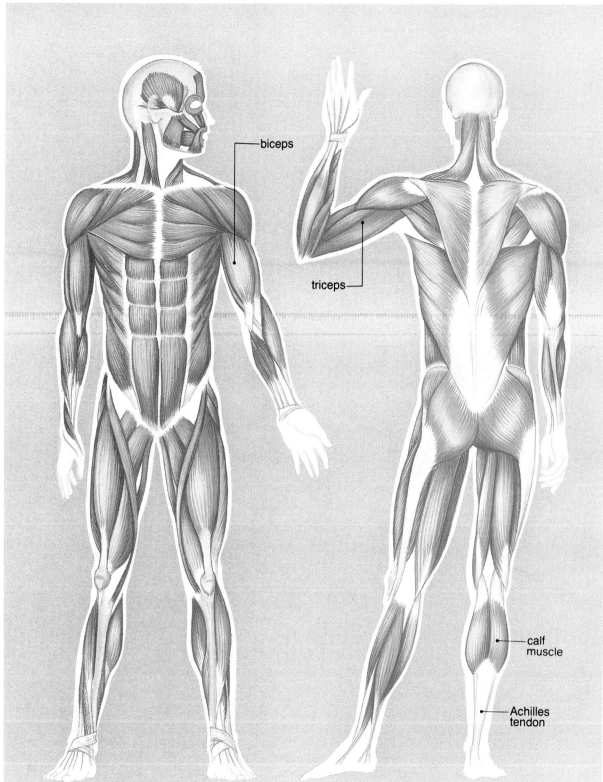

biceps

triceps

calf
muscle

Achilles
tendon

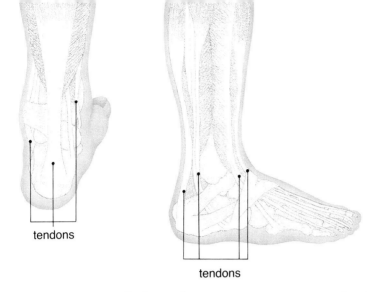

Tendons help you move because they connect muscles to bones.

tendons

tendons

Strong tissues called **tendons** connect your muscles to your bones. Some tendons are like cords. Some are more like flat straps. You can feel a tendon in the back of your ankle, just above your heel. You can also feel tendons in the back of your knee and in the bend of your elbow.

Not all of your voluntary muscles are connected to bones. Many small muscles in your face are connected to your skin. Some of these muscles help change the look on your face. They help you frown and smile. Some muscles are connected to your eyes. You are using these muscles right now to move your eyes as you read. The thinnest muscles in your body are the ones that open and shut your eyelids.

tendons (TEHN duhnz), tough tissues that attach your muscles to your bones.

STOP **REVIEW**
SECTION 3

REMEMBER?

1. What are the two main jobs of muscles?
2. What is the difference between voluntary muscle and involuntary muscle?
3. What happens to a muscle when it contracts?

THINK!

4. How can you have control but not have control over your cardiac muscle?
5. How are muscles important to the skeletal system?

Bionic Body Parts

Bionics is the science of designing and building new parts for the body. Some television and movie stories are about bionic creatures that look just like humans. In real life, no one has even come close to making such things. But scientists have made new body parts for almost every part in the body that can break or wear.

Most people know about lives that have been saved by artificial hearts. But other kinds of body-part replacements are not so widely known.

Scientists have been able to build new arms and legs, hands and feet, and fingers and toes. Almost 200,000 of these body parts are replaced every year.

A "bionic ear" has been developed for people who have hearing loss. A tiny device—something like a microphone—can be put inside a person's ear to create some hearing.

People who have been badly burned have benefited from receiving artificial skin. Scientists have also made bionic bones, veins, and even blood.

Today the body part that presents the greatest challenge to scientists is the human eye. The eye is joined to the brain by millions of tiny nerve threads. It would take more than one person's lifetime to connect that many nerve threads to an artificial eye.

Thinking Beyond

1. Besides the eye, what might be the most difficult body part or body system for bionic scientists to copy? Why?
2. Suppose scientists could make a whole human body. What might be some of the dangers of doing this?

■ *Replacements for body parts help some people be active.*

4 Your Digestive System

Although an apple is good for you, it is not much good to your body as an entire apple. Your body must change the apple into a form it can use. Your body breaks down food into the different nutrients that the body can use. **Nutrients** are the parts of food that give you energy, help you grow, or help you stay healthy.

How Does Digestion Begin?

Digestion begins when you chew food. Your teeth begin the work. Your thin, sharp incisors—your front teeth—cut up the food. Pointed cuspids next to the incisors tear the food. Wide molars at the back of your mouth grind and mash the food.

As you chew, your tongue moves the food around in your mouth. Your tongue helps mix the food with a digestive juice called *saliva*. Saliva in your mouth wets your food and makes it easy to swallow. Saliva also begins to break down the food into a liquid form your body can use.

When you swallow, muscles in your mouth and throat push the food into your esophagus. This is the tube that carries the food to your stomach. Muscles around the esophagus squeeze and relax to move the food along. The squeezing happens first at one place on the esophagus, then next to that place, and so on, moving along like a wave. This wavelike squeezing motion is called **peristalsis.** Peristalsis moves the food through the digestive system.

nutrients (NOO tree uhnts) parts of food that give you energy, help you grow, or help you stay healthy.

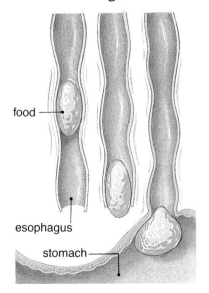

food

esophagus

stomach

■ *Peristalsis pushes food through the digestive system.*

peristalsis (pehr uh STAHL suhs), the wavelike squeezing motion of the digestive system.

THE DIGESTIVE SYSTEM

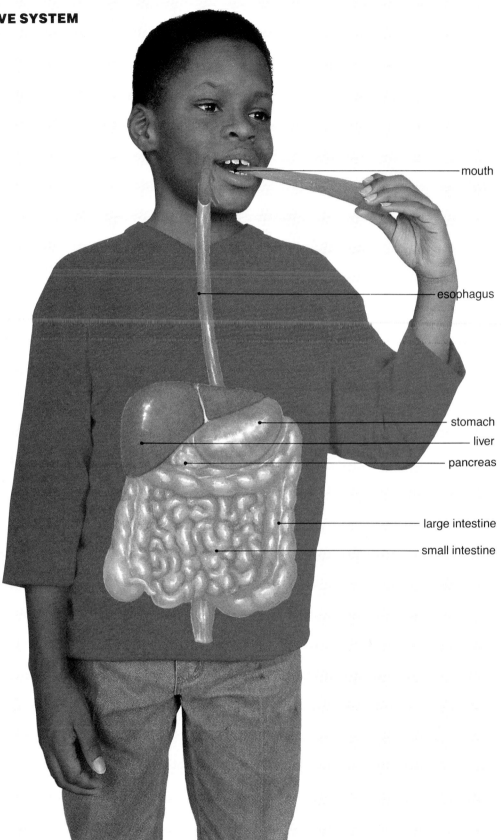

mouth

esophagus

stomach

liver

pancreas

large intestine

small intestine

When the food leaves your esophagus, it enters your stomach. The stomach wall is made of smooth muscles. Your stomach keeps squeezing and relaxing while food is inside it. This action helps mix and move the food. At the same time, juices pour out from the wall of your stomach. These juices are made of water, acid, and enzymes. An **enzyme** is a substance that helps a chemical reaction happen in the body. Some enzymes play an important part in the digestion of food. They help break down the food into its nutrients, which can then be used by cells.

Most kinds of foods stay in your stomach for about four hours. In that time, the foods become a thick liquid called *chyme*. As chyme forms, it moves into your small intestine.

Your small intestine is a long, coiled tube. It is only about as thick as your thumb. But for a person your age, it would measure about 15 feet (4 meters) in length.

How Do Nutrients Get to Your Cells?

Most digestion happens in the small intestine. This organ has a wall made of smooth, involuntary muscles. The muscles squeeze and relax to move your food along. The squeezing also mixes in the digestive juices that break your food into still smaller pieces.

In your small intestine, other juices also mix with the food as it moves through the digestive system. They help break down the nutrients in the food so that the nutrients can pass into the blood.

Two other organs—the pancreas and the liver—also make digestive juices. The juices are carried into the small intestine by small tubes from each organ. The liver is the largest organ inside the body. Your liver makes a juice called *bile*. This juice is stored in the **gallbladder.** Bile helps you digest fats in food. It is a salt solution that breaks down the fats into tiny particles. When bile is needed, the body senses this and some bile leaves your gallbladder. The bile enters your small intestine. Your **pancreas** is an organ near your stomach. It secretes digestive juices that break down carbohydrates, proteins, and fats.

enzyme (EHN zym), a substance that helps a chemical reaction happen in the body.

gallbladder (GAWL blad uhr), the pear-shaped organ lying under the liver; stores bile.

pancreas (PANG kree uhs), an organ near the stomach that makes juices for digesting foods.

47

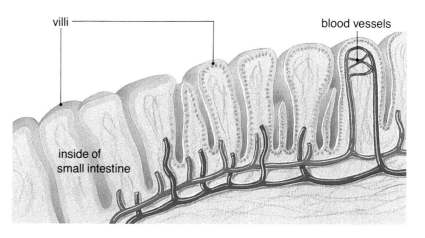

villi — blood vessels

inside of small intestine

■ *Villi line the wall of the small intestine. They let nutrients pass into the blood.*

villi (VIHL eye), tiny fingerlike growths inside the small intestine; nutrients pass into blood vessels inside them.

Look at the picture of the small intestine. Find the tiny fingerlike growths pointing in from the walls. These little "fingers" are called **villi.** Each one, called a villus, has a tiny blood vessel with a very thin wall. The nutrients from food pass through these walls and into your blood. The nutrients then move with your blood to every living cell in your body. Each cell takes out the nutrients it needs.

STOP REVIEW
SECTION 4

REMEMBER?

1. What does the esophagus do?
2. What makes food move through the digestive system?
3. Where does most of digestion take place?
4. How do nutrients get from your small intestine to your cells?

THINK!

5. What happens if a digestive organ, such as the pancreas or liver, fails to work as it should?
6. How is your muscular system important to digestion?

48

5 Your Excretory System

When you finish a meal, is there anything left on your plate? Most often there is. For example, you do not eat the bones from chicken or the peel from a banana. These are wastes, and you must get rid of them.

Your body has to get rid of wastes, too. The wastes form because you cannot use all parts of what you eat. Some wastes form in your cells as the cells use up nutrients. Other wastes never reach your cells. These are the parts of food that you cannot digest. You cannot digest fruit seeds, grain hulls, or the stringy parts of vegetables.

Certain organs in your body work to get rid of wastes from your blood, tissues, and cells. These organs make up your excretory system. Organs of the excretory system are found in several parts of your body. These organs are the kidneys, bladder, large intestine, skin, and lungs.

How Do Your Lungs Get Rid of Waste?

Your cells need **oxygen** to stay alive. You bring oxygen into your body every time you take a breath. The air you breathe reaches your lungs. These are two large spongelike organs inside your chest. From your lungs, oxygen moves into your blood. Your blood then takes the oxygen to all your cells.

KEY WORDS

oxygen
kidneys
urinary bladder

oxygen (AHK sih juhn), a gas needed by your cells.

■ *Every time you breathe out, your body gets rid of carbon dioxide, a waste gas.*

The air that you breathe out has a gas called carbon dioxide in it. Your cells make this gas as they work. Carbon dioxide is a cell waste. Your cells cannot use carbon dioxide and must get rid of it. Your blood carries carbon dioxide from all your cells to your lungs. There it passes out of your blood. It leaves your body when you breathe out.

How Do Your Kidneys and Bladder Get Rid of Wastes?

When a lot of wastes pile up in your house, you set them outside and someone takes them away. Your cells do almost the same thing. The wastes from cells are chemical wastes. Cells push wastes out, and your blood carries them away.

Cell wastes must not stay in your blood. They have to leave your body, or they will make you ill. Most of these chemical wastes are removed from your blood by your **kidneys.** These are two small, bean-shaped organs in your back, above your waist. Each is about the size of your fist.

kidneys (KIHD neez), bean-shaped organs in your back and above your waist; remove chemical wastes from your blood.

THE EXCRETORY SYSTEM

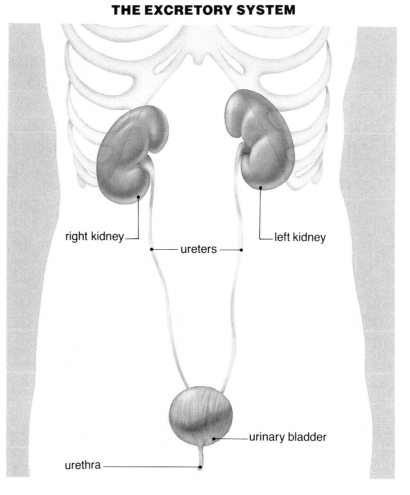

right kidney — | — ureters — | — left kidney

urinary bladder

urethra —

■ The kidneys and urinary bladder help the body get rid of wastes.

50

Your kidneys screen out certain cell wastes. They also remove extra water from your blood. From these wastes and water, your kidneys make a liquid called *urine*. It flows out of your kidneys through two narrow tubes called *ureters*. Urine goes into a baglike organ called the **urinary bladder.** Your urinary bladder is below your kidneys and close to the front of your body. The bladder has a layer of smooth muscle around it so it can stretch as it fills with urine and then contract when the urine is gone. Urine is stored in your bladder until it leaves your body. The urine flows through another tube, called the *urethra*, and passes out of your body.

urinary bladder (YUR uh nehr ee • BLAD uhr), the baglike organ that holds urine.

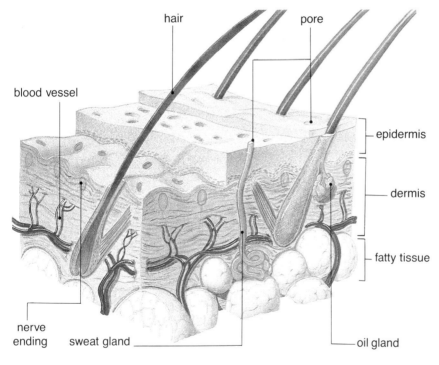

Some cell wastes and some excess water leave the body through pores in the skin.

hair

pore

blood vessel

epidermis

dermis

fatty tissue

nerve ending

sweat gland

oil gland

How Does Your Skin Get Rid of Wastes?

Some of your cell wastes and some extra water leave your body through your skin. Sweat glands in your skin take water, salt, and other wastes from your blood. When you sweat, these wastes leave your body.

Sweat, or perspiration, leaves your body through very small openings in your skin. These openings are called *pores.*

The sweat moves wastes out of your body and onto your skin. The water in sweat evaporates. The other wastes stay on your skin until you wash them away. Sweating is also a way your body cools itself.

How Does Your Large Intestine Get Rid of Wastes?

The wastes from undigested food move through your small intestine into your large intestine. The large intestine is wider and shorter than the small intestine. It is about 1 inch (2.5 centimeters) across and a little more than 3 feet (1 meter) long.

The undigested food that enters your large intestine is a thick liquid. In the large intestine most of the water in this thick liquid is removed and the wastes become solid. As the wastes become solid, they push against the wall of the large intestine. Muscles in the intestine's wall then contract. The muscles push the wastes out of the body. This action is called a *bowel movement*. It may happen up to 20 hours or more after you eat. What you eat and drink can change this amount of time.

STOP **REVIEW**
SECTION 5

REMEMBER?

1. What are the chief organs of the excretory system?
2. What happens to wastes that move out of your body and onto your skin in the form of sweat?
3. Where is carbon dioxide made in the body? How does the body get rid of it?

THINK!

4. Why does your urinary bladder have a smooth layer of muscle around it?
5. Why are properly working sweat glands important to having good health?

6 Your Respiratory System

Squeeze a sponge in your fist. While still squeezing, put your fist into a bowl of water. Then open your fist so the sponge can expand. After a minute, take the sponge out of the water. Squeeze it over an empty pan. Notice how much water the sponge took up when it had room to expand. The way the sponge acted in water is very much like the way your lungs act when they fill with air. This action of your lungs happens when you breathe.

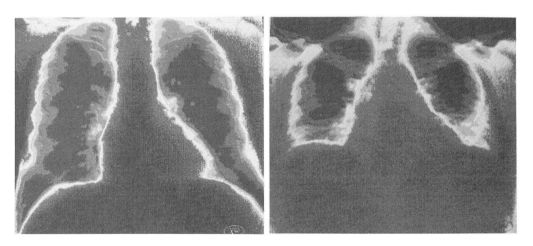

The system that you use for breathing is your respiratory system. Breathing is one of the most important jobs of your body. You can go for several days without eating food. You can go for many hours without drinking water. But you can live only a few minutes without breathing.

■ These X rays show the lungs when the person has breathed in, left, and when the person has breathed out, right.

How Do You Breathe In and Out?

Your lungs have no muscle tissue. They cannot draw in air on their own. Muscles around your lungs help you breathe.

Think of your chest as a box that holds your lungs. Your shoulders form the top of the box. Your ribs and the muscles connected to them form the sides. A sheet of muscle called the **diaphragm** is the bottom of the box. It lies under your lungs.

diaphragm (DY uh fram), the sheet of muscle at the bottom of your chest, under your lungs; helps you breathe.

53

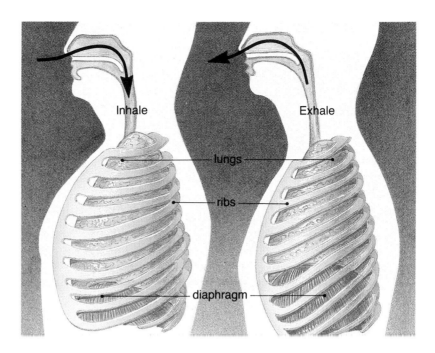

■ *When you breathe in, the diaphragm contracts, pulling air into your lungs. When you breathe out, the diaphragm relaxes, forcing air out of your lungs.*

Inhale   Exhale

lungs
ribs
diaphragm

When you breathe in, your diaphragm contracts. It pulls down, away from your lungs. The muscles between your ribs contract to pull your ribs up and out, making the box larger. Your lungs have more room, so they fill up, like balloons, with air.

When you breathe out, your diaphragm and rib muscles relax. The box of your chest closes around your lungs. Air rushes out of your lungs and leaves your body through your nose or mouth.

How Is Air Prepared for Your Lungs?

The air you breathe is cleaned before it reaches your lungs. It is also warmed and made moist. Cold, dry, or dirty air can harm your lungs.

Your nose begins cleaning and warming the air you breathe. Hairs in your nose trap some of the dust and other matter.

Some dust and dirt get past your nose hairs. Most of this matter sticks to mucus in your respiratory system. *Mucus* is a sticky substance that lines your nose and the tubes that go to your lungs.

The tubes that go to your lungs are lined with tiny hairlike cell parts called **cilia.** Cilia act as a living brush.

cilia (SIHL ee uh), tiny hairlike parts of special cells that line the trachea and bronchial tubes.

54

They are always moving, brushing mucus up toward your throat and away from your lungs. At the same time, your cells make fresh mucus to replace what is brushed away.

From time to time, you swallow the mucus that builds up in your throat. Most often, you do not notice yourself doing this. The mucus and the matter trapped in it go into your digestive system. The matter is then removed from your body along with solid wastes from your food.

How Does Air Enter Your Body?

Air can enter your body through your nose. This air passes through hollow spaces in your nose called *nasal passages*. Air can also enter through your mouth. Air moves from your mouth or nasal passages into a tube called the **trachea,** or windpipe.

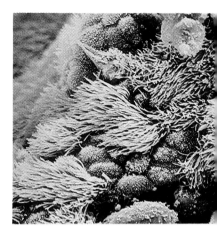

■ Cilia line the walls of the respiratory system.

trachea (TRAY kee uh), the windpipe, or passage through which air moves.

THE RESPIRATORY SYSTEM

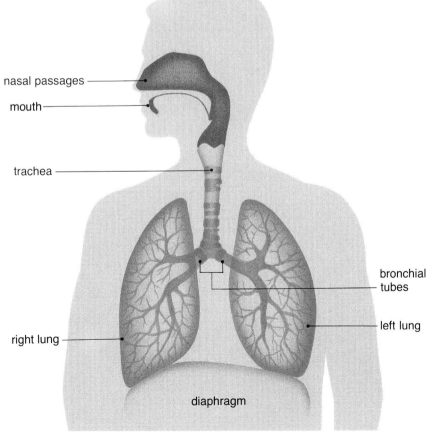

nasal passages

mouth

trachea

bronchial tubes

left lung

right lung

diaphragm

■ Air passes through the trachea and bronchial tubes to reach the lungs.

55

bronchial tubes
(BRAHNG kee uhl •
TOOBZ), two tubes at the
bottom of the trachea;
lead into the lungs.

alveoli (al VEE uh ly),
hollow pockets where
respiration takes place in
your lungs.

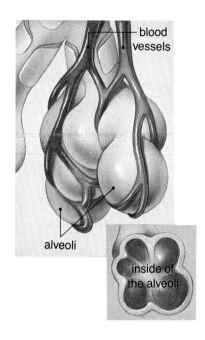

The alveoli allow
oxygen to move into the
blood as carbon dioxide
leaves the blood.

The bottom of your trachea divides into two branches
called **bronchial tubes.** One bronchial tube, or bronchus,
goes into each of your lungs. In your lungs, the bronchial
tubes divide into smaller and smaller branches. These look
something like the branches of an upside-down tree.

The smallest branches end in hollow pockets in your
lungs. These hollow pockets are called **alveoli.** Under a
microscope, they look like bunches of grapes. Your lungs
have thousands of alveoli. When you breathe in, the alveoli
fill up like tiny balloons.

The walls of the alveoli are very thin. The walls of the
blood vessels beside the alveoli are also very thin. Oxygen
from the air moves through these walls into your blood. At
the same time, carbon dioxide moves from your blood into
your alveoli. The exchange of these two gases is called
respiration.

STOP REVIEW
SECTION 6

REMEMBER?

1. What body parts does air pass through to reach the
   alveoli?
2. Why are the walls of the alveoli thin?
3. What happens when you breathe in and out?

THINK!

4. Why do other body systems depend on the respiratory
   system?
5. How might breathing smoke over a long time affect the
   respiratory system?

7 Your Circulatory System

Your circulatory system has three important parts. They are the blood, the blood vessels, and the heart. Blood is the liquid that picks up cell wastes and moves nutrients and oxygen all through your body. Blood vessels are the tubes that carry your blood. Your heart is the organ that pumps your blood to keep it moving.

Your circulatory system carries what your cells need to all parts of your body. This system picks up oxygen from your lungs and nutrients from your small intestine. It carries the oxygen and nutrients to all your cells. Your circulatory system takes everything to your cells that they need to stay alive. It also carries wastes away from your cells.

What Is in Your Blood?

One part of blood is called *plasma*. It is pale yellow and made mostly of water. It carries nutrients to your cells.

Blood is filled with different kinds of cells. The red color of your blood comes from *red blood cells*. These carry oxygen from your lungs to the cells throughout your body. Red blood cells also carry carbon dioxide from your body's cells to your lungs.

▦ *The solid part of blood contains white blood cells, left; platelets, center; and red blood cells, right.*

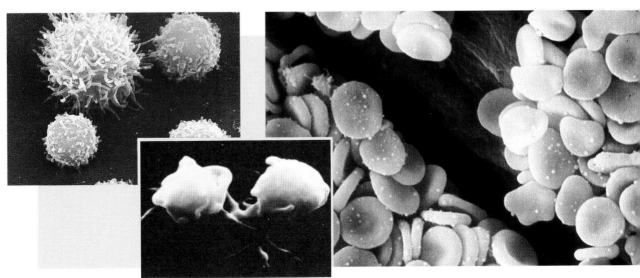

Each beat of your heart pushes blood into the arteries with force. Blood in arteries flows away from the heart. Blood cannot flow backward. Blood in veins does not flow with the same force as blood in arteries. Valves in veins keep slow-moving blood from flowing backward.

White blood cells are large cells in your blood that help your body fight microbes that have entered the blood. These microbes are tiny living creatures that can make you ill when they are inside your body. White blood cells work to destroy the microbes before they have a chance to start multiplying.

The cell fragments in your blood are called *platelets.* They help make your blood get thick, or clot, if you get a cut. The thick blood makes a scab, which seals the cut. The scab helps keep you from bleeding while your cut is healing.

■ *This photograph of a scab forming over a wound was taken through an electron microscope.*

How Does Blood Move Throughout the Body?

You have three kinds of blood vessels. **Arteries** carry blood away from your heart. **Veins** carry blood back to your heart. **Capillaries** connect arteries to veins. Capillaries are thinner than the hairs on your head. They wind among all your body's cells. Every cell in your body is near a capillary.

THE CIRCULATORY SYSTEM

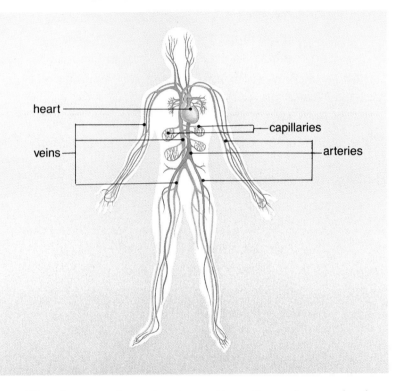

■ *Blood travels throughout the body in arteries, capillaries, and veins.*

Blood moves in a circular pattern through your body. Blood is pumped out of your heart and enters your arteries. The blood flows into smaller and smaller arteries. Finally, the blood flows into your capillaries. Blood from your capillaries empties into tiny veins. These veins join larger veins. Near your heart, the veins are very large. They carry the blood right into your heart. The heart then pumps the blood out again through your arteries.

Capillaries have very thin walls. Nutrients and oxygen can pass through the walls. Capillaries in your lungs let oxygen into your blood. Capillaries in the villi of your small intestine let digested nutrients into your blood. Blood carries the nutrients and oxygen to other capillaries, which in turn let the nutrients and oxygen out into your cells. These capillaries also pick up wastes from your cells. The blood then carries the wastes to the organs in your body that remove wastes.

How Does Your Heart Work?

Your blood never stops moving through your body. If it stopped, you would die in a few minutes from not having oxygen in your cells. Your blood keeps moving because your heart never stops pumping it.

Your heart is the hardest-working muscle in your body. It constantly receives blood from the veins that connect to it. A part of the heart fills with blood. With each beat, the heart forces the blood out through your arteries.

After each beat, your heart rests for less than a second. It fills with blood while it rests, and then it beats again. It has more power than any other muscle in your body. Therefore, the heart is considered the strongest muscle in the body.

Your heart is really two pumps in one. The left and right sides of your heart are separate pumps. The right side receives blood from all over your body and pumps it to your lungs. The left side receives blood from your lungs and pumps it to the rest of your body.

■ *Blood enters the right side of the heart from the body. Then it leaves the right side of the heart and goes to the lungs for oxygen. It returns to the left side of the heart and then is pumped to the rest of the body.*

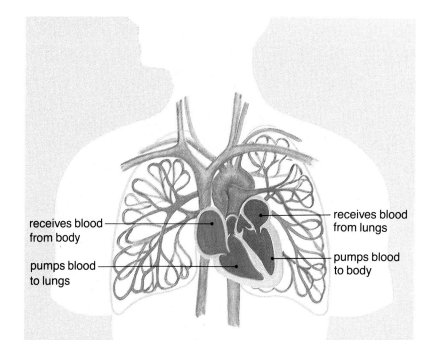

receives blood from body

pumps blood to lungs

receives blood from lungs

pumps blood to body

Your blood goes out the right side of your heart, through your lungs, and then to the left side of the heart. Then it goes out the left side of your heart, through the rest of your body, and back to the right side. The process of blood moving from the heart, through the body, and back to the heart is called *circulation*.

REVIEW
SECTION 7

STOP

REMEMBER?

1. What are the parts of blood?
2. Name three kinds of blood vessels.
3. How does your heart work?

THINK!

4. What happens to cells that do not get a good supply of blood?
5. Which blood vessels, do you think, contain the most oxygen? Why?

Thinking About Your Health

Check Your Health Habits

Answer the following questions to learn how proper health habits are related to your wellness and your body systems:

■ What body systems have an effect on good posture? How might good posture have an effect on your appearance and wellness? How might posture affect your internal organs?

■ What body systems are affected by a habit of regular exercise? How do your exercise habits contribute to both your appearance and your wellness?

■ What body systems are affected by healthful eating habits? How do eating habits that are healthful contribute to your appearance and wellness?

An Interview with an Internist

Ray Henderson helps people care for their body systems. He is a physician who practices internal medicine in Indianapolis, Indiana.

What is an internist?

An internist is a physician who has a certain interest in the health of the body systems. Many internists study only one body system. They learn all they can about how that system works. They also learn the many ways to care for that system.

I am a cardiologist. That means I study how the heart and the rest of the circulatory system work. Another internist might study the respiratory system or any of the other body systems. Some internists study more than one body system because the systems work so closely together. They might study the cardiorespiratory system, which is the circulatory and respiratory systems together.

How do all the body systems work together to keep a person healthy?

When all your body parts are healthy, the body works well as a whole. All the systems are needed for the whole body to work at its best. The body cannot work properly unless all the systems in the body work properly.

What happens when one body system does not work well?

A person might feel pain or become ill. That person might visit an internist, who would try to find out what is causing the problem. Once the cause is found, the internist can tell the person ways to treat the problem. Sometimes an operation is needed. Because the person has a problem, he or she often learns more healthful ways to care for the body systems.

What are some healthful ways to care for the body systems?

A daily schedule of exercise, rest, and sleep is good for all the systems. So is eating healthful foods. It also helps to avoid doing things that might directly

■ Dr. Henderson helps people who have hearts that do not work properly.

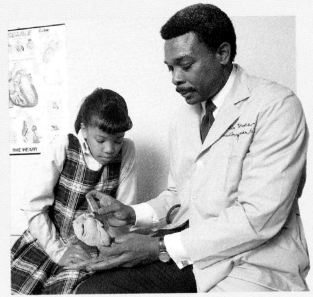

Dr. Henderson tells his patients how to prevent heart problems in later life.

What do you like best about your work?

I like to solve problems. When a person who is ill comes to see me, I have to find the reason for the illness. That is one problem I have to solve. Then I have to find a way to make the person well again. That is a second problem I have to solve. It makes me feel good to know I can solve these problems most of the time and help people get well and stay healthy.

harm the body systems. Using tobacco, alcohol, and illegal drugs can damage some of the body systems. Once they are damaged, they may never work properly again.

Was there some reason you chose to become an internist and not some other kind of physician?

A person who is thinking about becoming a physician has to make many choices. One choice is what kind of physician to become. My main interests were practicing internal medicine or being a surgeon. A surgeon operates to correct health problems of the body systems. An internist treats people with medicines. I wanted to treat people with medicines.

What kind of person makes a good internist?

Someone who is curious and likes to learn new things will make a good internist. It also helps to be good at problem solving. And if you cannot solve a problem right away, you should be willing to keep working hard until it can be solved.

Learn more about people who work as physicians of internal medicine. Interview an internist. Or write for information to the American Medical Association, Department of Allied Health Education and Accreditation, 535 North Dearborn Street, Chicago, IL 60610.

Main Ideas

- All parts of your body must work together to keep your whole body working smoothly.
- Your skeletal system forms a framework to hold your body up and give you your general size and shape.
- Your muscular system helps your body move, gives your body shape, and protects certain organs.
- Your digestive system breaks down foods into nutrients your cells can use.
- Your excretory system gets rid of wastes that your body cannot use.
- Your respiratory system helps your body take in oxygen and get rid of carbon dioxide.
- Your circulatory system carries oxygen and nutrients to your cells. It also carries wastes away from your cells.

Key Words

Write the numbers 1 to 15 in your health notebook or on a separate sheet of paper. After each number, copy the sentence and fill in the missing term. Page numbers in ( ) tell you where to look in the chapter if you need help.

tissues (31)
body system (32)
ligaments (34)
cartilage (35)
marrow (38)
voluntary muscles (39)
involuntary muscles (40)

tendons (43)
peristalsis (45)
enzyme (47)
urinary bladder (51)
diaphragm (53)
trachea (55)
alveoli (56)
arteries (59)

1. Tough bands of tissue that hold the bones together are ___?___ .

2. Muscles that you have control over are ___?___ .

3. A baglike organ called the ___?___ holds urine in the body.

4. Air moves from your mouth and nasal passages into a tube called the ___?___ .

5. Cells work together in groups called ___?___ .

6. Tough tissues that attach your muscles to your bones are ___?___ .

7. Hollow pockets where respiration takes place in the lungs are ___?___ .

8. A sheet of muscle that helps you breathe and is under your lungs is the ___?___ .

9. Food is moved down your esophagus by a wavelike squeezing motion called ___?___ .

10. The soft tissue in the shaft of a bone is ___?___ .

11. Blood vessels that carry blood away from your heart are ___?___ .

12. Several organs working together for one purpose make up a ___?___ .

13. Tough, stiff tissues that are found between the bones of most joints are ___?___ .

14. Muscles that you do not have control over are ___?___ .

15. An ___?___ helps a chemical reaction happen in the body.

Write the numbers 16 to 31 on your paper. After each number, write a sentence that defines the term. Page numbers in ( ) tell you where to look in the chapter if you need help.

16. cells (31)
17. organs (32)
18. skeleton (34)
19. joint (34)
20. vertebrae (35)
21. pelvis (37)
22. nutrients (45)
23. gallbladder (47)
24. pancreas (47)
25. villi (48)
26. oxygen (49)
27. kidneys (50)
28. cilia (54)
29. bronchial tubes (56)
30. veins (59)
31. capillaries (59)

Remembering What You Learned

Page numbers in ( ) tell you where to look in the chapter if you need help.

1. What kinds of joints are your shoulders? Your elbows? (34)

2. What makes it possible for your spine to bend? (35)

3. What organ in your body is made of cardiac muscle? (41)

4. How does food get from your small intestine into your blood? (47–48)

5. What organs in your body work to get rid of waste? (49–52)

6. What happens at the same time oxygen moves from your alveoli into your blood? (56)

7. Where does undigested food go from your small intestine? (52)

8. What muscles in your chest help you breathe in and out? (53–54)

9. What are four main parts of your blood? (57–58)

10. What different jobs do the right and left sides of your heart do? (60)

Thinking About What You Learned

1. How would you be affected if your bones were made of only compact bone?

2. What kinds of muscle keep working even while you sleep? Why?

3. Why are fluids important in digesting foods?

4. Why is sweat a waste product?

5. How are capillaries important to your muscular system, digestive system, and respiratory system?

Writing About What You Learned

Write three paragraphs describing ways you can protect and care for your body systems. You may include safety actions to prevent harm. You may include daily habits and other regular activities that help your systems.

Applying What You Learned

MATHEMATICS

Your hand has many joints in it. Count how many joints you use in your hand when you make a fist. How many joints in your whole body can you safely move at once?

Modified True or False

Write the numbers 1 to 15 in your health notebook or on a separate sheet of paper. After each number, write *true* or *false* to describe the sentence. If the sentence is false, also write a term that replaces the underlined term and makes the sentence true.

1. The main job of your digestive system is to get rid of wastes that your body cannot use.

2. Your bones are held together at the joints by ligaments.

3. The cranium is the only bone in your skull that moves.

4. The muscles lining your digestive system are voluntary muscles.

5. Food is moved through the digestive system by peristalsis.

6. When you sweat, your body gets rid of cell wastes and extra water.

7. The tubes to your lungs are lined with tiny hairlike cell parts called alveoli.

8. The hollow space inside the bone shaft contains marrow.

9. Your heart is cardiac muscle.

10. Bile is stored in the pancreas.

11. Urine leaves the body by the villi.

12. The circulatory system takes needed nutrients and oxygen to the cells.

13. Muscles are attached to bones by tendons.

14. The vertebrae support your upper body when you sit.

15. Your respiratory system helps your body move.

Short Answer

Write the numbers 16 to 23 on your paper. Write a complete sentence to answer each question.

16. Why are cells the most important parts of your body?

17. Why does your body need muscles?

18. In what ways do your respiratory and circulatory systems work together?

19. How do the nutrients in your small intestine reach your cells?

20. What is the purpose of your rib cage?

21. How are striated muscle and smooth muscle alike?

22. What happens to food when it is in your stomach?

23. What happens to food that you cannot digest?

Essay

Write the numbers 24 and 25 on your paper. Write paragraphs with complete sentences to answer each question.

24. Explain how you can be more responsible for your own health if you know how your body works.

25. Describe the path that food follows from the time you put it in your mouth until 20 hours later.

ACTIVITIES FOR HOME OR SCHOOL

Projects to Do

1. Hold your hands together with the palms apart and the fingertips touching. Your hands should make a shape like an upside-down letter *V*. Have a classmate gently push his or her hand between yours, starting from between your palms. Then have your classmate try the same thing starting from your fingertips. Which is easier? Your hands will be acting like a valve in one of your veins. Your classmate's hand will be acting like your blood. What does this investigation tell you about how your valves work?

2. Pretend you are holding a tennis ball in your hand. Your fingers will be slightly curled in this position. Squeeze your fingers shut one by one, in order, until you have made a fist. Then open your fist and start over. Squeeze your fingers shut again in the same order. Repeat this action quickly and smoothly many times. Try to make it look as if waves are moving through your hand. You will be making movements something like the peristalsis that moves food through your digestive system.

Information to Find

1. What treatment is a physician likely to give to a person who tears a ligament or "pulls" it (stretches it too far)? What is the treatment for a damaged tendon? To find out, ask a physician or your school nurse.

■ These students are showing how a one-way valve works.

2. Scientists continue to study the actions of different kinds of white blood cells that help fight illness. These cells and their actions are part of the body's *immune system*. Find out about the body's immune system. Your librarian can help you find magazine or newspaper articles about this topic.

Books to Read

Here are some books you can look for in your school library or the public library to find more information about your body systems and how to care for them.

Crump, Donald J. *Your Wonderful Body!* National Geographic Society.

Donner, Carol. *The Magic Anatomy Book.* W. H. Freeman.

GROWING AND CHANGING

You are always growing and changing. You started growing even before you were born. Sometimes you grow much faster than at other times. You will soon be reaching a time in your life when your body will grow and change quickly.

Growing up can be very exciting. Many changes happen. Some of the changes are physical. Other changes are emotional. You will also change intellectually and socially. Knowing how you and all other people grow will help you better understand the changes that are taking place. Taking good care of yourself by using good health and safety habits will help you grow up healthy.

GETTING READY TO LEARN

Key Questions

- Why is it important to learn how your body grows?
- Why is it important to know how you feel about the way your body grows?
- What can you do to help yourself feel good about your body's growth?
- How can you take more responsibility for helping your body grow as it should?

Main Chapter Sections

1 Stages of Growth
2 How You Grow
3 How Two Body Systems Change
4 How You Control Your Body

1 Stages of Growth

KEY WORDS

prenatal growth
infancy
childhood
adolescence
adulthood

Janice, her baby brother, and her mother are at her great-grandmother's birthday party. Janice's great-grandmother is 80 years old. Many changes can take place in the body in 80 years. Janice can see many physical differences between her baby brother and her great-grandmother. She can also see differences between herself and her great-grandmother. Janice often wonders what she will be like when she is an adult and when she is old. She wonders if she will live as long as her great-grandmother. Perhaps she will live even longer!

The members of this family are in many different stages of growth.

How Have You Grown?

You may not know it, but you have already passed through some important stages of growing. To someone younger than you, like a brother or sister, you seem very grown-up. To other people, like your parents and teachers, you still have a lot of growing up to do. All people go through the same stages of growing. The stages come at slightly different ages for different people, however.

Prenatal Growth. You began growing inside your mother's body as one tiny fertilized cell. That one cell was about the size of the period at the end of this sentence. You

Jarmaine is older and much taller than his sister.

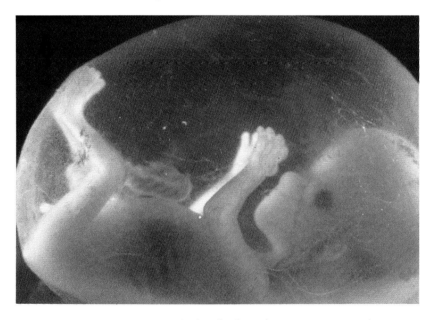

Prenatal growth occurs rapidly inside the mother's body.

grew inside your mother's body for about nine months, until you were born. The stage of growth inside the mother's body is called the **prenatal growth** stage. The word *prenatal* means "before birth."

You grew and developed faster during the prenatal stage than you *ever* will again. Your body grew from one cell. That one cell divided again and again into many cells. After about two weeks, your body was made up of more than 1 million cells. And you were still growing!

Many changes took place during your prenatal growth. Cells formed the tissues that make up the organs of your body.

prenatal growth (pree NAYT uhl • GROHTH), the stage of human growth that takes place inside the mother's body; usually lasts nine months.

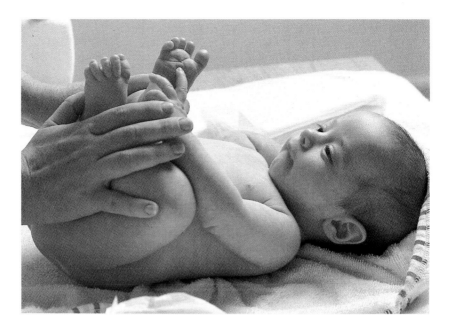

All the major organs of your body, such as your heart, brain, stomach, and lungs, formed before you were born. Groups of organs formed body systems, which also developed during your prenatal growth.

Most human babies weigh between 5 and 10 pounds (between 2.3 and 4.5 kilograms) when they are born. At birth, you were about 3 million times bigger than the first cell of your body!

infancy (IHN fuhn see), the second stage of human growth; begins at birth and lasts two years.

Infancy. The day you were born was the beginning of your second stage of growth. This is called the **infancy** stage. Infant is another word for baby. Your infancy lasted from your birth until you were about 2 years old.

Many changes take place during infancy. Babies grow very rapidly. By the time most babies are one year old, they often weigh three times as much as when they were born. During infancy, your body became stronger and better controlled. As time passed, you learned to move your head from side to side. You also learned to sit up and stand alone.

Along with physical changes, many other changes took place during your infancy. You learned to recognize people, places, and the things around you. You learned to understand what was said to you. You learned to make sounds and talk. Parents and others close to your family helped shape your emotional development. All infants need to be cared for and to learn to trust people. They also need to have people show them that they are loved. Even though you most likely do not remember your time as an infant, your infancy prepared you for the next stage of growth.

As a baby grows he or she learns to recognize faces and to walk.

Childhood. By age 2, you were no longer a baby. You were entering the next stage of growth, called **childhood.** Childhood lasts about ten years—from about age 2 to about age 12.

Physical changes keep taking place during childhood. You grow in size at a slow and steady rate. Your body becomes stronger, and you develop more control over the way it moves. Catching a thrown ball and using paintbrushes and pencils are skills you learn in childhood. Other changes also take place during childhood. For example, your primary teeth fall out, and most of your permanent teeth grow in.

childhood (CHYLD hud), the third stage of human growth; lasts for ten years, from age 2 to 12.

73

During childhood, you continue to grow intellectually, emotionally, and socially. You learn to talk, read, and write so that you can communicate with other people. You earn new responsibilities and privileges in your family. Some families use allowances to help children learn to finish chores and to manage money. You make friends with other boys and girls. Making friends is an important part of your emotional and social growth.

■ *Social growth, as well as physical, emotional, and intellectual growth, occurs during childhood.*

During childhood you learn many health skills that become habits. You learn how to take care of your body: how to brush your teeth; how to wash your hands, hair, and body; and how to care for your body systems. You also learn how to keep from becoming ill. The good health habits you learn as a child can help you the rest of your life. Poor habits, such as not washing your hands at certain times and not eating a balanced diet, make it more likely that you will become ill.

How Will You Grow?

You have already passed through three stages of growth. But your growth does not stop here. More changes are yet to come. You will soon be entering a new stage of growth.

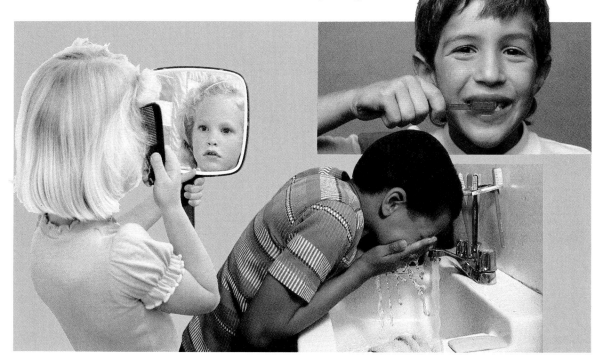

Adolescence. The next stage of growth you will go through is called **adolescence.** Adolescence most often lasts from age 10 or later to about age 18. During adolescence, your body once again grows very quickly and changes in many ways.

During adolescence, the body starts to develop many of the physical characteristics of an adult. For example, new hair begins to grow on different parts of the body. The body also changes as you begin to look more like an adult. This time of change is called *puberty.*

Adolescence, however, is more than just the physical changes you can see or feel. You will learn to do more things on your own and will make more choices on your own. You will earn more privileges by showing adults, especially your parents, how well you can handle tasks, finish jobs, and be trusted. You may start earning money by doing extra jobs. The changes that take place during

Good health habits, such as cleaning your body, brushing your teeth, and combing your hair, are developed during childhood.

adolescence (ad uhl EHS uhns), the fourth stage of human growth; lasts from about age 10 to age 18.

75

■ *Privileges are earned during adolescence by being responsible for tasks.*

adulthood (uh DUHLT hud), the last stage of human growth; follows adolescence.

■ *Being an adult often means taking on the responsibilities of being a parent.*

adolescence can be exciting. They make you feel that you are really growing up. The changes also mean you have more responsibilities and more choices. They help prepare you for the next stage of growth.

Adulthood. The growth stage that follows adolescent growth is **adulthood.** When are you really an adult? There is no one sign showing that a person has reached adulthood. You might look like an adult as adolescent growth ends. At that time, you will have reached your full height. All your body systems will be fully formed.

But there is more to adulthood than just looking like an adult. You will keep growing in other ways. You will keep growing emotionally, intellectually, and socially. If you marry, you will share many responsibilities with your partner. If you and your marriage partner have children, you both will have more responsibilities. You will make many important choices about where to work, where to live, how to spend money, and how to raise a family.

You will keep growing and changing in adulthood. As you become an older adult, your body will once again change physically. The good health habits you have been using all your life, however, will still help keep you healthy.

You can look forward to a lot of growth in adolescence and adulthood. Think about the question "How long does it take to grow up?" The answer is "Your whole life." People are always growing, no matter what their ages are.

STOP REVIEW
SECTION 1

REMEMBER?

1. What are the major stages of growth?
2. Describe what makes each stage different from the others.

THINK!

3. How might knowing how to make decisions help you as an adolescent?
4. How does an older adult keep growing?

Arranging a Sequence

Place the following stages of growth in the proper sequence from the first to the last:
- adolescence
- prenatal growth
- childhood
- adulthood
- infancy

Thinking About Your Health

What Are You Doing to Care for Your Growing Body?

In the picture is a package that represents your body. The package represents all the changes you have experienced or will go through as you grow. Use cardboard to make a copy of the package. Cover the outside of the package with pictures from magazines or with your own drawings and words. The pictures and words should show what you are doing to take care of your growing body. Cover the whole package with pictures and words as if you were wrapping it as a gift.

2 How You Grow

You cannot tell, but you are growing right now. Thousands of new cells are being made every minute. Your body grows by making more cells. Your body will make new cells all your life, even after you stop growing taller. In most body systems, new cells take the place of old cells that wear out.

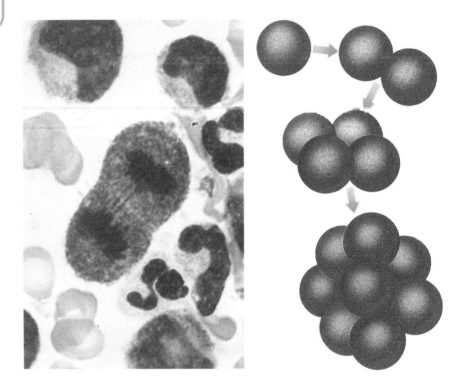

■ *Your body grows because it makes new cells. The long cell in the left photograph is dividing into two cells. During cell division, right, one cell becomes two.*

How Does Your Body Grow?

One cell turns into many cells through cell division. One cell divides and becomes two cells. The two new cells grow to a certain size, and then they both divide. They become four cells. In this way, the cells can increase in number. But all cells do not keep multiplying as fast as they can.

Cells divide at different speeds, depending on what kind of cells they are and where they are in the body. Some cells, such as skin cells, divide quickly and form all during your life. Bone cells, however, stop forming new cells after a

Milk provides many nutrients needed for bones to grow and become strong.

bone reaches a certain size. For example, the bones of the middle ear stop growing at a very young age. The body sends certain signals to cells to tell them when to stop dividing.

When one cell grows to a certain size, it divides. The two new cells are small. Cells grow by using nutrients to help cell parts grow. Your body uses nutrients to build all your cells. In this way, nutrients build your tissues and organs, which are made up of many cells. For example, bone cells turn certain nutrients into bone matter. In that way, your bone cells grow and multiply in number. This growth causes your bones to become stronger.

How Does Your Body Control Your Growth?

One system in your body controls your physical growth. It is your **endocrine system.** It controls the way most of your cells change and the way they use nutrients. It balances the working of your tissues and organs.

endocrine system (EHN duh kruhn • SIHS tuhm), the body system that controls your physical growth.

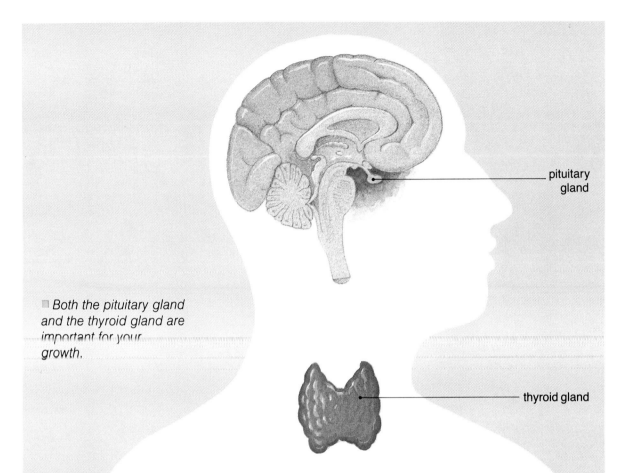

pituitary gland

thyroid gland

Both the pituitary gland and the thyroid gland are important for your growth.

gland, any organ that makes, stores, or gives off a certain substance inside the body.

hormones (HAWR mohnz), chemical messengers that control the actions of cells and certain organs in your body.

thyroid (THY royd), an endocrine gland; makes a hormone that controls the rate at which your cells get energy from nutrients.

Your endocrine system is made up of organs called endocrine glands. A **gland** is any organ that makes, stores, or gives off a certain substance inside the body. Endocrine glands are found in many different parts of the body. They make hormones.

Hormones are substances that control cells and certain organs in your body. Hormones are like chemical messengers. They are carried to parts of the body where they have very specific effects. The endocrine glands put their hormones into the circulatory system. The blood then carries the hormones to the cells of the body.

You have an endocrine gland in your neck that is called the thyroid. The **thyroid** makes a hormone that controls the rate at which your cells use the energy from nutrients. This hormone also makes sure that you have some nutrients to build new cells. The hormones from the thyroid can change your weight and the way you feel.

Some endocrine glands make more than one hormone. For example, one small gland connected to your brain makes 15 hormones. It is called your **pituitary gland.** One of the hormones your pituitary gland makes is called *growth hormone.* That hormone controls how fast your skeleton and muscles grow. It also helps determine your adult height.

pituitary gland (puh TOO uh tehr ee • GLAND), an endocrine gland attached to the brain; makes 15 hormones.

When Does Growing Speed Up?

At certain times, you grow very fast. You go through a quick **growth spurt** after growth hormone is released by your pituitary gland. You most likely went through one growth spurt during childhood, before you were 5 years old. Soon you will go through a second growth spurt, when you enter adolescence.

growth spurt, a period in which you grow very fast.

Take a look around your class. The physical growth spurt is easy to notice. Not everyone begins a growth spurt at the same time. Most girls begin their adolescent growth spurt when they are about 10. Their growth spurt lasts about two years. Many girls are taller than most boys their age for a year or two. Boys often start their adolescent growth spurt later than girls, at about age 12. The growth spurt of boys lasts about three years. Most boys catch up with most girls in height, and many grow taller.

Many children experience a growth spurt before the age of five. Another growth spurt occurs during adolescence.

In What Other Ways Will You Grow?

Understanding the many different ways you grow can help you accept the changes you will experience as you grow. At times you will see changes in your friends or classmates before you see them in yourself. Your physical growth, however, is only one way you will grow as you enter adolescence. You will also have intellectual, social, and emotional changes. Some of these changes will seem sudden. Others will happen slowly.

Intellectual growth involves becoming interested in new things. As you grow in this way, you might start a collection of something, such as stamps, baseball cards, or shells. You might explore new subjects by reading on your own. You might watch other people or ask them to teach you new skills, such as cooking, making crafts, or playing new games.

Your social growth shows in changes in the way you act with your family and friends. As you grow socially, you learn about being fair and honest with people. Friendships change a lot as you grow, too. This is because each friend enters adolescence at his or her own rate. You may have more arguments with other people at this time. However, disagreements and making up are important to learning the way to have real, long-lasting friendships. The ways you disagree without hurting yourself or others are important social skills.

As you grow, you will learn skills that will help you do many different things

82

Your emotional growth fits in with other physical, intellectual, and social changes. Just as you grow, have new ideas, and find new ways of acting with others, you will feel more strongly about many things. You may feel angry about being teased or feel let down by a parent. You may never have had such feelings before.

How Can You Feel Good About Changes As You Grow?

There are many things to like about your changing self. First, keep in mind that *everyone* goes through the same kinds of changes. Talking to a parent or older brother or sister helps you know what changes to expect.

Second, balance the new with old, familiar parts of your life. Your parents already know that some days you will act more grown-up and other days you may act as you did a few years ago. Moving forward some and back a little helps you go through adolescence slowly.

Third, keep sharing ideas with others. Show your family the new things you can do and make. Talk about new ideas with people your age. Ask your teacher or librarian for books or other items to help you find a new interest.

Scientists have learned how to make many human hormones in the laboratory. Physicians can order the hormones as medicines for people whose bodies do not make enough of those hormones.

STOP **REVIEW**
SECTION 2

REMEMBER?

1. What is cell division?
2. What does the endocrine system do?
3. How do growth hormones affect your body's growth?
4. In what four ways do people change during adolescence?

THINK!

5. Why do some people start their growth spurts sooner than other people?
6. Why should 12-year-old boys not worry about their height?

Many Things Affect Your Growth

Growth does not depend only on hormones. The way you grow also depends on heredity and environment.

Heredity is the passing on of certain traits from a parent to a child. Some traits can make a grandparent, parent, and child look alike, perhaps in the color of their skin or hair. Some traits cannot be seen, such as a tendency to develop a disease. Parents can pass on a growth pattern to their children.

Heredity affects the way you grow because your traits for growing were passed to you from your parents. Among those traits are the size and shape of your nose, your ears, and your feet. The rate at which you grow may be the same as the rate at which one of your parents grew. When you are fully grown, your size may be like the size of one of your parents. But you may also be bigger or smaller than either of your parents.

Your environment also affects your growth. Your *environment* is everything that surrounds you. Eating healthful foods, for example, helps your growth.

Living in a safe place with clean air and water also helps your growth. When you are healthy, your body has more energy for growing. It does not need to use its energy to fight off illness or repair injuries.

One of the most important parts of an environment is the people in it. People—such as family members, teachers, and older students—can help you learn how to grow and develop well in all areas. As you grow older, you will need to make choices that will help you stay healthy. You will need to choose to live in a healthful environment.

Thinking Beyond

1. Why might you be about the same size as your parents when you become an adult?
2. How are other people important to your intellectual, social, and emotional growth?

■ *Because of heredity, a person has many of the same characteristics as other members of his or her family.*

3 How Two Body Systems Change

When babies are born, they have all of the body systems. Some of the systems are not very well developed, however. As the babies grow, the body systems grow and change. Two systems in particular become larger and stronger. These are the skeletal and muscular systems. Their growth is the easiest way to see your body's growth.

KEY WORDS

growth plate
exercise

How Does Your Skeletal System Grow?

When you were born, your skeletal system was made of two kinds of tissue. One of these was bone. However, your bones were small and soft when you were born. At that time, your bones were made mostly of another tissue, called cartilage. The tip of your nose and the stiff part of your ears are made of cartilage. Feel those parts of your body. They are like what some of your bones were like at birth.

As you grew, bone-forming cells quickly took the place of the cartilage and formed bone. Layers of new cells formed around the outside of your bones, too. In that way, the bones grew thicker.

A person gets taller as bones add new cells and grow longer.

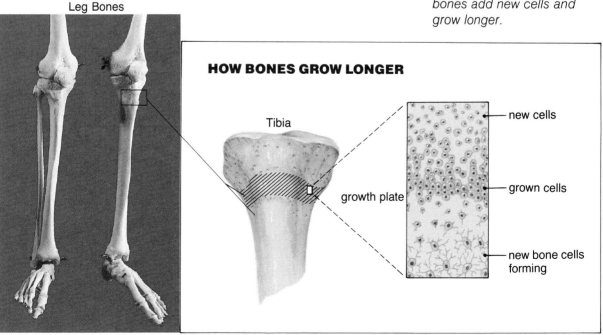

Leg Bones

HOW BONES GROW LONGER

Tibia

growth plate

new cells

grown cells

new bone cells forming

Your bones are still growing thicker. They are also growing longer. The long bones in your body grow longer because they have a growth plate near each end. The **growth plate** is a thin layer of cartilage between the shaft and the knob of the bone.

Bones become longer because the part of the growth plate near the end of the bone keeps making cells. Those cells grow and become part of the growth plate. The cells form bone tissue near the shaft of the bone. While this happens, new cells are still made in the part of the growth plate near the knob. Because of this, the shaft grows longer.

By the time you reach your late teens or early twenties, all the cells in your growth plates will have been replaced by bone tissue. After that, your bones will not grow any longer, and you will not grow any taller.

growth plate (GROHTH • PLAYT), a thin layer of cartilage between the shaft and the knob of bone.

exercise (EHK suhr syz), any activity that makes your muscles work hard.

▪ Exercise helps your muscles grow and get stronger.

How Do Your Muscles Grow and Change?

Once your bones stop growing, your muscles do not grow any more in length. However, they can always grow thicker and stronger. Your muscles grow stronger only if you use them a lot and make them work hard enough to get tired. Muscles that you do not use become weaker and smaller.

Any activity that makes your muscles work hard is called **exercise.** Exercise that tires your muscles wears them down a little. Then your muscles use the nutrients in the food you eat to repair themselves. The muscles then become a bit stronger than they were before. When you

have exercised regularly for a while, you have to exercise even more to tire your muscles. Then your muscles become still stronger. They may become thicker and heavier, too.

Strong, healthy muscles and bones can work together to help keep your whole body fit and well as you grow. You help your bones and muscles by eating a balanced diet and exercising. Nutrients are needed to build bone and muscle tissue. Exercise helps move nutrients from the blood to the cells that make bone and muscle tissues grow.

 **REVIEW**
SECTION 3

REMEMBER?

1. What kinds of tissues make up your skeletal system?
2. How do your long bones grow?
3. What is needed to help muscles grow thick and strong?

THINK!

4. How might your body be affected if you do not exercise regularly?
5. How might eating foods low in nutrients keep bones from growing properly?

MYTH
AND
FACT

Myth: Weight lifting is the best exercise for making muscles strong.

Fact: Weight lifting can be harmful for young people. Lifting incorrectly can lead to poor muscle develop-ment and injury. It is best to wait until the teenage years before beginning weight training. At that time, be sure to have a coach who knows about lifting.

Making Wellness Choices

Sandra is looking at some old family pictures. She notices how much she looks like her mother did as a young girl. She has red hair like her mother's. Even her posture and her smile are like her mother's. As Sandra looks for other shared traits, she wonders if her mother ever worried about growing up. She wonders if her mother worried as much about growing up as she does.

? Should Sandra talk with her mother about growing up? Why? Explain your wellness choice.

87

4 How You Control Your Body

KEY WORDS

neurons
brain
cerebrum
cerebellum
brain stem
spinal cord
nerves

Messages must be sent from both inside and outside your body for it to work properly. Your nervous system and its sensory organs put together the many messages.

The nervous system controls all the other systems of your body. It makes your fingers, your hands, and all your other parts move the way you need them to move. It keeps your lungs breathing and your heart beating. The nervous system makes all the parts of your body work together smoothly even as you grow. The nervous system senses and responds to messages from the world around you. It also sends and receives messages to and from different parts of your body.

Your nervous system is made up of three main parts: the brain, the spinal cord, and the nerves. All the parts of the nervous system contain certain cells called nerve cells, or **neurons.** The job of neurons is to carry messages.

neurons (NOO rahnz), nerve cells.

■ *Your nervous system makes your muscles work together to allow you to move in certain ways.*

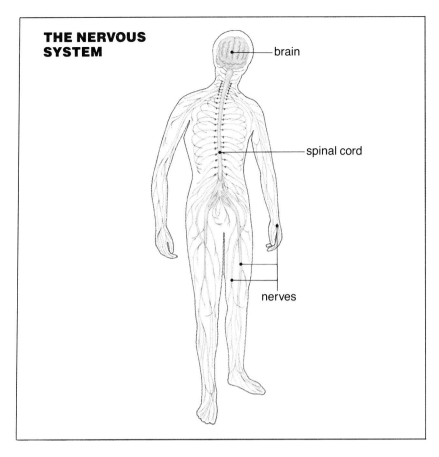

THE NERVOUS SYSTEM

brain

spinal cord

nerves

■ *Your nervous system is made up of parts that work together.*

How Do Your Brain and Spinal Cord Work?

The main part of your nervous system is your brain. Your **brain** is the control center of your nervous system. Each area of your brain has a specific job, but no area can work alone. Your brain is made up of many billions of neurons. An adult's brain is about the size of a grapefruit and weighs about 3 pounds (about 1.5 kilograms). Your brain is covered with many folds and grooves. They allow many neurons on your brain's surface to be together in a rather small space. The grooves also divide your brain into different parts with separate purposes.

There are three major parts of your brain. Each part controls different activities of your body. The first, your **cerebrum,** is the part that controls your ability to think, remember, dream, and feel. It also receives and interprets information from your eyes, your ears, your nose, your mouth, and your skin. The cerebrum lets you plan your voluntary actions, such as speaking.

brain (BRAYN), the control center of your nervous system.

cerebrum (suh REE bruhm), the part of your brain that controls your ability to think, remember, dream, and feel.

89

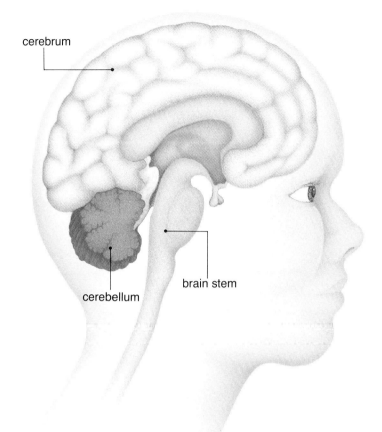

cerebrum

cerebellum

brain stem

■ *Each part of your body is controlled by a certain area of your brain.*

cerebellum (sehr uh BEHL uhm), the part of your brain that coordinates muscle action for voluntary movements.

brain stem (BRAYN • STEHM), the part of your brain that controls your involuntary movements.

Another part of your brain is the cerebellum. Your **cerebellum** coordinates your voluntary movements. Walking, running, and painting a picture are kinds of voluntary movements. Find out what your cerebellum does by trying to balance a ruler on end on the palm of your hand. Notice how you have to move your hand back and forth to keep the balance. You make the same kind of back-and-forth adjustment when you walk. But you no longer have to think about it. Your cerebellum sends the messages that keep you in balance. Your cerebellum took over this job after you had learned to walk. Until then, you had as much trouble walking as you now have balancing a ruler.

A third part of your brain, the **brain stem,** controls your involuntary movements. This part of your brain is like a basic life-support system. It keeps your heart beating and keeps you breathing.

How Do Your Nerves and Senses Work?

Another main part of your nervous system is the spinal cord. Your **spinal cord,** which is connected to your brain stem, forms the main path for messages entering and leaving your brain. The brain and the spinal cord make up the *central nervous system.*

The third main part of your nervous system is the nerves. **Nerves** are bundles of wrapped nerve-cell fibers. Nerves are long and thin, like threads. Your nerves carry messages throughout your body. Nerve fibers leave your central nervous system in nerve groups. A nerve has many branches at its ends. However, each fiber is continuous from its beginning to its end. Some nerves carry messages only from your brain to other parts of your body. Others carry messages from the parts of your body to your brain.

The nerves that carry messages from your brain to other parts of your body are called *motor nerves.* They tell each part of your body to move. Your brain controls all the actions of your body through your motor nerves.

The nerves that carry messages to your brain are called *sensory nerves.* They bring messages from all parts of your body, including your *sense organs.* Sense organs are body parts that can sense, or pick up, certain information about the world around you. They may also pick up information about your own body. Your eyes, your ears, your nose,

spinal cord (SPYN uhl • KAWRD), the part of your nervous system that forms the main path for messages entering and leaving your brain.

nerves (NURVZ), bundles of individually wrapped nerve-cell fibers that carry messages in your body.

FOR THE CURIOUS

You have other senses besides your five main senses. Your sense of balance keeps you from falling over. You also have
- a sense of direction.
- a sense of time.
- a sense of body position.

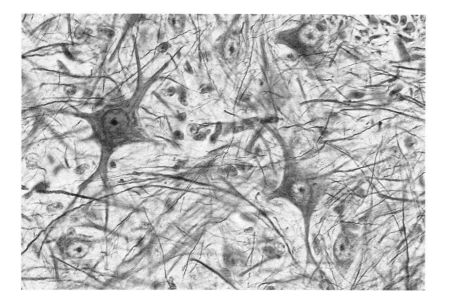

Sensory nerves in your eyes, ears, nose, tongue, and skin allow you to sense the conditions around you.

91

SENSE ORGANS OF THE BODY AND THEIR FUNCTIONS

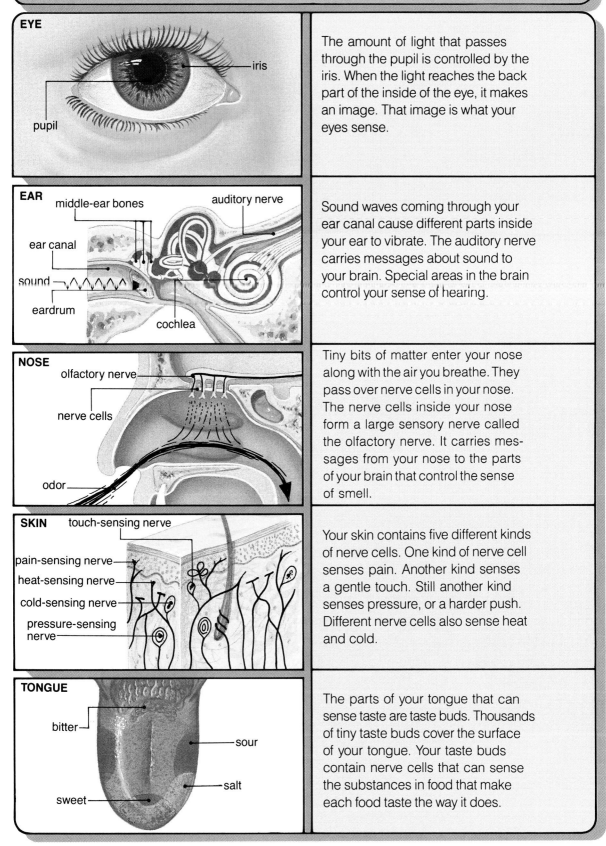

EYE

iris

pupil

The amount of light that passes through the pupil is controlled by the iris. When the light reaches the back part of the inside of the eye, it makes an image. That image is what your eyes sense.

EAR

middle-ear bones

auditory nerve

ear canal

sound

eardrum

cochlea

Sound waves coming through your ear canal cause different parts inside your ear to vibrate. The auditory nerve carries messages about sound to your brain. Special areas in the brain control your sense of hearing.

NOSE

olfactory nerve

nerve cells

odor

Tiny bits of matter enter your nose along with the air you breathe. They pass over nerve cells in your nose. The nerve cells inside your nose form a large sensory nerve called the olfactory nerve. It carries messages from your nose to the parts of your brain that control the sense of smell.

SKIN

touch-sensing nerve

pain-sensing nerve

heat-sensing nerve

cold-sensing nerve

pressure-sensing nerve

Your skin contains five different kinds of nerve cells. One kind of nerve cell senses pain. Another kind senses a gentle touch. Still another kind senses pressure, or a harder push. Different nerve cells also sense heat and cold.

TONGUE

bitter

sour

salt

sweet

The parts of your tongue that can sense taste are taste buds. Thousands of tiny taste buds cover the surface of your tongue. Your taste buds contain nerve cells that can sense the substances in food that make each food taste the way it does.

your tongue, and your skin are your main sense organs. Your eyes sense light. Your ears sense sounds. Your nose senses smells. Your tongue senses taste. Your skin senses pain, heat, and cold. Your sensory nerves carry messages, and your brain figures out what is happening in and around your body.

A healthy nervous system is important for proper growth and development. You can do many things to protect your nervous system from damage. In which of the pictures are the children protecting their nervous systems?

Think of other ways to protect your nervous system.

(STOP) REVIEW
SECTION 4

REMEMBER?

1. What are the three main parts of the nervous system?
2. What are the three main parts of the brain?

THINK!

3. Describe the differences between motor nerves and sensory nerves.
4. How might you protect your nervous system from harm?

An Interview with a Nurse Practitioner

Rubén D. Fernández knows about ways to help people with their health needs. He is a nurse practitioner who is in charge of nursing at a hospital in Newark, New Jersey.

What is a nurse practitioner?

A nurse practitioner is a registered nurse who has certain extra training. Because of this education, nurse practitioners can offer some of the services that physicians offer. For example, a nurse practitioner may order certain medicines.

Most nurse practitioners have a *specialty*. That means they are able to provide health care in a special field.

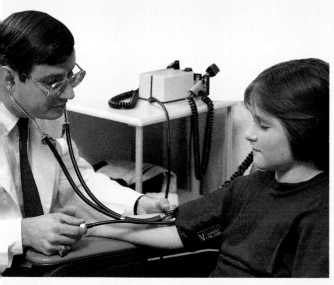

■ *Mr. Fernández helps young people stay healthy.*

For example, some nurse practitioners specialize in children's health. Nurse practitioners work in hospitals, in clinics, in schools, and in patients' homes.

How might a nurse practitioner help with children's growth and development?

Parents might worry if a young child has a problem walking or is not growing. A nurse practitioner can test the child for possible problems. A nurse practitioner can watch how the child walks or how the child works puzzles. Then the nurse practitioner can compare the child's development with that of other children who are the same age. If a child has a problem, the nurse practitioner can send the child to see a physician.

How do nurse practitioners in your hospital help children?

My hospital has something very unusual. There is a department for children that is run entirely by nurse practitioners. The department is for children who are having an operation and going home the same day. The department is called the Same-Day Surgery Unit. A child who will be in the Same-Day Surgery Unit meets a nurse practitioner a few days before the operation. They talk and get to know each other. They may talk about worries the child is having. Often the child and the nurse practitioner become friends. A few days later, the same nurse

interested in nursing need to study science. In college I earned a degree in nursing. This allowed me to take the state test so I could be called a registered nurse. As a registered nurse, or RN, I chose to work at a hospital. After working a while, I decided to go back to school. I went to college and took classes to become a nurse practitioner. I earned another diploma, this time for a master's degree in nursing.

How is the career of nursing changing?

I believe that more nurses will become nurse practitioners. That means that nurses will provide more health services for more of the public's health needs. More nurse practitioners and physicians will work with other nurses and health care team workers. Nurse practitioners will handle some of the duties of today's physicians. There will be more jobs in which nurse practitioners can use their new skills.

■ *Nurse practitioners at the hospital where Mr. Fernández works run a special department for children.*

practitioner will help prepare the child for the operation. Then he or she will visit the child after the operation.

What did you have to do to become a nurse and a nurse practitioner?

I first went to college, where I took a lot of science classes. Students who are

Learn more about nurse practitioners and the work they do. Interview a nurse practitioner. Or write for information to the National Association of Pediatric Nurse Associates and Practitioners, 1000 Maplewood Drive, Suite 104, Maple Shade, NJ 08052.

Main Ideas

- All people pass through the same stages of growth. The stages of growth include prenatal growth, infancy, childhood, adolescence, and adulthood.
- Your body will continue to make new cells all your life, even after you stop growing in size.
- Body systems grow and develop as a person passes through the stages of growth.
- Your endocrine system helps control your physical growth with hormones.
- Your nervous system controls all the other systems in your body.
- The three main parts of your nervous system are your brain, your spinal cord, and your nerves.

Key Words

Write the numbers 1 to 11 in your health notebook or on a separate sheet of paper. After each number, copy the sentence and fill in the missing term. Page numbers in ( ) tell you where to look in the chapter for help.

prenatal growth (71)
infancy (72)
adolescence (75)
adulthood (76)
endocrine system (79)
growth plate (86)
neurons (88)
brain (89)
cerebrum (89)
brain stem (90)
spinal cord (91)

1. The ___?___ stage lasts from birth until about age 2.
2. Rapid physical growth that happens between age 10 and age 18 is the growth stage of ___?___ .
3. The nervous system is made of special cells called ___?___ .
4. The growth stage that follows adolescence is ___?___ .
5. Messages enter and leave your brain through the ___?___ .
6. The ___?___ controls your ability to think, remember, dream, and feel.
7. The stage of growth before birth is called ___?___ .
8. A thin layer of cartilage between the shaft of a bone and the knob is the ___?___ .
9. Your ___?___ is the control center of your nervous system.
10. The ___?___ controls the way most of your cells change and the way they use nutrients.
11. The ___?___ controls your involuntary movements.

Write the numbers 12 to 20 on your paper. After each number, write a sentence that defines each term. Page numbers in ( ) tell you where to look in the chapter if you need help.

12. childhood (73)
13. gland (80)
14. hormones (80)
15. thyroid (80)
16. pituitary gland (81)
17. growth spurt (81)
18. exercise (86)
19. cerebellum (90)
20. nerves (91)

Remembering What You Learned

Page numbers in ( ) tell you where to look in the chapter if you need help.

1. List, in order, the five stages of growth. (71–76)

2. What kinds of physical changes take place during childhood? (73)

3. What are two ways that hormones can affect your cells? (80)

4. When does a second growth spurt usually happen in boys and girls? (81)

5. How do your bones grow longer? (86)

6. What system controls all the other systems of your body? (88)

7. Describe how the brain looks, and tell how much it weighs. (89)

8. What is the difference between sensory nerves and motor nerves? (91)

9. What are the main sense organs? (92)

Thinking About What You Learned

1. How long does it take to grow up? Explain your answer.

2. Describe two responsibilities an adult has that you do not have.

3. How might a body be affected if it had half the amount of growth hormone that it should have?

4. Why is the brain called the body's control center?

5. Why would a person lose all feeling and movement in the legs if the lower part of the spinal cord were crushed?

Writing About What You Learned

1. Predict what you will be like as an adult. Imagine yourself at a certain age. Tell your age, and describe how you look. What kind of job do you have? Where do you live? Do you have a family? What are your hobbies? What do you like most and least about being an adult?

2. Write a three-paragraph story. Describe yourself at three different times in your life: infancy, in your early school years, and during the current year. Write at least one sentence for each kind of change in you: physical, intellectual, social, and emotional.

Applying What You Learned

MATHEMATICS

Each student in your class should measure his or her height. Figure the average height of all the boys. Then figure the average height of all the girls. On the average, which group is taller? Explain your findings.

Modified True or False

Write the numbers 1 to 15 in your health notebook or on a separate sheet of paper. After each number, write *true* or *false* to describe the sentence. If the sentence is false, also write a term that replaces the underlined term and makes the sentence true.

1. Your <u>nervous</u> system controls all the other systems in your body.

2. A period in which you grow very fast is called a <u>growth plate</u>.

3. <u>Infancy</u> is the stage of growth that follows prenatal growth.

4. The <u>cerebellum</u> coordinates muscle action for voluntary movement.

5. Your body never stops making <u>cells</u>.

6. Childhood lasts about <u>16</u> years.

7. Cells grow by using <u>nutrients</u> to help cell parts grow.

8. How fast your skeleton and muscles grow is controlled by the <u>thyroid</u>.

9. Learning to play an instrument is a sign of <u>emotional</u> growth.

10. Any activity that makes your muscles work hard is called <u>growth spurt</u>.

11. Involuntary movement is controlled by the <u>brain stem</u>.

12. Your brain controls all the actions of your body through the <u>motor nerves</u>.

13. The rate at which your cells use the energy from nutrients is controlled by the <u>pituitary</u> gland.

14. The stage of growth during the first two years of life is <u>infancy</u>.

15. Your <u>emotional</u> growth is controlled by the endocrine system.

Short Answer

Write the numbers 16 to 23 on your paper. Write a complete sentence to answer each question.

16. How do your bones grow?

17. How is adolescence different from adulthood?

18. Describe how hormones control the body.

19. How does your brain receive messages from other parts of the body?

20. How can you help your body grow as it should?

21. Why does the body never stop growing?

22. Why does the body need glands?

23. How is the thyroid involved in the growth spurt?

Essay

Write the numbers 24 and 25 on your paper. Write paragraphs with complete sentences to answer each question.

24. Summarize how the endocrine system is related to human growth.

25. Suppose a friend of yours is unhappy because of his or her size. What could you say to your friend? Explain your answer.

ACTIVITIES FOR HOME OR SCHOOL

Projects to Do

1. Using a steel measuring tape or wooden yardstick secured to a wall, work with a partner to measure each other. Your teacher may plot everyone's height on a graph. The graph will show how much difference there can be in a class of students in your age group. Remeasure in six months. Is the new graph similar to the old graph?

2. Get a turkey neck from a butcher shop or a food store. With the help of an adult, cut it open. You can see the neck bones inside. Find the hole through which the spinal cord runs in the middle of each neck bone. Then look for the spinal cord itself. It is like a soft rope about ¼ inch (0.6 centimeter) across.

Dogs can be trained to help people who cannot see or hear.

Information to Find

1. Talk to a parent or guardian. Ask what he or she remembers about the growth spurt in adolescence. At what age did he or she start to grow more quickly? How did he or she feel about the physical and emotional changes?

2. People who are blind or deaf are often helped in their daily lives by dogs. Seeing Eye dogs help blind people move around safely. "Hearing-ear" dogs help deaf people respond to sounds. Write to an organization for the blind or for the deaf in your community. Ask for information about how those special dogs are trained.

Books to Read

Here are some books you can look for in your school library or the public library to find more information about the way you grow and about your nervous system and sense organs.

Baldwin, Dorothy, and Claire Lister. *How You Grow and Change.* Franklin Watts.

Sharp, Pat. *Brain Power! Secrets of a Winning Team.* Lothrop, Lee & Shepard.

van der Meer, Ron and Atie. *Your Amazing Senses.* Macmillan.

CHAPTER 4

TAKING CARE OF YOUR HEALTH

You are learning how your body works. As you learn about your body you take more responsibility to care for it. As you grow older, your family and teachers expect you to live up to your responsibility by practicing good daily health habits. Being more responsible for your own body also makes you feel good about yourself.

GETTING READY TO LEARN

Key Questions

- Why is it important to learn how to care for your body?
- How does the way you feel about taking care of your body affect your health habits and safety?
- How can you learn to make wise choices about health products and services?
- What can you do to take more responsibility for the care of your own body?

Main Chapter Sections

1 Getting Ready to Care for Your Health
2 Taking Care of Your Teeth and Gums
3 Taking Care of Your Eyes and Vision
4 Taking Care of Your Ears and Hearing
5 Taking Care of Your Hair and Nails

1 Getting Ready to Care for Your Health

KEY WORDS

health consumer
myths
advertising
sunscreen

Amy was two years old when she was given her first toothbrush. Her father brushed her teeth gently each morning and before she went to sleep. Amy's father explained why toothbrushing is an important habit to follow all through her life. As Amy grew older, she began brushing her own teeth after eating and before going to sleep. Amy's family encouraged her to practice this good health habit. They knew it was important to Amy's personal health.

■ *Many products have been developed to help people care for their health.*

Amy's family has been her first source of information about personal health. Soon, however, she will be getting advice from many different sources. She will get it from friends and other peers. She will also get it from health workers, from advertising, and even from labels on health products. Some of the health facts and figures will be correct.

Others may not be correct. Amy will need to study the health information she gets. She will need to understand it to make important choices about caring for her health. She will become a health consumer. A **health consumer** is someone who buys things to care for his or her health.

Who Influences Your Health Behavior?

You often act the way you do because other people have an influence on you. You learn many of your health behaviors from watching and listening to your family. You see that your family acts in certain ways. This behavior is familiar to you. You hear your parents' or guardians' opinions about what health practices are important. Your family's health behaviors or habits often become yours.

Friends and other peers may also influence a person's health behaviors. If a person's friend behaves a certain way and nothing bad seems to happen, the person will often try behaving the same way. The behavior may be good, such as eating healthful foods, or bad, such as taking dares. A person may form both healthful habits and risky habits because of the influence of peers.

health consumer
(HEHLTH • kuhn SOO muhr), a person who buys things to care for his or her health.

■ *Learning the proper way to trim fingernails is the start of a healthful habit.*

■ *Dependable sources of information help a person make healthful decisions.*

As you grow older, you will take more responsibility for your own personal health. You will need to base your health choices on dependable sources of health facts and figures. Dependable information is complete and scientifically correct.

What Are Dependable Sources of Health Information?

Rick was visiting Dr. Tracy's office. He saw a school diploma and a state license hanging on the wall. Rick had seen them on past visits. But he did not know what they meant. Rick's mother explained, "They tell us something about Dr. Tracy's training. The diploma tells us where and when he studied to become a dentist. The license tells us that Dr. Tracy passed a state test to be able to treat people's teeth and gums."

■ *A diploma can tell you where a health care worker was trained.*

A dentist is one of many kinds of health workers that Rick and his family depend on for health information. The following chart lists some of the health workers Rick and his family see. The information that these workers offer is based on their training and experience. *Training* is knowledge a person gains by going to school. *Experience* is knowledge a person gains from working.

A variety of groups provide dependable information about health care.

SOME DEPENDABLE SOURCES OF HEALTH INFORMATION	
Health Worker	**Kind of Health Information**
Audiologist	ears and hearing
Dentist	teeth and gums
Dermatologist	skin, hair, and nails
Ophthalmologist	eyes and vision
Pediatrician	children's health
Pharmacist	medicines and health products
Physician	diseases and disorders
School nurse	general health

Sources of Health Myths
- claims made by certain people
- beliefs passed from generation to generation
- wrong information from different sources

How to Avoid Health Myths
- consider the source of every health claim you hear or read
- talk to a parent, teacher, school nurse, or other health worker
- read dependable books and magazines

■ *There are many health myths. You should consider only the facts when making a health decision.*

myths (MIHTHS), false beliefs.

Many groups of health workers also give out health information. The American Dental Association, for example, is a group of dentists. It gives out information about proper care of teeth and gums. The American Red Cross gives out information on safety and health protection. Groups like these print booklets, teach classes, and give people health tips. You and your family can use this information to help you make choices about your personal health.

What Is a Health Myth?

Most people have heard some health **myths,** or false beliefs. You may have heard, for example, that you should put butter on a minor burn, but this is wrong. People sometimes accept myths as facts without thinking.

Some people also accept myths without knowing the harm that might result. For example, putting butter on a burn would actually make the burn worse. Butter and other forms of grease hold heat in. This causes more pain and adds to the time it takes for a burn to heal.

You can check out health advice with a parent, guardian, or health worker. You can also learn more about health facts by reading certain books and magazines. Knowing what is myth and what is fact can help you make wise decisions about your personal health.

106

How Can You Separate Fact from Appeal in Advertising?

Advertising is one source of many health facts and figures. The main purpose of advertising is to get consumers to buy a product. Most advertising, however, does not give complete information. Often advertising gives only a message that is directed to selling something. The way the information is given can influence what item or service a person selects.

Advertising often aims a selling message directly at young people. Advertising tries to appeal to what young people like. For example, some advertising uses popular music to sell a product. Think about some of the advertising you remember. You might remember the music. The music might then make you think of the product.

Sometimes advertising says that a product will give you more energy. It may suggest that a product will make you more popular or will let you have more fun. This message appeals to most people. A wise consumer, however, is careful to think about what is said in advertising. Young people need to be able to separate the facts about a product from the appeal of the advertising.

advertising (AD vuhr tyz ihng), a common source of information, directed toward selling things.

■ Advertising can influence a person to buy certain products and services.

BE A WINNER
It whitens! It brightens!
It gives you confidence!

Brush with
GREATSMILE
toothpaste!

GREATSMILE'S
ingredients are specially made for young teeth.
Buy the toothpaste with confidence built in. GREATSMILE!

107

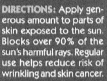

Labels on most health products provide information about using the products.

DIRECTIONS: Apply generous amount to parts of skin exposed to the sun. Blocks over 90% of the sun's harmful rays. Regular use helps reduce risk of wrinkling and skin cancer.

ACTIVE INGREDIENTS: Octyl Dimethyl PABA, Octyl Methoxycinnamate, Oxybenzone.

$5.48

RAYS OUT
S U N S C R E E N

ULTRA PROTECTION
SPF 15

PARK LOTIONS CO.

6 FL. OZ.

$3.89

BEACH & SUN

DEEP TANNING LOTION

SPF 4
MODERATE PROTECTION

4 FL. OZ.

How Can Label Information Help You in Making Choices?

A wise consumer needs to be able to tell the differences among health products. The labels on products can help you. You can use the labels to compare different products. That way, you can choose safe products for your needs.

Look at the pictures of labels for different sunscreens. A **sunscreen** is a lotion that blocks some or all of the sun's dangerous rays. It protects against sunburn, which can cause skin cancer. Each label tells you the

- kind of product.
- name of the product.
- name of the company.
- amount of product in that package.
- directions for use.
- ingredients used to make the product.

Notice the letters *SPF*. These letters stand for *sun protection factor*. The SPF levels on these labels are all different. What might that tell you?

SPF levels are usually given in numbers from 0 to 15. The higher the number, the more protection is given from the sun. How can knowing the SPF level help you choose the right sunscreen for your needs?

sunscreen, a lotion that blocks the sun's dangerous rays and protects your skin against sunburn.

REAL-LIFE
SKILL

Selecting Sunscreens

Physicians say that a sunscreen with SPF 15 is the most effective kind. Sunscreens with higher SPF numbers do not block significantly more sun. They cost much more, however.

108

THE ABC'S OF SPF (SUN PROTECTION FACTOR)

SPF Levels	Amount of Protection
SPF 0 to 3	no protection
SPF 4 to 6	mild protection for skin that tans easily and rarely burns
SPF 7 to 8	extra protection that still permits tanning
SPF 9 to 10	excellent protection for skin that burns easily
SPF 11 to 15+	total protection to block the sun's rays

A good way to learn about health products is by talking about them with a parent, guardian, or teacher. Your school nurse can help you find out about most kinds of health products. He or she can also explain personal health habits you can practice. Having information and skills to take care of your health helps raise your self-esteem. You feel you have some control of your body as it grows.

A trusted adult can often provide dependable information about health products.

STOP REVIEW SECTION 1

REMEMBER?

1. What people may have an influence on your health behavior?
2. How can you tell what health information is a myth?
3. What kind of information does most advertising give?

THINK!

4. Why do you need to be careful about gathering health information?
5. What products have you seen advertised that seem "too good to be true"?

109

SECTION 2 Taking Care of Your Teeth and Gums

KEY WORDS

plaque
cavity
fluoride

Many young people know that teeth and gums affect their appearance. They realize that not brushing their teeth or not seeing a dentist for a toothache can cause serious problems. Dentists know many things that young people can do to help their teeth and gums be as attractive and healthy as possible.

Healthy teeth and gums can help a person look and feel good.

What Can Cause Tooth Problems?

The major cause of tooth loss among young people is tooth decay. Tooth decay is caused by microbes, or germs, in your mouth. The microbes mix with a clear, sticky film that forms on the teeth. This film is called **plaque.** When the microbes in plaque mix with sugar, they make strong chemicals called *acids.* The acids erode, or eat away, the tooth *enamel,* the hard coating on the teeth. In time, the acids make the enamel soft and wear part of it away. Then more microbes enter and form a **cavity,** or hole, in the tooth.

plaque (PLAK), a clear, sticky film in which microbes live; forms on the teeth.

cavity (KAV uht ee), a hole that forms in a tooth because of decay.

110

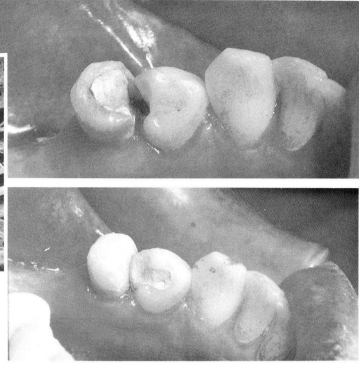

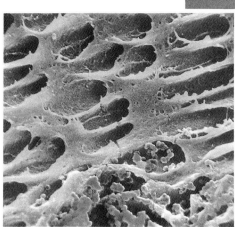

■ *Microbes in plaque, above, can cause a cavity to form, right top. All cavities need to be filled by a dentist.*

If a cavity in a tooth is not filled, it can grow bigger and deeper. Acids eat through the *dentin*, the thick layer under the enamel. They reach the tooth *pulp*, in the middle of the tooth, and attack the pulp tissue. When this happens, the tooth hurts. If you have a toothache, you should see a dentist as soon as possible. If you do not see a dentist, the pulp infection can cause tooth loss.

To stop the cavity from becoming bigger, a dentist can remove all the decayed material. Then the dentist can fill the hole with a metal or quartz mixture that becomes hard, like enamel.

If a cavity is taken care of early, the tooth can remain healthy. Some people seem to get more cavities because of the kinds of microbes in their mouths. If you take care of your teeth, you may not get any cavities.

What Can Cause Gum Problems?

The roots of your teeth fit into your jawbone. But your teeth still need the help of your gums to stay in place. Gums help protect the roots of your teeth from disease.

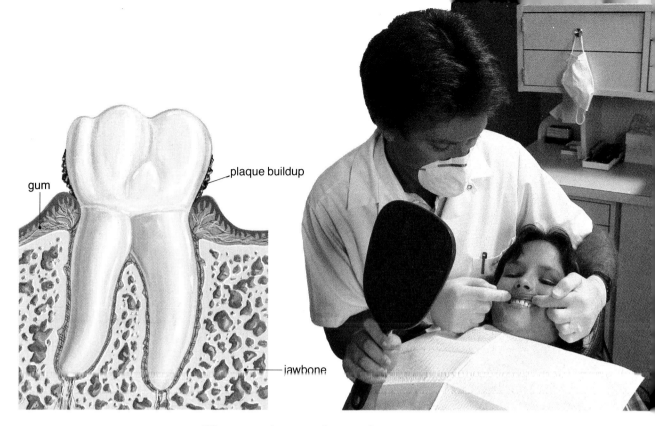

gum

plaque buildup

jawbone

■ *Plaque can build up between teeth and gums, left, causing gum disease. Preventing gum disease is necessary for healthy teeth.*

The microbes in plaque that cause cavities can also harm your gums. Plaque on your teeth hardens if you do not clean them daily. Plaque on teeth and under gums can push your gums away from your teeth. Microbes can grow in that space. Then your gums become sore and may bleed when brushed. Most people's gums get sore if the teeth are not brushed well at least once daily. Brushing gums, as well as teeth, helps the cells in gum tissue stay healthy.

When toothbrushing causes gums to bleed or when bad breath lasts all day, gum disease is often the cause. Gum disease in an early stage is called *gingivitis*. If you think you have gum disease, a school nurse or a dental hygienist can tell you if a dentist needs to help you or whether you can help yourself. Sometimes gentle brushing and flossing can help your gums become healthy again. If gum disease is not treated, teeth can become loose and may even fall out. Gum disease can cause a person to lose healthy teeth that never had a cavity!

Gum disease can begin when a person is young. You can actually help prevent much gum disease by removing plaque from your mouth before it becomes hard. You can take responsibility for daily care of your teeth and gums.

How Can You Care for Your Teeth and Gums?

Tooth care begins with cleaning your teeth. If you clean your teeth properly, plaque has less of a chance to form. Without plaque, the microbes that cause cavities cannot stick to your teeth.

Missy has several ways of cleaning and protecting her teeth. One way is to use a fluoride toothpaste on a soft-bristled toothbrush. Toothbrushes come in many shapes and sizes. There are also different kinds of toothpastes. Fluoride toothpastes that are accepted by the American Dental Association (ADA) are best for protecting the teeth from decay. **Fluoride** is a substance that helps tooth enamel stay hard. Dentists recommend the use of fluoride for people of all ages.

fluoride (FLUR yd), a substance that helps tooth enamel stay hard and protects against tooth decay.

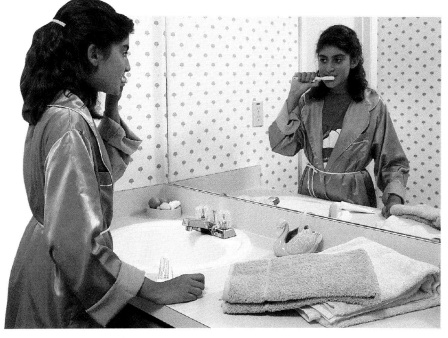

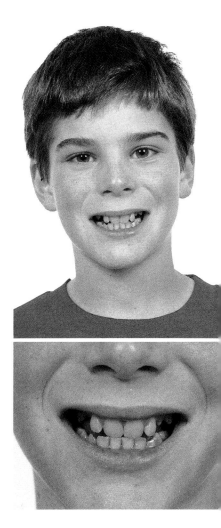

Missy tries to brush after every meal. When she cannot brush after a meal or snack, she rinses out her mouth with water. Some communities add fluoride to the drinking water. Missy's drinking water has safe amounts of fluoride. Missy's cousin lives in a town with too little fluoride in the water. The family uses a rinse solution ordered by the dentist. The school nurse also has a fluoride rinse that students can use if parents or guardians permit.

■ How do you know if your teeth are clean? "Disclosing tablets" can show whether plaque is still present.

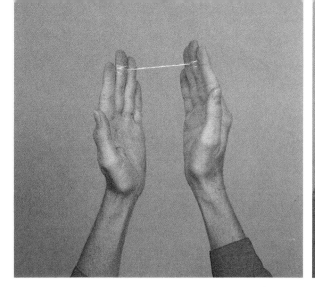
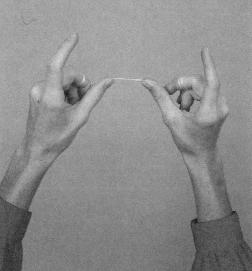

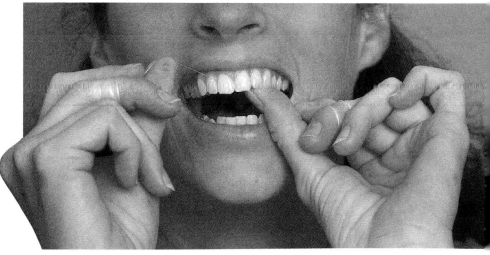

■ *Dental floss can be used to remove plaque between teeth. The floss is wrapped around the fingers and held between the thumbs.*

Brushing and rinsing cannot remove all the plaque and food from teeth. That is why Missy also uses dental floss. *Dental floss* is a kind of soft thread used for cleaning between teeth. Missy's dentist recommends unwaxed floss. Flossing removes plaque and food that stick where toothbrush bristles cannot reach.

Flossing finishes the job that brushing and rinsing start. Your dental hygienist can teach you safe and useful ways to brush and floss your teeth.

Visiting a dentist every six months for checkups is an important part of caring for your teeth. Your dentist and dental hygienist can find and treat dental problems just as they are starting. Using special tools, the dentist or hygienist can clean plaque from your teeth. Some dentists apply a plastic sealant on molars or other teeth that have deep grooves. The grooves are hard to keep free of plaque.

Dentists have ways to help keep your teeth and gums healthy when you cannot control dental problems. For example, dentists called *orthodontists* can straighten crooked teeth. They put braces on these teeth. Over several months or years, the teeth become straighter and fit better in the mouth. Straight teeth are important for chewing food and for appearance. People who have crooked teeth often have more cavities than people with straight teeth because crooked teeth are harder to keep clean.

You can help your teeth and gums with healthful eating habits. Foods rich in calcium—such as milk, cheese, and yogurt—help make your teeth strong. A diet with daily vitamin C helps keep the gum tissue healthy. Avoid eating sticky, sugary foods. Having these foods in your mouth for a long time can increase the effects of harmful acids. Eating crunchy foods, such as celery and carrots, can help scrub your teeth as you eat.

Ask your dentist or school nurse for other advice about how to take care of your teeth and gums. It is never too soon to begin. You can protect your teeth and gums so that they will stay healthy all your life.

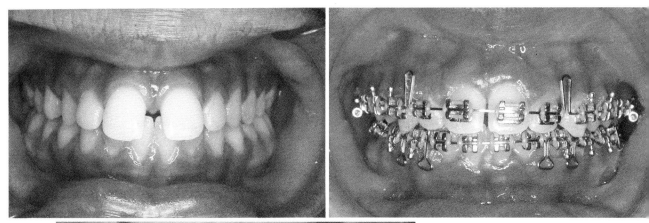

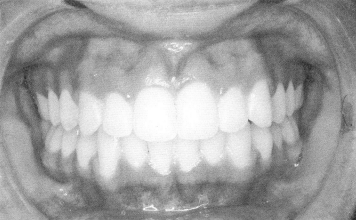

■ *Braces can help improve the health and appearance of teeth.*

115

REMEMBER?

1. What is the most common dental health problem?
2. What can happen to gums if teeth are not cared for properly?
3. What are four important habits for caring for your teeth?

THINK!

4. Why does a person need to form good dental habits at an early age?
5. Besides preventing cavities, how might keeping your tooth clean help you?

Thinking About Your Health

How Do You Care for Your Teeth and Gums?

How do you know if you are making wise choices in caring for your teeth and gums? You might not be if you say "sometimes" or "never" to any of the following statements. You might need to talk with your parent, guardian, school nurse, or teacher about caring for your teeth and gums.

- I brush my teeth at least once a day.

- I use dental floss every day.
- I use a toothpaste that contains fluoride.
- I eat foods that keep my teeth strong.
- I snack on crunchy foods instead of soft and chewy foods.
- I tell my parent or guardian if I think I have a problem with my teeth or gums.
- I get regular dental checkups.

116

3 Taking Care of Your Eyes and Vision

Your eyes are organs that send messages to the brain for vision. Your eyes do a lot for you. They let you see objects that are close and objects that are far away. They let you see in bright light and even in dim light. They let you read. You need to protect your eyes to keep them healthy and safe.

KEY WORDS

cornea
iris
pupil
lens
retina
optic nerve

Protecting your vision means preventing harm to your eyes.

How Do You See?

You can see only things that either give off light or reflect light. Your eyes need to take in some of the light to let you see. When light from an object hits your eyes, the light forms an image, or picture, of the object inside your eyes. That image is what your eyes sense.

Light first passes through the clear layer of each eye, called the **cornea.** The cornea forms the bump on the front of the eye. It covers and protects two other parts of the eye. The **iris** is the colored middle part of the eye. It is made of smooth muscles. These muscles control the amount of light that passes through the pupil. The **pupil** is also covered by the cornea. The pupil is a hole in the center of the iris.

cornea (KAWR nee uh), the clear cover that protects the front of the eye.

iris (EYE ruhs), the colored middle part of the eye.

pupil (PYOO puhl), an opening in the eye, leading to the lens.

117

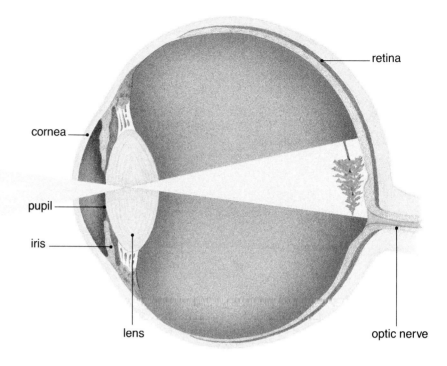

cornea

retina

pupil

iris

lens

optic nerve

■ *The human eye is a complex organ.*

lens (LEHNZ), the part of the eye that bends light to make an image sharp and clear.

retina (REHT uhn uh), a tissue made of two kinds of cells that sense light; covers the inside of the eye at the back.

optic nerve (AHP tihk • NURV), the sensory nerve that takes messages about the image on the retina to the brain.

The pupil is always wide open when you are in dim light. It closes slightly in brighter light.

After going through the cornea and the pupil, light passes through the lens of the eye. The **lens** bends light to make an image that is sharp and clear. The lens can change shape because of little muscles connected to it. The lens adjusts its shape to the distance of the things you see. It forms sharp images of things that are near or far.

When light reaches the back of the eye, it falls onto the retina. The **retina** is a tissue made of two kinds of cells that sense light. One kind of cell senses color. Those cells are called *cones* because of their shape. The other cells sense only the brightness of light. They are called *rods*, also because of their shape.

When light reaches cells on the retina, the cells make chemicals. The chemicals make electrical messages that are carried by nerve cells. Those nerve cells form a bundle of nerves called the optic nerve. The **optic nerve** takes the messages about the image on your retina to your brain.

Your brain plays an important part in helping you see. As light passes through the lens in each eye, the lens bends it. It makes an upside-down image on the retina in each eye. When your brain gets the messages about the image, it lets you see right-side up. Your brain also figures out what you are seeing.

How Are Your Eyes Protected?

Your body has certain features to protect your eyes from harm. Most of each eye is protected by the bones of the skull. The bones of the nose and cheek, around the eyes, act like the face mask of a football helmet. They keep large objects that might hit the face away from the eyes. The front part of each eye is also protected by other parts of your face.

If your retina had only rods, you would see everything in black, white, and shades of gray. The world would look much as it does on a black-and-white television.

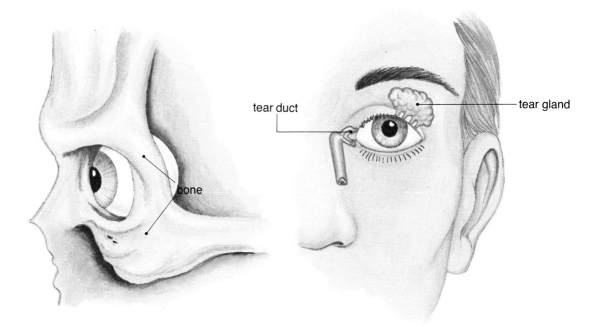

tear duct

tear gland

bone

Tear glands at the outside corner of each eye help wash your eyes. They make the watery liquid you know as *tears*. Some tears come out of your tear glands all the time. Each time you blink, you spread the tears across your eyes. Then they flow down, washing away dust and dirt. Tears leave the tear glands through little tubes, called *tear ducts*, at the inside corner of each eye.

■ Bones and tear glands help protect parts of your eyes.

Suppose dirt blew into one of your eyes. The tear gland in that eye would suddenly make a lot of tears. Your eye would begin to "water." The tears would help wash out the dirt. Tears can also kill microbes in the eye that could cause an infection.

The eyes are protected in still other ways. For example, you have a blink reflex. When the eyes sense a very close object or any harm, the lids close quickly without your thinking about it. Another kind of protection is from your eyelashes. They act like screens. They keep dust and dirt from reaching the eyes.

How Can You Protect Your Eyes?

You can protect your eyes by following some eye-care tips. Some of these may help prevent discomfort. Others may help you keep your vision.

- Wear sunglasses outdoors on bright days. Wearing sunglasses, especially near snow or water, cuts down the glare that can hurt your eyes.
- Wear safety glasses or goggles when mowing the lawn, working with tools, or playing certain contact sports.
- Keep sharp objects away from your eyes.
- If you feel something in your eye, ask an adult for help. Blink quickly to help increase the flow of tears. Do not try to remove the particle yourself. You might scratch the cornea of your eye.

MYTH
AND
FACT

Myth: Reading in dim light will cause vision problems.

Fact: Eyestrain is a muscle strain, not a problem with the eyeball. Eyestrain is caused by squinting when reading in dim light. Eyestrain does not harm the eyes, but it does make them feel tired. If you want to enjoy reading without becoming tired, be sure you have enough light.

If you have something in your eye, ask an adult for help. If you try to remove the object yourself, you might scratch the cornea.

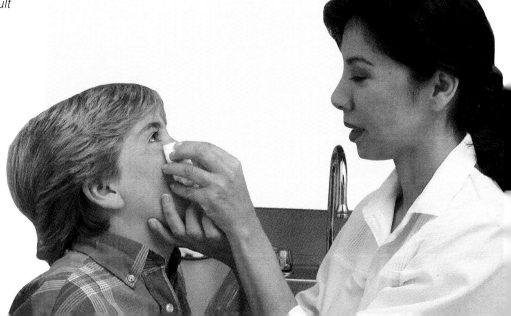

You can also help your eyes by taking care of your whole body. Remember that each part of your body affects how other parts work. If you have not had enough sleep, your eyes may feel irritated. Eating healthful foods can also help.

How Do You Know If You Have an Eye Problem?

Most vision problems begin very slowly. In school, one student may have trouble seeing words close up in books. Another student may have trouble reading words far away on the chalkboard. As vision problems get worse, people often start to squint to focus a blurry image. Some people may tip their heads to see more clearly. These are signs that their eyes and vision should be tested by an eye-care professional, such as an *ophthalmologist.*

To a nearsighted person, left, objects far away appear blurry. To a farsighted person, right, objects nearby appear blurry.

Most often, vision problems are caused by a change in the shape of the eye. The shape affects the way light rays focus on the retina. A change in the eye's shape happens slowly and may go on for several years. For this reason, a person may need to get new glasses each year for several years in a row.

Wearing eyeglasses allows many people to see things clearly. The ability to see well makes people feel good about themselves.

Sometimes the eye becomes too long. If it does, images focus before reaching the retina. Faraway things look blurry. Nearby things remain clear. A person with this kind of vision is *nearsighted*.

Sometimes the eye becomes too short. Then images reach the retina before coming into focus. Nearby things look blurry. Faraway things remain clear. A person with vision like this is said to be *farsighted*.

Sometimes the cornea of the eye is shaped unevenly. If it is, both nearby and faraway things may look blurry. This kind of vision problem is called *astigmatism*.

Eyeglass lenses or contact lenses can usually correct these vision problems. The lenses bend the light entering each eye so that the light focuses where it should, on the retina. Then the person can see sharp, clear images.

Young people should feel good about wearing glasses when they need them. With glasses, people have a better appearance. They do not have to squint or tip their heads to see. Some people who are nearsighted do much better in sports when they use their glasses. When needed, glasses let people see things clearly that they might otherwise miss.

REVIEW
STOP
SECTION 3

REMEMBER?

1. What parts of the eye does light pass through before it reaches the retina?
2. What are two kinds of cells in the retina that sense light?
3. What are three eye-care tips to help you protect your vision?

THINK!

4. Why is sleep important for good vision?
5. If a person needs to wear glasses but does not wear them, how might he or she be taking a risk?

Health Close-up

Contact Lenses

Contact lenses are very small lenses that correct vision problems. Unlike eyeglass lenses that are held in frames, contact lenses float over the corneas on tears.

Contact lenses are made of very thin plastic. They can be either hard, semi-soft, or soft. A hard lens is very small and looks like a tiny plastic bowl. A semi-soft lens looks like a hard lens but is a little softer. Both kinds can be worn only while the wearer is awake. A soft lens looks like a round piece of cellophane and is soft enough to roll up between your fingers. Some soft contacts can be worn only while the wearer is awake. Others can be left in for several days before they need to be taken out and cleaned.

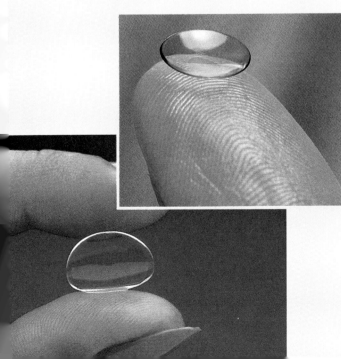

■ *Contact lenses are made of either hard or soft plastic.*

Like eyeglasses, contacts bend light rays to focus them on the retina. Contacts have some advantages over eyeglasses, though. Many people who wear contact lenses have better vision at the sides than with eyeglasses. Contacts are sometimes easier to wear when playing sports, but protective goggles or safety glasses should also be worn.

Contact lenses can correct vision problems of people who are nearsighted or farsighted. Contacts can correct special vision problems, too. For example, people with astigmatism whose corneas are bumpy are helped by contacts. To these people, straight lines look wavy. Special contacts can get rid of this problem.

Contacts need more care than eyeglasses and are usually more expensive. Because they are so small, they are easier to lose. Special liquids are used to clean and to maintain the lenses. Users must wash their hands well before handling their contacts. If contacts are not cleaned well, bacteria on them can cause an eye infection. If contacts are not worn properly, they can scratch the cornea.

Thinking Beyond

1. What are some advantages of wearing contact lenses?
2. What are some disadvantages of wearing contact lenses?

4 Taking Care of Your Ears and Hearing

Knowing about your ears and how to care for them can help you protect your hearing. Knowing how people hear can help you avoid hearing problems. Some people, however, are born with hearing problems or lose some of their hearing due to illness, aging, or too much noise.

How Do People Hear?

Irene is playing the guitar. Louis watches her pluck the strings. He hears the music. He sees the strings moving back and forth. They move so fast that they look blurred. This kind of quick back-and-forth motion is called *vibration*. The vibration of the strings makes the air vibrate. Sounds are made by vibrations of the air.

■ *You are able to hear music because the ear can change sound vibrations into nerve messages.*

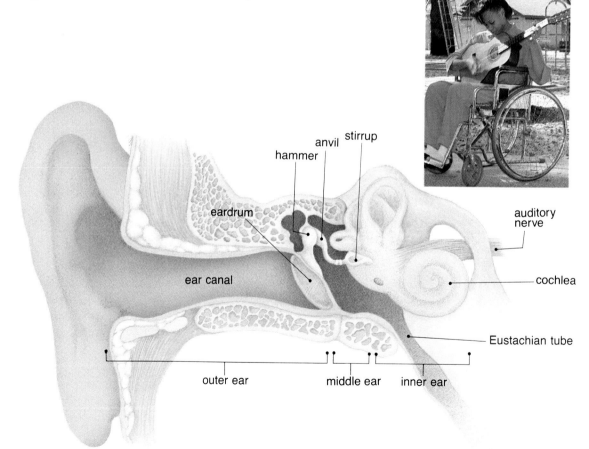

- anvil
- stirrup
- hammer
- eardrum
- auditory nerve
- ear canal
- cochlea
- Eustachian tube
- outer ear
- middle ear
- inner ear

Before you hear a sound, a vibration of tiny bits of air must reach the outer ear. The outer ear is made up of a tube called the *ear canal*. The outer ear funnels and directs sound to the middle ear. Between the outer ear and the middle ear are layers of delicate tissue that form the *eardrum*. The sound vibrations push against your eardrum and cause it to vibrate.

Tiny hairs inside the cochlea transfer vibrations to nerve endings. The brain interprets messages from the nerves as sounds.

There is a group of three small bones behind the middle ear attached to the eardrum. These bones are called the hammer, anvil, and stirrup because of their shapes. They are the smallest bones in your body. They pick up the vibrations from the eardrum. And they pass the vibrations to the inner ear.

The stirrup is the last of the small bones. It connects to the cochlea in the inner ear. The **cochlea** is a coiled tube that is filled with a liquid much like seawater. When the stirrup vibrates, it makes the liquid in the cochlea vibrate.

The cochlea has about 17,000 tiny hairs that are connected to specialized cells. Vibrations in the liquid make the hairs move. The special cells sense the movement. These special cells send messages about the sound to the brain through the auditory nerve. You have one auditory nerve coming from each ear. The auditory nerves go to the parts of the brain that control hearing. There the brain figures out what the messages mean.

cochlea (KOH klee uh), the liquid-filled, coiled tube in the inner ear.

125

How Are Your Ears Protected?

Your body has some parts that help keep your ears working well. One of these is the *Eustachian tube.* Air in the spaces of the middle ear passes through this tube. The Eustachian tube protects your ear by keeping the correct air pressure inside it. At the correct pressure, the tiny bones vibrate well. Quick rises or drops, such as in an elevator or an airplane, do not allow the pressure in the middle ear time to change. Swallowing or yawning often helps open the tube and correct the pressure. Sometimes, however, allergy or illness causes swelling at the opening of the tube.

How Can You Protect Your Hearing and Your Ears?

Many hearing problems can result from loud noise. Even a short, loud sound—such as from a firecracker—can injure the tiny hairs in the cochlea, causing hearing loss. A softer noise over a long time can also cause a hearing loss. The loudness of a noise and how long it lasts affect hearing loss.

decibels (DEHS uh behlz), units of measure for the loudness of a sound.

The loudness of a sound is measured in **decibels.** A scale of decibels from 0 to 200 works like this: A sound at 20 decibels is 10 times louder than a sound at 10 decibels. A sound at 30 decibels is ten times louder than a sound at 20 decibels, and so on. The chart shows how loud some sounds are. Wearing ear protection is one way to help keep hearing loss from happening.

LOUDNESS OF SOUNDS

Source	Decibels	Possible Hearing Loss
Space shuttle blast-off Jet take-off	180 140	immediate
Rock concert, thunderclap Chain saw, jackhammer Traffic, noisy home appliances	120 100 80	gradual
Normal speech Quiet living room Whisper at 5 feet (1.6 meters)	60 40 20	none

You can protect your outer ears and your eardrums by following some simple health habits. Here are two habits you can form to care for your ears every day:

- Never put anything into your ears, including cotton-tipped swabs. Cotton-tipped swabs can pack earwax into the auditory canal, forming a plug.
- Clean your ears when you wash your face. Cleaning your ears more often is not necessary. Drying behind your ears with a towel helps prevent skin irritation.

How Do You Know If You Have a Hearing Problem?

There are signs that let you know that friends or family members may have hearing problems. (People most often do not recognize their own hearing problems.) Sometimes people do things that show they are trying to hear better. They may need to turn toward a sound to hear more clearly. They may often say "huh?" or "what?" They often may need to ask people to repeat what was said.

A hearing aid helps a person hear sounds that he or she would otherwise miss.

If a person complains of an earache or has a watery liquid in the ear, that may be a sign of a serious problem. Feeling as if your ears are "stuffed" or "stopped up" may also be a sign of a hearing problem. Ringing, buzzing, or other noises in one or both ears also can be a warning sign. Finally, people with a hearing problem may talk more loudly than is necessary.

Each sign of a hearing problem means that the ears and hearing need to be tested. People often do not know they have hearing problems until they have their ears tested. Find out if you are hearing well. Anyone with a hearing problem should see a physician.

STOP REVIEW SECTION 4

REMEMBER?

1. How do you hear a sound?
2. What are two habits to follow every day to care for your ears?
3. What are three signs that show that a person may have a hearing problem?

THINK!

4. How might knowing about different decibel levels help you protect your hearing?
5. Why does an earache need to be checked by the school nurse or your physician?

Making Wellness Choices

Robert and his friend Eric are at Robert's home one day after school. Both boys are watching a funny show that Robert had recorded. As the tape plays, Robert laughs at what is being said. Eric could not hear what was said. Eric asks Robert what is funny. Robert explains the joke and makes the volume a little louder. Robert laughs again, and Eric again asks what was said. Robert makes the volume a little louder. After a third joke, Eric asks Robert to make the volume even louder.

? What might Robert say to Eric? Explain your wellness choice.

5 Taking Care of Your Hair and Nails

Rona had her hair trimmed yesterday. She had about 2 inches (5 centimeters) cut off. Then she cut and filed her fingernails. Even though those parts of her body were cut, Rona did not feel any pain. There are no nerves in the hair or fingernails.

KEY WORD

hair follicle

Having your hair trimmed regularly will help keep it healthy.

The hair and nails that you can see are made of dead cells. Live hair cells and nail cells are made inside your body, just under the top layer of your skin. By the time your hair cells and nail cells come out of the body, they are dead. The dead cells are pushed out as the new cells form inside the skin. More cells are always being made inside your body. That is why your hair and your nails keep growing.

What Is Hair?

Use a magnifying glass to look at your arm or at the top of your hand. You can see little pits all over the surface. Now look a little closer. Almost every pit has a hair growing out of it. Each hair grows out of a tiny sac called a **hair follicle.** The main parts of a follicle lie below the surface of your skin. You can see the shape of the whole follicle in the picture.

hair follicle (HAIR • FAHL ih kuhl), a tiny sac from which a hair grows out of the skin.

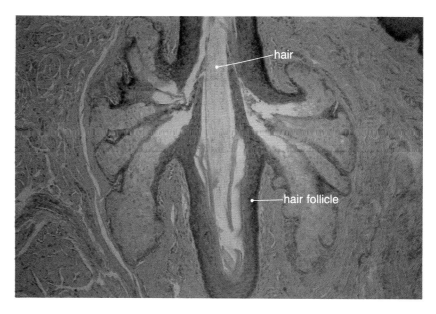

hair

hair follicle

■ Each hair grows from a follicle, a tiny sac in the skin.

Hair texture and color are inherited. The feel or shape of the hair strands determines how curly your hair is. Hair color is caused by a coloring matter called *pigment* in the cells. Dark hair has a lot of pigment. Lighter hair has less pigment. White hair has no pigment.

Your hair does several jobs. It brings oil to the surface of your skin. It also helps keep you warm. Hair traps a layer of air next to your skin. The air warms up from being next to your body.

How Can You Care for Your Hair?

The oil from the oil glands near your hair follicles keeps the hair on your head shiny and healthy. But the oil also makes your hair a little sticky. Your hair catches dirt from the air.

Shampoos work best for washing hair. The suds from shampoos are easy to rinse out. Suds from a bar of soap can be hard to rinse out. They can also take out too much oil and leave your hair dull looking and too dry.

Many people need to wash their hair only two or three times a week. That keeps it looking clean but does not dry it out. The hair follicles of most people your age do not yet give off as much oil as in teenagers and adults. For this reason, you may not need to wash your hair as often as they do. Talk with a parent or guardian about how often you should wash your hair. Talk about what kind of shampoo is best for you. A parent or a pharmacist can help you choose a shampoo that meets your needs.

Brushing your hair helps keep it healthy, too. Brushing makes the roots of your hair more active. It draws oil to the ends of the hairs, which usually do not get as much oil. Long hair often needs brushing more than short hair does because long hair tangles easily. Tightly pulled ponytails and cornrows can actually break hairs. Even if you brush every day, the ends of your hairs may split and break. Every four to eight weeks, you most likely need to have the ends trimmed.

■ *Caring for your hair includes brushing and combing as well as shampooing regularly.*

The way your hair looks is often a sign of how you feel about yourself. There is much advertising for hair-care products because many people feel that hair care is a way to express themselves. You have many choices to consider in hair care. Ask an adult for help.

What Are Nails?

Your nails protect the delicate tissues at the ends of your fingers and toes. These tissues are easily bruised or scraped. Without nails, your fingers and toes could be easily injured. Doing simple things, such as scratching your skin, could be very painful.

■ *Fingernails need to be cleaned, trimmed, and filed to keep them healthy.*

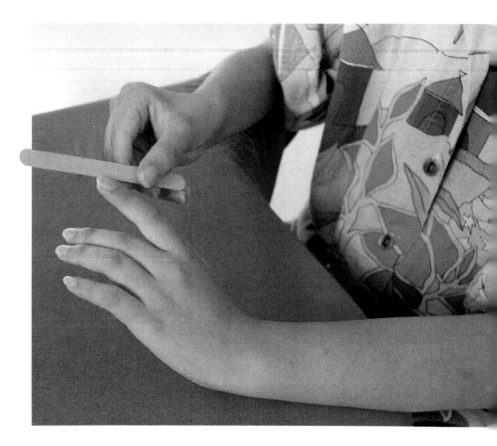

Your nails grow more slowly than your hair. Your nails may grow about 1/4 inch (6 millimeters) a month. In that same time, your hair may grow 1/2 inch (12 millimeters) or more. The speed at which hair and nails grow is different for different people.

Keeping the skin under your fingernails clean is an important health habit. Doing this removes dirt and microbes from under your nails. Clean fingernails can help you stay safe from disease. Scrubbing your nails when shampooing your hair or washing your hands helps keep the nails clean.

Clean, trimmed nails show others how you feel about your appearance and yourself. Nail care is something that you can do with a few simple tools. A nail clipper for fingernails, a clipper to cut toenails straight across, and an emery board to smooth rough nail edges cost little money.

If your nails grow too long, they can catch on objects and break. Long nails are also hard to keep clean. You need to keep your nails trimmed. But do not cut them too short or bite them. Biting your nails allows the dirt and microbes on them to get into your mouth. Live tissues connect your nails to your skin. These tissues will hurt if you cut into them or bite them. Also, nails that are too short will not do their job of protecting your fingertips and toes.

REAL-LIFE
SKILL

Caring for Your Toenails

Toenails need to be cut carefully. The largest toenail can become *ingrown* by growing at the side and cutting into the skin. An ingrown toenail is painful. Cutting the toenail straight rather than rounding the sides often helps prevent an ingrown nail.

STOP **REVIEW**
SECTION 5

REMEMBER?

1. Why can you cut your hair and nails without feeling pain?
2. What three things can you do to care for your hair?
3. Why do you need to keep your fingernails clean?

THINK!

4. What should you think about when choosing a shampoo?
5. How can a person break the habit of nail biting?

People in Health

An Interview with a Dentist

Mary Fisher, D.D.S., knows about treating and preventing dental problems. She is a dentist in West Bloomfield, Michigan.

What does a dentist do?

A dentist checks and treats the teeth and the tissues of the mouth. A dentist takes X rays, cleans teeth, fills cavities, fixes damaged teeth, and treats gum disease. When it is needed, a dentist will also remove teeth. The most important part of a dentist's job, however, is to help people prevent dental problems and preserve their natural teeth.

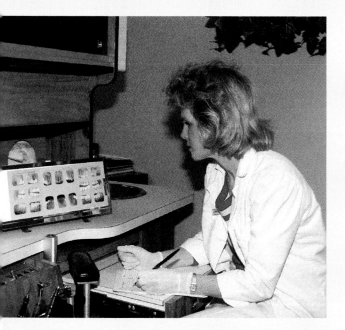

■ *Dr. Fisher uses X-ray photographs to check for cavities in the teeth.*

What does D.D.S. after your name mean?

D.D.S. stands for *Doctor of Dental Surgery*. When I graduated from dental school, I received the degree of Doctor of Dental Surgery. Other dental schools give the degree Doctor of Dental Medicine. Dentists who have that degree use D.D.M. after their names.

Are there different kinds of dentists?

Yes, some dentists are specialists. That means those dentists do only certain kinds of dental work. For example, an orthodontist straightens teeth. A periodontist treats the gums. There are other kinds of dental specialists, too.

What kind of dentist are you?

I am a *general practitioner*. That means I give many kinds of dental care. I do not specialize in only one area. My dental practice centers around family care. I treat both children and adults.

What do you like best about being a dentist?

I enjoy helping people feel better about themselves. Sometimes people are not happy with the way they look. Their teeth may be discolored or not healthy. I can repair their teeth and tell

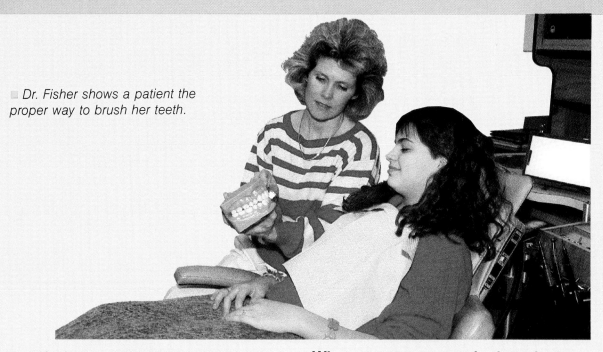

■ *Dr. Fisher shows a patient the proper way to brush her teeth.*

people how to take care of them. It is rewarding to know that my work can help people feel better about themselves.

How many years of school did you need to become a dentist?

I had to finish four years of college and then four years of dental school. After dental school, I had to take a state licensing test. I must renew my license every year.

What qualities should a dentist have?

A dentist should enjoy working with people and be able to put them at ease. Like an artist, a dentist should also enjoy working with his or her hands. Because teeth are so important to health, a dentist must be able to make good decisions about treatments and procedures.

What can young people do to keep their mouths healthy?

It is wonderful that there are so many ways now that young people can protect their teeth and gums. Young people need to be responsible for taking care of their own teeth. They should brush their teeth at least once a day with a fluoride toothpaste. They should also floss their teeth once a day. They should try to eat balanced meals. Eating nutritious, low-sugar foods is important for good dental health. Young people should have a dental checkup every six months.

> *Learn more about people who work as dentists. Interview your family dentist. Or write for information to the American Dental Association, 211 East Chicago Avenue, Chicago, IL 60611.*

Main Ideas

- You need to gather correct information to make important decisions about caring for your health.
- Many people may influence your behavior and give you advice about staying healthy.
- Good dental habits include brushing and flossing your teeth each day and visiting a dentist for checkups.
- You can protect your vision by wearing safety glasses during certain activities, keeping sharp things away from your eyes, and getting help when something gets in your eye.
- You can protect your hearing by staying away from sudden noises or long periods of loud noises.
- You can keep your hair clean by using a shampoo that meets your health care needs.
- You care for your nails by cleaning under them and trimming them.

Key Words

Write the numbers 1 to 8 in your health notebook or on a separate sheet of paper. After each number, copy the sentence and fill in the missing term. Page numbers in ( ) tell you where to look in the chapter if you need help.

health consumer (103)	cavity (110)
myths (106)	fluoride (113)
advertising (107)	lens (118)
sunscreen (108)	decibels (126)

1. The loudness of a sound is measured in ___?___ .

2. A person who uses health information to make decisions about caring for his or her health is a ___?___ .

3. False beliefs are ___?___ .

4. A lotion that blocks the sun's strong rays and protects against sunburn is a ___?___ .

5. A hole in a tooth is a ___?___ .

6. A source of much health information is ___?___ .

7. The ___?___ bends light to make an image sharp and clear.

8. A substance that helps tooth enamel stay hard is ___?___ .

Write the numbers 9 to 16 on your paper. After each number, write a sentence that defines the term. Page numbers in ( ) tell you where to look in the chapter if you need help.

9. plaque (110)	**14.** optic nerve (118)
10. cornea (117)	**15.** cochlea (125)
11. iris (117)	**16.** hair follicle (130)
12. pupil (117)	
13. retina (118)	

Remembering What You Learned

Page numbers in ( ) tell you where to look in the chapter if you need help.

1. What are two kinds of behaviors that come from the influences of others? (103–104)

2. What are some good sources of health information that are easy to get? (104–106)

3. What is the main purpose of advertising? (107)

4. What is the difference between fact and appeal? (107)

5. What are four kinds of information that you can find on the label of a health product? (108)

6. What do microbes do when they live in plaque? (110)

7. What can happen when plaque builds up on the teeth near the gums? (112)

8. How can you prevent gum disease? (113–115)

9. How often should you brush and floss your teeth? (113)

10. What is the difference between *rods* and *cones* in the retina? How are they similar? (118)

11. What should you do to get something out of your eye? (120)

12. What is astigmatism? (122)

13. How can a person know whether he or she has experienced a hearing loss? (127)

14. What are two jobs of hair on your body? (130)

15. What can happen to the hair on your head if you wash it with a bar of soap? (131)

Thinking About What You Learned

1. Why might your health habits be similar to those of your family?

2. How might believing in a myth have an effect on a person's health?

3. Why is music added to some advertising?

4. Why should you compare labels on similar products before you buy one?

5. How is it possible to have a tooth with decay in it and not know about it?

Writing About What You Learned

1. In your health notebook or on a separate sheet of paper, write the name of a health product you have seen advertised on television. Write about the way the health product is advertised. Should the product be used by all people or just by people with a certain health problem? Write about the information given for the health product. Is enough information given to persuade you to buy the product? Why or why not?

2. Write a story about a person your age who forgot to take dental-care items on a camping trip. Describe what decisions the person needs to make to keep his or her teeth clean.

Applying What You Learned

SCIENCE

Make an ear trumpet to show how the outer ear works.

Modified True or False

Write the numbers 1 to 15 in your health notebook or on a separate sheet of paper. After each number, write *true* or *false* to describe the sentence. If the sentence is false, also write a term that replaces the underlined term and makes the sentence true.

1. Microbes in <u>plaque</u> mix with sugar to make acids that can cause cavities.

2. Gum disease in its early stage is called <u>fluoride</u>.

3. If you did not have an <u>optic nerve</u>, you would not be able to see.

4. If a sound has a very <u>low</u> decibel level, it may damage your hearing.

5. The amount of light that passes through the pupil is controlled by the <u>cornea</u>.

6. Cells that sense the brightness of light in the eye are called <u>rods</u>.

7. <u>Calcium</u> helps make your teeth strong.

8. If nearby and faraway objects look blurry, you may have <u>farsightedness</u>.

9. The <u>stirrup</u> is one of the smallest bones in your body.

10. Listening to a loud noise over time can cause <u>hearing loss</u>.

11. If you buy toothpaste with fluoride, you are a wise <u>health consumer</u>.

12. Hair grows out of <u>follicles</u>.

13. If you have <u>light</u> hair, the cells in the hair have a lot of pigment.

14. Keeping your <u>fingernails</u> clean can help you stay safe from disease.

15. The <u>anvil</u> is a coiled tube in the inner ear, filled with a liquid much like seawater.

Short Answer

Write the numbers 16 to 23 on your paper. Write a complete sentence to answer each question.

16. How does your body protect your eyes?

17. How do cavities form?

18. Why is it important to use dental floss even if you brush your teeth daily?

19. How does hearing loss happen?

20. Why do adults and teenagers need to shampoo their hair more often than people your age?

21. What are three signs of a vision problem?

22. What information can you get from an advertisement?

23. How should you care for your ears?

Essay

Write the numbers 24 and 25 on your paper. Write paragraphs with complete sentences to answer each question.

24. Write an essay describing what things you do each day to take care of your own health.

25. List the people who are involved in your health care. Explain how these people help you maintain good health.

ACTIVITIES FOR HOME OR SCHOOL

Projects to Do

1. Go someplace where the light is dim. For example, you can stand in a closet with the door almost shut. Have a classmate hand you several pieces of paper or cloth of different colors. Can you tell the color of each piece while you are in the dim light?

2. Place a row of marbles in a cardboard channel to show how the energy of sound moves through air. Space the marbles apart rather than touching. Hit the first marble hard into the others. Then hit the marble lightly. Which way does a quick, loud sound move through the air? How might that sound affect the ear?

■ *The movement of sound energy is something like the movement of these marbles.*

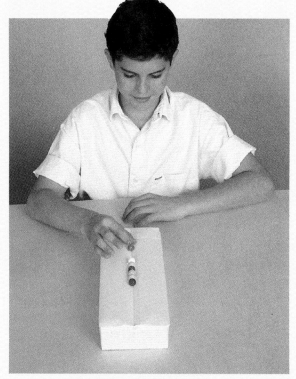

Information to Find

1. A tooth that is knocked out of the mouth sometimes can be put back in place. The tooth needs to be kept moist. Ask your school nurse, a dentist, or a dental hygienist what you would need to do to protect a tooth that has been knocked out.

2. Some people say that cats can see in the dark. Can a cat really see in complete darkness? Is a cat's night vision better than yours? If so, why? Look in books about cats to find out how cats' eyes work.

3. Many television stations show certain programs with captions. The captions are for people who have hearing loss. Write or telephone a television station that broadcasts near your community. Ask what captioned programs the station shows.

Books to Read

Here are some books you can look for in your school library or the public library to find more information about caring for your body.

Bains, Rae. *Health and Hygiene.* Troll Associates.

Iveson-Iveson, Joan. *Your Skin and Hair.* Franklin Watts.

Settel, Joanne, and Nancy Baggett. *Why Does My Nose Run?* Atheneum.

Silverstein, Alvin and Virginia. *The Story of Your Mouth.* Putnam.

CHAPTER 5

FOOD FOR A HEALTHY BODY

Young people usually have changes in their nutritional needs when they start their adolescent growth spurt. The changes of adolescence often cause young people to think about balanced food choices to help them maintain health and stay active. This is also the time when young people start making more food choices on their own.

An important part of good nutrition is knowing what foods to put into your body. Some foods are more healthful than others. Choosing your foods wisely helps you grow. Healthful foods give you energy and keep you strong. Wise food choices also help you reach and maintain wellness.

GETTING READY TO LEARN

Key Questions

- Why is it important to learn about food?
- What can you do to have more healthful eating habits?
- How can you learn to make healthful food choices?
- How can you take more responsibility for the foods you choose to eat?

Main Chapter Sections

1 Your Body Needs Food
2 Variety and Balance in What You Eat
3 Influences on Your Food Choices

KEY WORDS

energy
carbohydrates
glucose
sucrose
calories
fats
proteins
minerals
vitamin
fiber

energy (EHN uhr jee), the ability your body has to grow, be active, and stay healthy.

◼ A healthful breakfast gives you the energy nutrients you need for school and play.

1 Your Body Needs Food

Melody and Jean always plan their morning so they have breakfast. They both have a busy day ahead. At school they will read and talk and work out problems. After school Melody has a dance class. Jean is going to play softball.

Both girls are growing fast. Growing is hard work for their bodies. The girls need a lot of *energy* every day. **Energy** is the ability your body has to grow, be active, and stay healthy. The girls need a good breakfast to get them started. Healthful foods help their bodies grow. Foods help make them healthy and give them energy. The way your body uses food is called *nutrition*.

The parts of food that help you stay healthy are nutrients. Some nutrients give you energy. Some give you the material your body needs to build cells. Your body grows by making new cells. Your body also has to replace dead cells and repair worn-out cells. Your body needs about 40 different kinds of nutrients to stay healthy. Eating a variety of foods gives you many of those nutrients.

Which Nutrients Give You Energy?

Carbohydrates should be your main source of energy each day. Carbohydrates are in foods that come from plants, such as fruits, vegetables, and grains.

There are two kinds of carbohydrates that give you energy. *Sugar* is one kind of carbohydrate. There are many kinds of sugar, and your body gets energy from all of them. These sugars, however, must be broken down into a sugar called glucose before the body can use them. **Glucose** is a simple sugar that contains energy for your cells to use. Most of the sugar in canned or packaged foods is a kind of sugar called sucrose. **Sucrose,** or table sugar, is made from sugarcane or sugar beets. Eating too much sucrose can cause tooth decay.

Starch is another kind of carbohydrate. Plants have a lot of starch in them because that is the form in which they store food. Your body uses starch as another way to get energy. Foods such as potatoes, rice, corn, and noodles all have starch in them. Carbohydrates from starchy foods should make up about half of your daily calories. **Calories** are measured amounts of energy. Foods that have starch are your body's most important source of energy because they also have other nutrients important for good health. Most sucrose-rich foods, such as candy, have few other nutrients in them.

Your body's next most important way to get energy is from fats. **Fats** are the nutrients that give you the greatest number of calories for the amount of food eaten. Foods such as margarine, mayonnaise, and vegetable oils are high in fats. Eggs, cheese, and whole milk all have fats as well as other nutrients in them. Frying adds fats to food.

carbohydrates (kahr boh HY drayts), nutrients that should be your main source of energy each day.

glucose (GLOO kohs), a simple sugar that contains energy for your cells to use.

sucrose (SOO krohs), table sugar; made from sugarcane or sugar beets.

calories (KAL uh reez), measured amounts of energy in food.

fats, the nutrients that give you the greatest number of calories for the amount of food eaten.

■ Foods containing fats supply the greatest number of calories for the amount eaten.

Fats give you twice as many calories per ounce as carbohydrates or proteins. When you do not use all the calories, your body stores the extra energy as fat.

Which Nutrients Help You Grow?

proteins (PROH teenz), nutrients that give you energy and help build and repair cells.

Proteins, too, are nutrients that give you energy to help you grow. But proteins are also important nutrients for building and repairing cells. In fact, all cells in your body are made of proteins. You can get proteins from red meat, chicken, fish, eggs, grains, cheese, and milk. However, you should eat only red meat that does not have a lot of fat.

Milk gives you proteins. It also gives you important minerals. **Minerals** are another kind of nutrient that helps the body grow and work. Calcium and phosphorus, two of the minerals in milk, help build strong bones and teeth.

minerals (MIHN uh ruhlz), nutrients, such as calcium and iron, that help the body grow and work.

■ Foods containing minerals help your body grow and work .

144

You may know about a mineral called iron. Iron in certain forms is used to make buildings and cars. Your body also has a tiny amount of iron. You could not stay alive without that small amount of iron. Iron is a mineral that helps your red blood cells carry oxygen to all your body cells.

The chart "Some Minerals for Good Health" lists some of the minerals you need. It shows some of the foods that can give you each mineral. The chart also tells how each mineral can help you grow and stay healthy.

SOME MINERALS FOR GOOD HEALTH

Mineral	Sources	What It Does
Calcium	milk and dairy foods, soybeans, tofu, some leafy vegetables, canned salmon	builds bones and teeth; helps blood to clot
Iodine	fish, iodized salt	is used by thyroid gland to make two kinds of hormones
Iron	liver, green leafy vegetables, dried fruit, molasses, food cooked in an iron pot	carries oxygen in blood
Magnesium	milk and dairy foods, whole grain cereals, leafy vegetables, nuts, meat	builds bones; helps body use energy
Phosphorus	meat, chicken, fish, milk, peas, beans, whole grains, egg yolks	builds bones and teeth; helps body use energy
Potassium	baked potatoes, lima beans, oranges, bananas, squash (Most foods have some.)	helps muscles and nerves work
Sodium	table salt, milk, seafood, additives, processed foods	helps muscles and nerves work
Zinc	eggs, seafood, meat, grains, cheese, nuts, soybeans	helps wounds heal

Which Nutrients Help You Use Other Nutrients?

Your body also needs a group of nutrients called vitamins. Each **vitamin** helps cause specific reactions to happen in the body. Eating the right amounts of vitamins keeps the chemical processes in your body working properly. There are several kinds of vitamins. Each kind helps your body in a different way.

vitamin (VYT uh muhn), a nutrient that helps cause a specific reaction in the body.

■ *Fruits and vegetables provide a variety of vitamins.*

Oranges, tomatoes, and broccoli have a lot of vitamin C. Many other red, orange, or green fruits and vegetables also have this vitamin. Vitamin C helps keep your gums and blood vessels healthy. It helps your body fight off illness. Vitamin C helps your body use the iron in your diet.

An important group of vitamins is the B-complex vitamins. The different forms of vitamin B are needed by your body for releasing energy and for fighting infections. Milk, cheese, grains, and most vegetables contain the B-complex vitamins.

Milk is a source of protein, vitamins, and minerals.

Vitamin D is an important vitamin for young people. It helps build strong bones. Vitamin D is sometimes called the "sunshine vitamin" because your body can make it when sunshine reaches your skin. Vitamin D is also found in butter, egg yolks, and fortified milk. *Fortified* means that a vitamin has been added to that food. Milk fortified with vitamin D had the vitamin added to it when the milk was packaged. The added vitamin helps you use the minerals in milk. Vitamin D helps get the calcium and phosphorus from food into your bones and teeth.

The chart "Some Vitamins for Good Health" lists some of the vitamins you need. It also lists some foods that can give you each kind of vitamin. The chart also tells how each vitamin can help your body.

SOME VITAMINS FOR GOOD HEALTH

Vitamin	Sources	What It Does
Vitamin A	milk, butter, egg yolks, green and yellow vegetables	helps vision in dim light; keeps skin healthy
Vitamin B$_1$ (thiamine)	pork, seafood, milk, whole grains, peas, nuts	helps body use energy; helps nervous system
Vitamin B$_2$ (riboflavin)	meat, cheese, eggs, fish	helps body cells use energy; keeps skin, eyes, and nerves healthy
Vitamin B$_6$	chicken, fish, whole grains, cereals, egg yolks	helps body use proteins; helps nerve tissue work; helps produce red blood cells
Vitamin B$_{12}$	meat, fish	helps nervous system
Vitamin C	citrus fruits, raw broccoli, tomatoes, dark green and red vegetables	keeps gums and blood vessels healthy; helps body use iron
Vitamin D	fish, egg yolks, fortified milk	helps build strong bones and teeth by controlling calcium and phosphorus

Why Do You Need Water and Fiber?

Water is also a nutrient. Water is such an important nutrient because most of your body is made of water. Water is part of every single cell. If a person weighs 98 pounds, for example, 56 of those pounds are from water!

Your body needs about eight 8-ounce glasses (almost 2 liters) of water every day. You get some of this water by drinking plain water, fruit juices, milk, and other liquids. You also get water from fruits, vegetables, and other foods.

Water helps your body use other nutrients in food. First it helps your body digest food. Then blood, which is almost all water, carries nutrients to all your cells. Water also carries wastes out of your body.

Fiber is another part of certain kinds of food that helps in digestion. Fiber comes from the parts of a plant that give the plant shape. Fiber helps your digestive system work as it should. Without enough food fiber, digestion may slow down. This can cause wastes to build up in your intestines and stay there longer than normal. You will feel uncomfortable as a result.

Many people in the United States worry about the amount of fiber they eat. Most food processing breaks down or removes the fiber parts of raw food. As a result, people must now plan to get enough fiber in their diets each day.

Foods high in fiber include bran cereal, whole grains, seeds, and many fruits and vegetables. The skins of many fresh fruits and vegetables, such as apples and potatoes, are good sources of fiber, too. Most nutrition experts agree that people need to eat some foods with fiber every day. The chart "Fiber in the Food You Eat" on page 150 lists some foods that have healthful amounts of fiber. Depending on body size, an adult needs to eat between 20 and 35 grams of fiber each day.

fiber (FY buhr), a part of food that helps your digestive system work as it should.

MYTH
AND
FACT

Myth: Honey is more healthful for you than sugar.

Fact: Honey *is* sugar. The only advantage of using honey is that it actually tastes sweeter than table sugar.

Foods that are high in fiber and water help digestion. You can get fiber and water from many kinds of foods.

FIBER IN THE FOOD YOU EAT

Serving	Amount of Fiber
Apple, 1 large	4.0 grams
Blackberries, 3/4 cup	6.7 grams
Bran cereal, 100%, 1 cup	8.4 grams
Broccoli, 1/2 cup	3.5 grams
Brown rice, 1/3 cup	1.6 grams
Cherries, 20 large	2.2 grams
Corn flakes, 3/4 cup	2.6 grams
Lettuce, 1 cup	0.8 gram
Oat bran, 1/3 cup uncooked	4.0 grams
Oatmeal, 1/3 cup uncooked	3.0 grams
Pear, 1 medium	4.0 grams
Potato with skin, 1 medium	4.0 grams
Rye bread, 1 slice	0.8 gram
Strawberries, 1 cup	4.0 grams
Tomato, 1 small	1.5 grams
White rice, 1 cup	1.5 grams
Whole-wheat bread, 1 slice	1.3 grams
Whole-wheat crackers, 6	2.2 grams

STOP REVIEW SECTION 1

REMEMBER?

1. How are carbohydrates, fats, and proteins alike?
2. What mineral helps your blood carry oxygen to all your cells?
3. Why does your body need water every day?
4. What foods could you eat to get vitamin C?

THINK!

5. Why do you need to limit the fat you eat every day?
6. Why is water considered a nutrient?

150

Food Sources of the Future

Where does food come from? That question is likely to make you think of farms that grow crops such as wheat, corn, or soybeans. But nutrition experts are experimenting with many other possible sources of food.

The buffalo gourd, for example, is a kind of squash that grows in some wilderness areas in North America. Scientists have found that the seeds of the buffalo gourd contain oil and protein.

The buffalo gourd is uncommon today but may be a common food in the future.

This discovery could mean that farms in the future will grow the buffalo gourd for food. Several other unusual plants may have similar possibilities.

Other scientists work at creating food substitutes in laboratories. Substitutes for orange juice, milk, and sugar have become popular products during the past several years.

Recently food companies have introduced such products as a cheese substitute that contains no fat, a meat substitute made from soybeans, and an egg that has no yolk.

Another new development involves a fish called surimi. Surimi is a very nutritious fish that has been popular in Japan for hundreds of years. Now it is being used to make imitations of such foods as hot dogs and salami.

Surimi has very little flavor, so it can be flavored to taste like almost anything. If it is ground into a paste and then flavored, it can pass for chocolate, potato chips, steak, butter, or almost anything else.

Thinking Beyond

1. How might the development of manufactured foods help people eat a balanced diet?
2. How might manufactured foods help people in places where many fresh foods are not available?

151

2 Variety and Balance in What You Eat

KEY WORDS

balanced diet
caffeine

balanced diet (BAL
uhnst • DY uht), food
choices that give you the
amounts of different
nutrients your body
needs

Think about all the foods you eat and drink at one meal. Each food has different nutrients. One food may have a lot of protein. Others may give you fats, carbohydrates, minerals, or vitamins. A healthful meal gives you many different nutrients, including water and fiber.

All your meals together make up your diet. To reach and maintain wellness, you need a balanced diet. A daily **balanced diet** gives you different nutrients in the amounts your body needs. Different foods have different combinations of nutrients. A diet with many different foods can give you all the nutrients you need.

■ Carefully making a grocery list is one way to plan a balanced diet.

Milk Group
[3 servings each day]

Fruit and Vegetable Group
[4 servings each day]

Grain Group
[4 servings each day]

Meat-Egg-Nut-Bean Group
[2 servings each day]

A food wheel can help you plan a balanced diet.

How Can You Plan a Balanced Diet?

Donna and her father are making a shopping list. They want to buy foods for balanced meals. They are not sure what to buy. Most foods have more than one nutrient. Donna and her father know which nutrients they need. But they wonder which nutrients are in which foods.

There is a simple answer to their question. Most foods belong in one of four basic food groups. Each of the four groups has its own special nutrients. Foods that are found in the same group are similar in their nutrient content.

Look at the picture of the food wheel. It shows how much you should eat from each group each day. It is easy to plan a balanced meal by choosing foods from each of the groups. All the foods together will give you most or all of the important nutrients you need.

You get minerals, vitamins, carbohydrates, and fiber from the Fruit and Vegetable Group. Food from the Meat-Egg-Nut-Bean Group will give you proteins, some minerals, vitamins, and fats. Foods in the Milk Group have vitamins, minerals, proteins, and fats. Any food from the Grain Group will give you carbohydrates, some vitamins and minerals, and fiber.

Even when eating in a restaurant, it is important to choose foods that provide a balance of nutrients.

You do not need food from every group in every meal. But if you leave a food group out of one meal, try to eat something from that group at another meal.

Shawn is looking over a restaurant menu to choose his dinner. He chooses not to eat meat. Shawn can have a balanced meal without eating meat. He can choose a different food from the Meat-Egg-Nut-Bean Group. On the food wheel, fish, eggs, dried beans, nuts, and dried peas are in the same group as meat. They give you many of the same nutrients that meat does.

Foods from the four basic food groups need to be your first choice in planning a balanced diet. Foods not in those groups are put together in their own group, the Fats and Sweets Group. Foods in that group contain a lot of sugar and fats. They do not have growth nutrients in amounts you need to stay healthy.

A GUIDE FOR DAILY FOOD CHOICES

Food Group	Number of Servings	Examples of One-Serving Sizes
Fruit and Vegetable	4	1 small bunch grapes 1/2 cup fruit juice 2 plums 1 medium-sized apple or banana 1 1/2 cups cooked vegetable 1 cup raw, leafy vegetable
Meat-Egg-Nut-Bean	2	2 tablespoons peanut butter 1/4 cup nuts (almonds) 1/2 cup cooked dry beans 1/4 cup sunflower seed kernels 2–3 ounces meat, fish, or poultry 1 egg
Milk	3	1 cup milk 8 ounces yogurt 1 1/2 ounces natural cheese (not cheese spread)
Grain	4	1 slice bread 2 large crackers 1 cup dry cereal 1/2 cup cooked rice, pasta, cereal, or grits

What Happens When Nutrients Are Missing from Your Diet?

Suppose a nutrient were missing from your diet. You might not see any difference for a few days. You might even go for weeks without any harm. But after a while, certain cells would be damaged. You would be able to feel the changes.

Each missing nutrient causes a different health problem. The chart "How Nutrients Help Keep You Healthy" gives information about some of these problems. Reversing the signs of a lack of nutrients is not easy. A physician can help if any of the given signs happen.

HOW NUTRIENTS HELP KEEP YOU HEALTHY

Nutrient	What Happens When the Nutrient Is Missing
Carbohydrates	poor growth, weight loss, lack of energy
Proteins	poor growth, weight loss, weakness
Vitamin A	night blindness; dry, rough skin
Vitamin B_1	numb feeling in toes, tingling legs, weak muscles, nervousness
Vitamin B_2	tender or sensitive skin, blurred vision, irritated eyes
Vitamin B_6	irritability, tiredness, cracked lips at corners of mouth
Vitamin B_{12}	weakness, tiredness, sores in digestive system tissue
Vitamin C	sore, bleeding gums; infections of minor cuts
Vitamin D	softened bones and teeth

How Can You Make Healthful Food Choices?

Sometimes what you eat is your choice. If your family allows snacking, you may choose what to eat after school. You need to find out about your different snack choices.

Talk with a parent about each snack. The best choices are low-fat, low-sugar foods that also contain other nutrients.

As you look into the food cabinet or refrigerator, ask yourself some questions. What is in this food? How can that food help keep me healthy? How is this food more healthful than that one? By answering questions like these, you get some of the information you need to make a healthful food choice. You can think about how eating each food might change your body.

■ *Adults can help you choose snack foods that are nutritious and taste good.*

Some people have cookies, candy, and sweetened soft drinks as snacks. Those foods have large amounts of sugar or fats and few other nutrients. Added sugar can cause tooth decay. Eating high-fat and high-sugar snacks as a habit can cause a person to gain more weight than needed.

The extra weight can make many organs, such as your heart and pancreas, work harder than they should. The pancreas is a body organ that makes digestive juices that help break down proteins, fats, and carbohydrates.

A piece of fruit or a bowl of sliced vegetables is a healthful, tasty snack. It has many of the nutrients you need to stay healthy. It also costs little money, considering all the nutrients it contains.

■ *Fruits or sliced vegetables make healthful, inexpensive snacks.*

caffeine (ka FEEN), a natural chemical found in chocolate, coffee, tea, and most cola drinks.

Some candy and soft drinks have caffeine in them. **Caffeine** is a natural chemical found in chocolate, coffee, tea, and most cola drinks. Too much caffeine in the diet can make people jittery. It can keep people awake when they need to fall asleep. It can cause a stomachache or a burning feeling in the stomach. Milk, water, and fruit juice are more healthful drinks than coffee, tea, or cola drinks.

After choosing a healthful snack, enjoy it. But also think about how you made your food choice. You can be proud of yourself for the way you made your choice. Making wise food choices shows that you are becoming a responsible person.

REVIEW
SECTION 2

REMEMBER?

1. How can you be sure to get all the nutrients you need each day?
2. What kinds of nutrients are found in the Fruit and Vegetable Group?
3. How many servings do you need each day from each of the four food groups?

THINK!

4. How might making a shopping list help you in your planning for a balanced diet?
5. How can healthful snacking help balance your diet?

Making Wellness Choices

Sarah and Betty Lou often spend Saturday mornings together. While at Sarah's house one Saturday, Betty Lou complains that she is hungry because she skipped breakfast. Betty Lou says that she often skips breakfast to lose weight. She says that she then drinks two or three glasses of water. She says the water helps get rid of the hungry feeling.

? What could Sarah say to Betty Lou? Explain your wellness choice.

159

3 Influences on Your Food Choices

KEY WORDS

ingredients
additives
food allergy

Have you ever wondered why you eat the foods you do? You may already know that your likes and dislikes influence some of your food choices. Knowing about your nutrient needs can help you make healthful food choices. But food choices are influenced by other things as well.

■ *Many influences affect your food choices.*

How Do Family, Friends, and Culture Affect Food Choices?

You probably like most foods prepared by your family. Those foods are familiar to you. You see that your family likes certain foods. The way members of your family feel about food is often the way you feel, too.

Your friends may also influence what you choose to eat. If your friends eat certain kinds of food, such as pizza or burritos, you are likely to eat those foods too. Positive and negative ideas about food come from a person's relationships with other people.

Certain foods are closely tied to the cultures of different parts of the United States. Barbecued pork, grits, and cornbread are tied to the culture of the South. Clam chowder, lobster, and other seafood are connected with New England. When people think of food and the Southwest, they often think of beef, beans, and chili.

Along with regional foods, there are food choices tied to certain national cultures. If your background is Greek, moussaka might be a well-liked food in your family. *Moussaka* is a food made of ground meat and sliced eggplant. Some families from a Spanish background often eat a food called *paella.* It is made of rice, meat, seafood, and vegetables.

Families have come to the United States from many countries. They have brought favorite food traditions with them. The tradition of eating those foods often stays with these families.

How Do Emotions Affect Food Choices?

Is there a kind of soup or drink that a parent prepares for you when you are ill? Is there a food you often eat after a busy day at school? Many people connect foods with certain feelings. In many families, certain foods are often used as a reward for good behavior. People learn to associate such foods with feelings of love or belonging.

Families often eat certain foods at holidays or other happy times. The foods may be part of their culture. In time such foods can become connected with feelings of happiness.

A parent may prepare certain foods for you when you are ill.

How Does Availability Affect Food Choices?

People tend to eat and enjoy foods that are familiar to them. Familiar foods are available to buy in food stores. Certain foods are in the stores near you because they are made in your state. The food selections vary among states and regions because different foods are grown in different parts of the United States. The climate or soil may be better for a certain food in one place than in another.

You may live in a state where large amounts of fruits and vegetables are grown. So you may eat more of such foods. However, foods grown in one state are often shipped to other states for sale.

Today freezing and canning are often done to keep foods from spoiling. When foods are frozen or canned, they can be shipped long distances. Because of this, many kinds of foods are available near you all year round. Preserved foods add to the variety of choices people can make.

Even if certain foods are available where you live, they may not always be available to you. Food availability includes the ability of people to pay the cost of the food.

■ *Fresh fruits and vegetables are available throughout the United States because of improved methods of farming and transportation.*

How Do Advertising and Food Labels Affect Food Choices?

Advertising affects many parts of your life. It tries to tell you what foods to choose and what foods to buy. Advertising can affect your food choices. You can test the influence of advertising the next time you go to a food store. See how many brand names you know. You most likely learned those names from advertising.

Advertising makes you familiar with the brand names on packages. A wise consumer studies the whole label on a food package, however. The label lists the ingredients inside the package. The **ingredients** are the materials that make up the food.

Ingredients are listed on the label in order, from the one used in the largest amount to the one used in the smallest amount. The list must include everything that was used to make the food. The label must show all the additives in the food. **Additives** are chemicals often used to keep food from spoiling or to improve the way it looks. Additives are necessary in some foods.

Sometimes a label lists the nutrient values of the food in the package. You can use the list to help you choose the foods with the most nutrients.

REAL-LIFE SKILL

Drawing Conclusions About Advertising

Are certain colors used more than others to help sell food products? Survey different brands of foods in one or two aisles of a grocery store. Some brands will use a combination of colors to "catch your eye." Which color is used most often? Why, do you think, do advertisers use this color?

■ *Knowing the ingredients of packaged foods can help you make wise food choices.*

ingredients (ihn GREED ee uhnts), the materials that make up a food.

additives (AD uht ihvz), chemicals often used to preserve food or improve the way it looks.

163

How Do Special Health Needs Affect Food Choices?

People sometimes make food choices because of special health needs. As a young person who is growing, you have a need for a wide variety of foods. The foods you eat should have large amounts of the nutrients you need to stay healthy. You need foods rich in carbohydrates to give you energy. You need proteins and minerals to help you grow. You need calcium, magnesium, and phosphorus to give you strong bones and teeth.

Some people avoid certain foods because of a health problem. They may have a food allergy. A **food allergy** is a disorder that causes a person to have a physical reaction to some foods. A food that affects a person with an allergy does not affect other people the same way.

An allergy to a food can begin at any age. After eating the food, the person usually reacts right away, but may react later. Headaches, intestinal cramps, and skin rashes are common reactions caused by food allergies.

food allergy (FOOD • AL uhr jee), a disorder that causes a person to have a physical reaction to a food.

Jennifer needs extra carbohydrates because she is very active. Foods such as spaghetti are rich in carbohydrates.

A physician can help a person with a food allergy learn which foods to avoid. Knowing the four basic food groups can help a person choose nutritious foods to replace the one to which the person has an allergy.

REVIEW
SECTION 3

REMEMBER?

1. What are three factors that influence your food choices?
2. In what order are the ingredients of a food listed on the label?
3. What are some special health needs that cause people to make certain food choices?

THINK!

4. How might food cost influence your decision to choose certain foods?
5. How can you use food labels to help you balance your diet?

Thinking About Your Health

Who or What Influences Your Food Choices?

Do you know what most influences the food choices you make? Make a list of the foods and beverages you eat or drink most often. Place each in a food group category—fruits and vegetables, meat-egg-nut-bean, milk, or grain. Then code each food or drink according to the categories listed here. The code system will help you answer the question "Who or what influences my food choices?" You may use one or all of these symbols in your coding:

P = peers, friends
F = family likes or dislikes
PP = personal likes or dislikes
A = advertisements
B = family background
FA = food availability
C = cost

165

An Interview with a Food Grower

Tommy Staley knows that healthful foods are important for being healthy. He grows vegetables on a large farm in Zellwood, Florida.

What do you do as a food grower?

I manage all the stages of food production, from planning which crops to grow to packaging and selling them. About 30 different vegetable crops are grown on this farm. We grow lettuce, cabbage, parsley, leeks, spinach, carrots, radishes, corn, beets, turnips, and cauliflower. Carrots are the major crop.

Who eats the vegetables you grow?

Most of this farm's produce is sold to people in major cities east of the Mississippi River. That means Chicago, Baltimore, Cleveland, Atlanta, Boston, New York, and Philadelphia. Certain vegetables, such as radishes and carrots, are shipped to the Netherlands, Ireland, and France. Many large food producers in the United States today grow food for the world. They are not just growing food to feed their families and neighbors.

What is one modern way to grow nutritious vegetables?

One way is growing plants by using a plastic ground covering. The plastic is laid on the ground. Then holes are punched in it. Plants are put through the plastic into the soil. Small tubes go under the plastic, next to the plants. The tubes have tiny holes to let water drip out. Only a small amount of water is used on each plant, and that water has nutrients in it. The nutrients are used in the exact amount each plant needs. The whole process is guided by a computer. This way no water or nutrients are wasted. No harmful substances reach the plants. The plastic keeps weeds from growing next to the plants. And it keeps rain from washing away the nutrients.

■ *Mr. Staley grows many different kinds of vegetables on his farm.*

After you harvest your vegetables, how do you keep them fresh on the way to market?

The vegetables are sprayed with water so they are damp. Then the vegetables are put into a machine that removes some of the moisture quickly. Removing moisture cools the vegetables and keeps them fresh. It is like putting water on your hand and blowing on it. Your hand feels cooler. The evaporation causes the cooling. To keep vegetables fresh during transport, they are cooled to just above freezing, about 35 or 36 degrees Fahrenheit [1.6 or 2.2 degrees Celsius].

Today a farmer needs to know many subjects, including biology, mathematics, and business.

What qualities and training should a person have to run a farm?

Today a person going into farming needs a lot of knowledge and must be a good planner. A college education helps. Farming is a business. It is also very competitive. A person in farming has to know about many subjects, such as chemistry, biology, mathematics, government, law, and business. That person also has to know about machinery and computers. In the past, a person who started a farm had often grown up on one. I did, and it is still possible to start that way. But farming is becoming more costly and complicated. It is becoming harder to start a farm, and the people who do will have to be smart to stay in farming.

What do you like best about your job?

I like the feeling of accomplishment I have every day. It gives me great pleasure to see a plant grow. I feel close to nature in this job. Whenever I see a plow turning soil, I want to be on that plow. I guess you can tell I love this work. I am proud to know my work is going to help feed people and keep them healthy.

Learn more about modern methods for growing food. Interview a food producer. Or write for information to the Science and Education Administration, United States Department of Agriculture, Room 432-A, Washington, DC 20250.

CHAPTER REVIEW

Main Ideas

- Your body gets both energy and the materials to make new cells from healthful foods.
- Some nutrients help you grow, and others help you use other nutrients.
- To reach and maintain wellness, you need a diet with many different nutritious foods.
- Your ideas about foods are shaped by your family, your friends, and your culture.
- Such factors as emotions, food availability, advertising, and special needs influence what people choose to eat.

Key Words

Write the numbers 1 to 9 in your health notebook or on a separate sheet of paper. After each number, copy the sentence and fill in the missing term. Page numbers in ( ) tell you where to look in the chapter if you need help.

energy (142)　　caffeine (158)
glucose (143)　　ingredients (163)
sucrose (143)　　additives (163)
calories (143)　　food allergy (164)
balanced diet
　(152)

1. Most of the sugar in canned and packaged foods is ___?___.

2. A natural chemical found in chocolate, coffee, tea, and most cola drinks is ___?___.

3. A disorder that causes a person to have a physical reaction to a certain food is called a ___?___.

4. The power your body needs to grow, be active, and stay healthy is called ___?___.

5. A ___?___ gives you different nutrients in the amounts your body needs.

6. Chemical ingredients often used to preserve food or improve its looks are called ___?___.

7. A simple sugar that contains energy for your cells to use is ___?___.

8. The things that make up a food are called ___?___.

9. Measured amounts of energy are called ___?___.

Write the numbers 10 to 15 on your paper. After each number, write a sentence that defines the term. Page numbers in ( ) tell you where to look in the chapter if you need help.

10. carbohydrates (143)
11. fats (143)
12. proteins (144)
13. minerals (144)
14. vitamin (146)
15. fiber (149)

Remembering What You Learned

Page numbers in ( ) tell you where to look in the chapter if you need help.

1. What two kinds of carbohydrates give your body energy? (143)

2. What are three sources of carbohydrates? (143)

3. How is protein different from fats and carbohydrates? (143–144)

4. List three minerals and their sources, and tell what each one does for your body. (144–145)

5. List three vitamins and their sources, and tell what each one does for your body. (146–148)

6. What do foods in the same food group have in common? (153–155)

7. What kinds of snacks are the most healthful? (157–158)

8. How do friends affect food choices? (160)

9. What is one way to get the information you need to make a healthful food choice? (163)

10. When can a food allergy begin? (164)

Thinking About What You Learned

1. How might having too much fat in your diet be harmful to your body?

2. Why should you not depend on sunshine to help your skin make vitamin D?

3. How might a fiber-free diet be harmful to your health?

4. How can you find out which snack foods are healthful for you?

5. How is it helpful to know the way in which ingredients are listed on food labels?

Writing About What You Learned

1. Interview an older adult to find out his or her favorite breakfast foods. What did the person eat for breakfast at your age? Then list your own favorite breakfast foods. How are they the same? How are they different? How might the ethnic backgrounds of you and the person you interviewed have an effect on the breakfast foods eaten? Share your findings with your classmates.

2. Write a story about how you or a friend could change one poor nutritional habit to a healthful nutritional habit. How could a parent help? Could a teacher or school nurse be of help?

3. Write a 30-second commercial for a nutritious food. Use the style of commercials for fast foods, but advertise some food that is low in fat and low in sugar and salt. You may advertise a ready-to-eat food or food cooked at home or in the school cafeteria.

Applying What You Learned

SOCIAL STUDIES

Draw a map of the United States. In each state, draw at least one food product that is grown or produced in that state.

Modified True or False

Write the numbers 1 to 15 in your health notebook or on a separate sheet of paper. After each number, write *true* or *false* to describe the sentence. If the sentence is false, also write a term that replaces the underlined term and makes the sentence true.

1. Margarine, mayonnaise, and oils are high in <u>fats</u>.

2. Iron is a <u>vitamin</u> that helps your blood carry oxygen to all your cells.

3. To find out what nutrients are in a food, you can check the <u>ingredients</u>.

4. If you have difficulty digesting food, you may not be eating enough <u>fiber</u>.

5. <u>Starch</u> is made from sugarcane or sugar beets.

6. <u>Caffeine</u> is a chemical found in coffee and most cola drinks.

7. The <u>five</u> basic food groups must be included in a balanced diet.

8. Your main source of energy should be <u>fats</u>.

9. All cells in your body are made from <u>protein</u>.

10. Vitamin <u>D</u> helps your body use the iron in your diet.

11. <u>Blood</u> is made almost entirely of water.

12. The Fats and Sweets Group <u>is</u> one of the four basic food groups.

13. Added <u>sugar</u> can cause tooth decay.

14. You may like a food because other members of your <u>family</u> like it.

15. One way people can eat certain foods all year is by <u>preserving</u> them.

Short Answer

Write the numbers 16 to 23 on your paper. Write a complete sentence to answer each question.

16. How can advertising affect your choices when you buy foods?

17. Explain how a vitamin is different from a mineral.

18. How can you make sure you are eating a balanced diet?

19. What is a food allergy?

20. Describe how snacking can help you have a balanced diet.

21. What would happen to your body if you drank no water?

22. Why is it important to know how many calories are in foods?

23. How do your family and friends affect your food choices?

Essay

Write the numbers 24 and 25 on your paper. Write paragraphs with complete sentences to answer each question.

24. You are going to the grocery store to buy food. Describe what you would buy, and explain how your choices would make up a balanced diet.

25. Describe what the positive and negative results of food additives might be.

ACTIVITIES FOR HOME OR SCHOOL

Projects to Do

1. In a small group and then with the class, discuss different ways schools raise money with food-related events. Prepare a list of nutritious foods that might be sold at such events. Share your class list with the principal or student council.

2. You can make a healthful snack to take with you on long car trips or on camping trips. Make the snack by mixing together healthful foods that do not need to be cooked. Choose foods that you think would taste good together. Many kinds of dried fruit might go on your list. Nuts and some unsugared cereals, such as wheat flakes or oatmeal, may be included. Some of the cereals may need to be toasted in the oven. Ask an adult to help you with that part.

■ Different foods can be combined to make a nutritious snack.

Information to Find

1. Use books in the library to find out how many calories are in different foods. Which foods have many calories for the weight of the food? Which foods have few calories? How many calories are in soft drinks with sugar (sucrose or corn syrup) and without sugar?

2. People in different parts of the United States have their own special ways of preparing food. Choose a part of the country other than your own. You might choose the Northeast, the Midwest, the South, the Southwest or another region. Get a book from the library that gives recipes for foods eaten in the part of the country you have chosen. Use the book to plan a meal that might be eaten in that part of the country. Remember to include something from each of the four basic food groups in your meal. Label each food with the name of the food group from which it comes.

Books to Read

Here are some books you can look for in your school library or the public library to find more information about food, diet, and your digestive system.

Gaskin, John. *Eating.* Franklin Watts.

Smaridge, Norah. *What's on Your Plate?* Abingdon Press.

Ward, Brian R. *Diet and Nutrition.* Franklin Watts.

171

ACTIVITY FOR A HEALTHY BODY

You know that to reach wellness, you need daily habits of personal care. You need a balanced diet. You also need balanced activity. Balanced activity means daily exercise, rest, and sleep. You will need balanced activity all your life.

Young people are more likely than adults to get the sleep they need without special effort. But some young people need to find ways to rest during times of extra work, extra study, or unusual problems. Many young people in the United States do not get enough exercise. With help, you can review your present habits and can make changes where needed. You can gain a balance of exercise, rest, and sleep.

GETTING READY TO LEARN

Key Questions

- Why is it important to learn about balancing exercise, rest, and sleep?
- How do you feel about the way you now exercise, rest, and sleep?
- How can you learn to make healthful choices about exercise, rest, and sleep?
- What can you do to have more healthful habits?
- How can you take more responsibility for choosing healthful ways to exercise, rest, and sleep?

Main Chapter Sections

1 Exercise and Your Health
2 Daily Practices for Fitness
3 Finding Out How Fit You Are
4 Balancing Activity with Rest and Sleep

173

Exercise and Your Health

physical fitness (FIHZ ih kuhl • FIHT nuhs), the condition in which your body works the best that it is able.

Exercising makes people feel good about themselves. It also helps them stay healthy.

Mrs. Raynes is very proud of each student in her class. Her fifth-grade class won many honors on Fun Day at King Elementary School. Fun Day is a day of races, jumping, tag, and other games. Each class member took part in all the events.

Even after all the Fun Day games, the students are still active. They walked around helping younger students. They drank water to replace what their bodies had lost during the games. The students in Mrs. Raynes's class did well because they are physically fit. **Physical fitness** is the condition in which your body works the best that it is able. People who are physically fit can play and work with less effort and for a longer time than people who are not physically fit.

Mrs. Raynes has another reason to be proud of her students. They spend time each day doing exercises. Exercise is activity that makes their bodies work hard. Regular exercise helped the students prepare their bodies for all the activities on Fun Day. Mrs. Raynes told her students that they were taking responsibility for their health by doing exercise. She also told them that exercising each day would help them feel good about themselves. Regular exercise will help them be healthy all their lives.

How Does Exercise Improve Physical Fitness?

Your body needs regular exercise to stay healthy. A daily habit of active play or work improves your physical fitness in three ways. Exercise builds up your ability to play or work for long periods without getting too tired. It makes your body strong. It helps your body move easily.

Hard exercise builds up your heart and the muscles that help you breathe and move. Daily exercise gives you endurance. **Endurance** means your body is able to be active for a long time without getting too tired. All the students in Mrs. Raynes's class have endurance. They are able to run, walk, and jump even after taking part in all of the games on Fun Day.

Exercise also builds up your muscle strength. **Muscle strength** means your body is able to apply force with its muscles. The more you work your muscles, the stronger they become. Many activities, such as carrying firewood or climbing stairs instead of using an elevator, help build strength in the muscles of your upper arms and your legs.

A physically fit person can play or work for long periods without feeling tired.

endurance (ihn DUR uhns), the ability of your body to be active for a long time without getting too tired.

muscle strength (MUHS uhl • STREHNGTH), the ability of the body to apply force with its muscles.

175

■ *Stretching your muscles improves your flexibility.*

Taking part in different kinds of hard exercise works different muscles. Doing many kinds of exercises makes all your muscles stronger. Strong muscles help your legs hold up your body. Strong muscles in your back and abdomen help hold your spine straight when you sit, walk, and stand. You need strong muscles to have good posture.

Daily exercise makes you flexible. **Flexibility** means you are able to move your body with ease. You can gain flexibility through exercise that stretches muscles, ligaments, and tendons at the movable joints. Those joints are places where your bones meet. Shoulders, elbows, and wrists are movable joints in your arms. The joints in your hips, knees, and ankles are also movable joints. Your neck and your back also have movable joints. The more flexible you are, the easier it is to move your joints.

Certain exercises help you develop balance and coordination between body parts as well as build strength and endurance. For example, you may have used a tricycle or a scooter when you were younger. Learning to ride them helped you become coordinated so that you could later handle a bicycle or a skateboard. Both bicycling and skateboarding also help make your leg muscles strong.

176

How Does Exercise Help Your Respiratory System?

When you exercise hard, your muscles use up a lot of energy. Your body needs more oxygen to use more energy. So you breathe deeper and faster when you exercise.

Deeper breaths draw more air into your lungs. The alveoli inside your lungs open to their greatest size. Then your lungs can hold more air. More air means more oxygen for your blood to carry to your cells.

Lungs that can hold more air help you each time you breathe out, too. Each breath gets rid of carbon dioxide, a waste given off by your cells. There is more carbon dioxide to get rid of when cells burn more energy.

The best exercises for your respiratory system are those that make you breathe deeply for 20 to 30 minutes. Such exercises should be done at least two or three times a week. Riding your bicycle is one such exercise. Swimming, walking fast, and jumping rope also make you breathe hard. Lively games, such as basketball and soccer, can help your respiratory system, too.

An improved respiratory system helps your body get more oxygen. More oxygen gives you more energy for work and play. By exercising to improve your respiratory system, you can help make your whole body work better. You will also feel more relaxed and feel better about yourself.

A machine that tests the respiratory system can show if a person's body is getting enough oxygen.

■ *Running up steps increases the heart rate. Jane is finding out her heart rate by checking her pulse.*

blood pressure (BLUHD • PREHSH uhr), the force of blood against the walls of your arteries.

How Does Exercise Help Your Circulatory System?

Exercise makes your heart beat faster and harder. Because your heart is a muscle, the hard work makes it stronger. As your heart muscle gains strength, it becomes easier for it to do its work. A strong heart can pump more blood each time it beats. Even during rest, a strong heart does not have to beat as often. It takes a longer rest between beats. The rest helps your heart work hard when it needs to do so.

Exercise that requires more oxygen for cells causes your blood vessels to open wider. Exercise keeps materials from building up on the inside walls of blood vessels. Plenty of exercise and clean blood vessels can help your blood pressure stay normal all your life. **Blood pressure** is the force of blood against the walls of your arteries, the blood vessels that carry blood away from your heart.

Active play or work can help your circulatory system. Fast walking, dancing, skating, swimming, cross-country skiing, and bicycling are all good exercises for your heart and blood vessels. So are games such as tennis and soccer.

How Does Exercise Improve Cardiorespiratory Fitness?

People with healthy circulatory and respiratory systems have **cardiorespiratory fitness.** This kind of fitness is reached only by doing hard exercise regularly. Only one kind of exercise helps build cardiorespiratory fitness: aerobic exercise.

Aerobic exercise means "exercise with oxygen." During aerobic exercise, your respiratory and circulatory systems work together to give your muscles the oxygen they need to keep working without stopping. You should be able to do aerobic exercises without becoming out of breath.

Swimming, cross-country skiing, and jogging are some good aerobic exercises. So are skating, bicycling, and jumping rope. Each activity should be done for at least 20 minutes without stopping. For example, jumping rope for 20 to 30 minutes at least three times a week is a good aerobic exercise plan. Aerobic exercise is a good way to build endurance.

How can you tell if an exercise is aerobic? Think of the word *FIT*. *F* stands for *frequency* (how often); the exercise should be done at least three times a week. *I* stands for *intensity* (how hard); the exercise should make you breathe deeply and break into a sweat. *T* stands for *time* (how long); the exercise should last at least 20 minutes without stopping.

cardiorespiratory fitness (KAHRD ee oh REHS puh ruh tohr ee • FIHT nuhs), a healthy condition of the circulatory and respiratory systems.

aerobic exercise (air OH bihk • EHK suhr syz), activities you do in which your muscles get enough oxygen to work without stopping.

■ *Almost everyone can benefit from a program of regular aerobic exercise.*

179

anaerobic exercise (an uh ROH bihk • EHK suhr syz), activities you do in which your muscles do not get enough oxygen to keep working without stopping.

■ *Short, fast bursts of running often leave a person out of breath.*

Anaerobic exercise is "exercise *without* oxygen." It is done in short, fast spurts. Running a 50-yard (46-meter) dash is a form of anaerobic exercise. Your body works very hard during anaerobic exercise. But the hard work only lasts a short time. Your heart and lungs cannot give your body as much oxygen as your muscles need. You need to rest for a short time after anaerobic exercise. Anaerobic exercise helps muscles become stronger.

People who do both aerobic and anaerobic exercises are working to improve their physical fitness. Many people do aerobic exercise one day and anaerobic exercise the next. Such people have a lower risk of health problems, and they feel better about themselves.

STOP **REVIEW**
SECTION 1

REMEMBER?

1. How does having strong muscles help you?
2. What does flexibility do for the body?
3. What two body systems can be improved by regular aerobic exercise?

THINK!

4. How might having physical fitness improve your self-concept?
5. What are two ways in which exercising can help you be healthy all your life?

SECTION 2 Daily Practices for Fitness

Many people your age exercise as part of a school physical education program or in family and social groups. Some of them exercise to help train for a sport. Most people, however, need to review their daily habits and add certain kinds of activities for physical fitness of the whole body.

People who want to become physically fit use a plan. A plan helps them stay organized and keep to a schedule. Exercise schedules help them remember when to exercise.

KEY WORDS

warm-up
cool-down

■ A schedule of regular exercise helps the members of this family meet their physical fitness needs.

The Bakers' Fitness Calendar

Sun	Mon	Tues	Wed	Thurs	Fri	Sat
2-mile walk	3-mile bicycle ride	2-mile walk (fast walk)	Rest	3-mile bicycle ride	2-mile walk	Rest
3-mile walk	Rest	2-mile bicycle ride	2-mile walk (fast walk)	3-mile bicycle ride	Rest	2-mile bicycle ride
Rest		2-mile walk	Rest	2-mile walk (fast walk)	Rest	2-mile bicycle ride
				bicycle ride		Rest

People plan how much they want to exercise to meet their goal. Families can discuss plans that include doing fitness activities together.

Maybe you have already talked with a parent or physical education teacher about a plan to improve your fitness. If you are just beginning to make a fitness plan, you need to think about some important points. Your plan for fitness should have activities to prepare you for lively exercises. Your plan should be fun to keep you interested. It should also have guidelines for your safety.

How Can You Get Ready for Exercising?

Paying attention in class and studying are two good ways to prepare for a test. If you do not do those things, you may not do well on the test. You need to prepare your body in a certain way before you exercise, too. A five-minute period of easy exercises that prepare your muscles to work hard is called a **warm-up.**

warm-up, exercises that prepare your muscles to work hard.

Warm-up exercises build up, little by little, the need that your muscles have for oxygen. A warm-up slowly increases your heartbeat for more blood flow to your muscles. Slow stretching as part of a warm-up also helps get your muscles ready to work. It gets your joints moving. The pictures show you three simple warm-up exercises. When

■ To do the first two exercises, move slowly from position 1 to position 2. Avoid jerky or bouncing movements. Hold still in position 2 while you count to four. Then move back to position 1. Do this five times for each exercise. To do the third exercise, start in position 1. Jump up and land in position 2. Then jump up and land in position 1 again. Repeat these moves quickly 20 times, keeping up a steady pace.

Exercise 1

Position 1   Position 2

you do warm-up exercises, try not to jerk or bounce. That can harm your muscles. Instead, move slowly and hold each stretching position for about five to ten seconds.

Stretching and doing other slow movements for five minutes after hard exercise acts as a **cool-down.** A cool-down is a way to slowly stop exercising. You can use many of the same exercises for cooling down as for warming up. Cool-down exercises, however, should be done fewer times than warm-up exercises. They should also be done more slowly. Riding a bicycle slowly or walking slowly before stretching is good for a cool-down. This lets your muscles slowly relax as your heart rate returns to normal. It lets the large amount of blood that has gone into your large muscles return to your heart.

You need to warm up and cool down before and after aerobic and anaerobic exercises. That way your muscles will not feel as sore the next day. It will help make your exercise healthful and safe.

cool-down, slow exercises done after hard exercise.

What Exercises Can You Choose for Fitness?

Doing different exercises is important to any exercise plan. Different exercises keep different muscles strong. Having different physical activities can make doing exercise interesting and fun.

The exercises on the next three pages can be enjoyed by young people with different abilities. These are only a few of the many exercises from which you can choose. You need to think about your choices. Choose exercises that you think you will enjoy. As you become skilled at or tired of one kind of activity, you can challenge yourself with new ones. The point is to do something active—keep moving. Do something you enjoy.

Exercises for Endurance. Endurance takes time to develop. It does not happen all at once. Building up your endurance can be simple and fun.

■ *Swimming builds endurance.*

Endurance exercises can be done by yourself, with a partner, or in a small group. Jogging and fast walking, for example, are endurance exercises you can do alone or with others. When you jog, you should start with warm-up exercises. Then you should walk slowly and build to a slow jog. You should keep the same pace for a set time, which should be about 20 minutes. While jogging, have fun and talk to your partner. If you cannot talk because you feel out of breath, you are jogging too fast. Slow down, and have a good time while you improve your physical fitness.

For most people, endurance is a personal goal. It is not a competitive sport. If you have not done any regular endurance exercise before, if you are overweight, or if you have a health problem such as asthma, talk with your teacher, nurse, or physician about your endurance plan. You may start by increasing your walking speed or by doing walk-and-run cycles with your arms swinging to build endurance. It is more important that you move steadily for 20 minutes than that you move fast.

Exercises for Strength. When choosing strength exercises, you need to be careful to avoid injuries. Because your body is growing rapidly, some kinds of strength exercise may be dangerous for you. Straining to lift heavy weights may cause injury to your bones and muscles.

One good strength exercise is the push-up. It helps build strong muscles in your upper arms and shoulders. You build strength by pushing a part of your body weight away from the ground. Then you slowly lower your weight back to the ground. One correct way to do the push-up is shown in the pictures below. The push-up is a good exercise to use all your life.

Jumping rope is an aerobic exercise.

Push-ups can help strengthen muscles.

Exercises for Flexibility. Young people your age are likely to be active and flexible. As you grow older or want to try certain sports, you should have flexibility exercises in your fitness plan.

Muscles in your legs and back that have not been exercised may feel tight. Stiff muscles can be stretched over time so that you can have good flexibility. Stretching exercises are good warm-up and cool-down exercises. One kind of stretching exercise is the sit-and-reach. The proper way to do the sit-and-reach exercise is shown in the picture.

■ The sit-and-reach is a stretching exercise.

Exercise helps you most if you do it at least three times a week. Regular exercise adds to your endurance, strength, and flexibility. Having physical fitness is your responsibility. You will have a good feeling about yourself when you are physically fit.

How Can You Be Safe While Exercising?

Staying safe while you exercise is important to any exercise plan. Injuries take time to heal and will keep you from doing exercise for a while. Being unable to exercise can discourage anyone who wants to be physically fit.

Some kinds of exercise call for special equipment. It is tempting to try to use exercise equipment if you see it. Ask your physical education teacher or coach how to use the equipment that is safe for your body size. Do not try to use any equipment you do not know how to use.

Fast walking and jogging are exercises in which injuries can happen. When fast walking or jogging, wear shoes that are made for the activity. The shoes should properly cushion your heels and support your ankles. Choose walking or running surfaces that are smooth and a little soft. Grass, dirt, or sand will give as you walk or jog. Using such surfaces may keep you from getting certain foot and leg injuries. Learn to look for surfaces that are not even as you walk or jog. Do not jog at night when you cannot see dangers. Do not exercise alone at night.

People want to be safe from traffic when they run, walk, or bike. For that reason, some communities build hike-and-bike paths. A person your age should exercise with a partner in a public place, such as a community park or hike-and-bike path, away from traffic.

■ *One way to be safe while exercising is to have a partner. Running on a soft, smooth surface may prevent injuries.*

You need to replace water that your body loses through sweating.

Part of being safe while exercising is drinking enough water. Water lost because of sweating during exercise must be replaced. People who exercise a lot in hot weather should drink water before they exercise. They may carry water to sip at times while they bike, run, dance, or play a sport. When they finish exercising, they always drink enough water to quench their thirst. Sometimes they drink fruit juice besides water.

STOP REVIEW
SECTION 2

REMEMBER?

1. What are two ways that having a plan for exercise can help you?
2. What are three important parts of an exercise plan?
3. What are two safety rules to follow while exercising?

THINK!

4. Why should your plan for physical fitness have many different exercises?
5. How might working out by yourself with exercise equipment be dangerous?

Making Wellness Choices

Manuel's older brother is a high school student who likes to exercise and lift weights. There is a set of weights in the basement of their home. Manuel, who is a fifth-grade student, likes to watch his brother when he lifts weights. Manuel has asked his friend James to come to his house and see the weights. James thinks it would be a good idea to have a contest to see who can lift the most weight.

 What should Manuel say? Explain your wellness choice.

3 Finding Out How Fit You Are

How do you know if you are physically fit? There are some simple tests to find out how fit you are. The tests will tell you two things. They will tell you in what ways you are already physically fit, and they will tell you which kinds of exercise you need to add to your daily schedule. *Do not take these tests if your physical activity is limited for any medical reason. Do not take the test for endurance unless you have been doing aerobic exercises for at least 8 weeks.*

How Can You Test Your Endurance?

When you test your endurance, you are also testing your cardiorespiratory fitness. A parent, a teacher, or your physical education teacher can help you by timing you with a watch while you jog.

Jog at a steady pace that can be maintained during the testing period.

Follow these steps for your endurance test:

1. Choose a measured course, such as a track around a football field.
2. Warm up for five minutes.
3. Start jogging when the person timing you says, "Go." Do not start too fast. Jog at a steady pace for 20 minutes. If you become too tired to keep jogging, try to keep walking quickly.
4. After 20 minutes, the person timing you will need to spot where you are on the course. The person will need to measure how far you went, to the nearest tenth of a mile.
5. Do not stop moving after 20 minutes. Cool down for five minutes by stretching or walking. This will help bring your heart rate to normal.

Jogging 1.8 miles (2.9 kilometers) or farther in 20 minutes is a sign of endurance fitness for a girl in fifth grade. Jogging 2 miles (3.2 kilometers) or farther in 20 minutes is a sign of endurance fitness for a boy in fifth grade.

How Can You Test Your Strength?

The muscles of the abdomen are the best muscles to test for strength in young people. It is safer to test those muscles than muscles in your arms or legs. This is because the bones in your arms and legs are still growing. Trying to lift a heavy weight may harm those bones.

The bent-knee curl-up is an exercise that you can do. To do the test for strength, follow these steps:

1. Lie on your back with your knees up. Place your arms across your chest. Keep your chin close to your chest.
2. Have a partner hold your feet flat on the floor.
3. When your partner says, "Go," curl up so that you are almost sitting. Your hips should touch the floor at all times. Touch your elbows to your thighs. Blow air out as you curl up. This helps you give power to the movement.
4. Finish the curl-up by lowering your shoulders to the floor. Breathe in as you do so. This is counted as one curl-up. Your partner will count your curl-ups.

5. The test will last for two minutes. Keep the same pace while doing each curl-up correctly. Try to do as many curl-ups as you can in two minutes.

Doing 36 or more curl-ups in two minutes is a sign of muscle-strength fitness for a boy or girl in fifth grade.

When doing bent-knee curl-ups, be sure to keep your hips in contact with the testing surface at all times.

How Can You Test Your Flexibility?

Good flexibility in your lower back muscles may help prevent problems in your lower back. Many adults have back trouble because they do not have good flexibility.

Testing your flexibility is easy. You will need someone to help you with the test. You will also need some equipment. The pictures show the equipment that is needed and the way the test is given.

1. Warm up by stretching your leg and back muscles.
2. Sit on the floor with your legs straight and your feet flat against the box. The person helping you will hold the yardstick on top of the box.

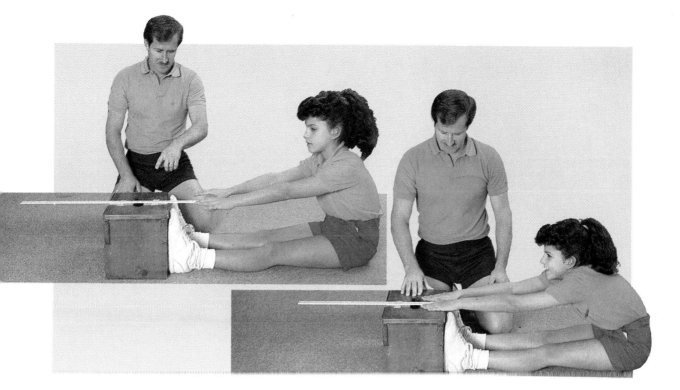

On each attempt of the sit-and-reach, hold your position for at least three seconds.

3. Place one hand on top of the other. Slowly lean forward and reach as far as you can. Hold your position while your helper marks the spot at the end of your finger. Reaching nine inches or more is a sign of flexibility fitness for a boy or girl in fifth grade.

STOP **REVIEW**
SECTION 3

1. What two body systems work hardest when you are being tested for cardiorespiratory endurance?
2. Which muscles are being tested when you do a bent-knee curl-up?
3. How can you tell if you have good flexibility in your lower back muscles?

4. Why should testing for fitness be a part of your physical fitness plan?
5. What would you do if the tests told you that you were not physically fit?

Health Close-up

Modern Technology for Measuring Fitness

Most professional athletes have to stay as physically fit as possible. For them, making a living depends on being in top physical condition.

That is why professional sports teams have trainers who help athletes stay in top physical condition. These trainers use modern equipment to measure the fitness of the athletes. Many training machines for athletes have built-in computers.

For example, one machine has been designed especially for testing the strength and flexibility of the knee. The physician or trainer straps a measuring device to a person's knee. The device is attached to a computer.

As the person moves his or her leg, the device measures what is happening to the knee. It sends this information to the computer. The computer records the information and displays it on a screen.

■ *Fitness can be measured by some computers.*

The computer also prints a record of all the information it gets. Of course, it will also store all the information in its memory. Studying this information allows the physician or trainer to decide whether the knee needs treatment.

Other machines can measure the effects that exercise has on various parts of the body. A stress machine, for example, shows how the body reacts to certain kinds of exercise. Stress machines are not new. However, many of the new ones have built-in computers.

If you were tested on a stress machine, you would have measuring devices taped to parts of your body. Then you would begin walking on a treadmill—a "path" that moves while you stay in the same place. The treadmill can be slanted to make you walk "uphill" and speeded up to make you walk faster. The machine shows how your circulation and respiration are affected as walking becomes more difficult.

Equipment like this is not just for professional teams. Some physicians have stress machines in their offices or in the hospital where they practice. Health and exercise clubs also use them to help their members plan safe fitness programs.

Thinking Beyond

1. Why is it important to know how exercise affects your body?
2. How have computers changed the way physical fitness is measured?

4 Balancing Activity with Rest and Sleep

After a day of being active, you may feel tired. Feeling tired helps your body protect itself from working too hard. It lets you know that your body needs rest. To help keep yourself physically fit, you need a balance of exercise, rest, and sleep.

What Does It Mean to Rest?

There may be times when you feel tired during the day. Your eyelids may get heavy. You may start yawning. Feeling tired is your body's way of telling you to rest a while.

You may feel tired for many reasons. Your muscles may feel tired after you exercise. Maybe you have been working for a long time. Your whole body may be tired. Strong emotions can also make you tired. Sometimes you have too much to do or to think about. You may start to worry and feel tense. The tension is called stress. Feeling too much stress can make you tired.

Rest can help your body and mind get back to normal. Everyone needs to rest for some time each day.

Some kinds of activity can help people relax. Some of these activities can be done by one person, such as listening to music, reading, writing in a diary, or thinking creatively. What do you do to rest and relax?

After exercising, you need to rest to regain your strength.

194

What Happens When You Sleep?

Sleep is a condition in which you are not aware of the things around you. Certain parts of your brain control your pattern of sleeping and waking.

When you sleep, most of your body systems slow down. The activities of your circulatory and digestive systems, for example, slow because they are doing less work. Your cells do not need as much oxygen because they are not as active. Your heart rate slows. Your body temperature is lower than when you are awake. When you sleep, your body can repair itself, grow, and store energy for the next day's activities.

This machine measures a person's brain activity during sleep.

Your muscles relax when you sleep. However, your brain does not stop working when you sleep. Dreaming and other brain activity continues.

How Much Sleep Do You Need?

You most likely have a certain time for going to bed. You may wonder why your parents or other adults stay up longer than you do. Young people are very active and are still growing rapidly. They need more sleep than most adults. There are times when you would rather stay up later. Your parents know that if you have too little sleep,

195

■ Doing a lot of school work can make you tired. Sleep is one way your body gets the rest it needs.

you will not feel well and may have trouble being alert the next school day.

Most adults need about 7 to 8 hours of sleep. Some need even less sleep. Most young people need between 10 and 11 hours of sleep. You may already sleep 10 to 11 hours because you have learned how much sleep you need to feel rested in the morning.

STOP **REVIEW**
SECTION 4

REMEMBER?

1. What are two reasons that a person may feel tired?
2. What happens to the activities of most body systems when you sleep?
3. About how many hours of sleep do you need each night?

THINK!

4. What activities and surroundings help you relax better?
5. How might not getting enough sleep affect your activities the next day?

A Daily Pattern for Total Health

For one day, make a list of each kind of activity you do. For example, you could list sleeping, eating, reading for pleasure, resting, exercising, studying, working around the house, and attending school. Record the amount of time you spend on each activity—for example,

     sleep—10 hours

     school—6 1/2 hours.

Then, on a large sheet of paper, draw a figure like the one shown here. Use a ruler to draw a figure that is 12 inches (30 centimeters) long and 2 inches (5 centimeters) tall. Draw lines to divide the figure into 24 parts. Each part equals one hour in the day.

Now use your list of daily activities and the time you spent on them to chart your day. Follow the example. Use the chart to help you think about the way your balance of activities affects your wellness—your physical, intellectual, social, and emotional health.

Hours of the Day

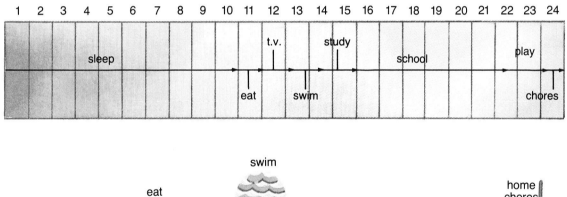

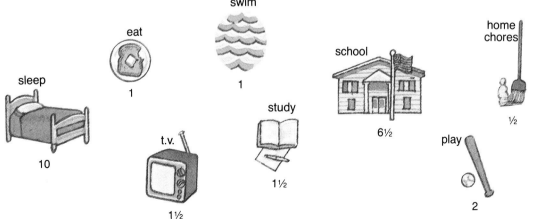

197

An Interview with an Athletic Trainer

Hazel Ando knows about sports and fitness. She is an athletic trainer at a large university in Irvine, California.

What is an athletic trainer?

Athletic trainers help people prevent injuries. They care for injured athletes and help them get better as soon as possible. They also help people become and stay physically fit.

How do athletic trainers do these things?

Athletic trainers help people prepare for playing sports. They help them plan exercises for building endurance, strength, and flexibility. Athletic trainers also give advice on diet. When it is needed during practice and games, they give first aid. They work hard to make sports safer. Football, for example, is safer today because athletic trainers have pointed out safety and health measures.

What is the difference between an athletic trainer and a coach?

The coach trains and drills an athlete in skills for a certain sport. The athletic trainer helps an athlete avoid or overcome any injuries.

Who are the athletes you help?

I help men and women who are on the sports teams at the University of California in Irvine. They are team members in basketball, volleyball, soccer, baseball, tennis, swimming, and other sports. Besides helping them, I work with dance students. I also give first aid to anyone else who may get hurt while exercising at the gym.

■ *Ms. Ando tapes an athlete's ankle to help prevent injury to nearby tissue.*

Athletic trainers are prepared to give first aid to injured athletes.

Does a person have to be an athlete to become an athletic trainer?

A person does not have to be an athlete to understand what each sport is about and what its dangers are. That is the kind of thing a person can learn. However, many people become interested in this kind of work because they like sports.

What does someone have to do to become an athletic trainer?

Most of us are members of the National Athletic Trainers Association, or NATA. NATA requires that athletic trainers graduate from an approved college. Athletic trainers must prove they know first aid and emergency procedures. They also must work at least 1,800 hours with an experienced athletic trainer.

Where do athletic trainers get experience?

Athletic trainers work in universities, junior colleges, and high schools. There are some working in junior high schools. Some trainers work in clinics. Most trainers get early experience working as student trainers.

What are student athletic trainers?

They are students who help athletic trainers. There are ten students who work in my training room at the university. They want to become athletic trainers, physicians, nurses, dietitians, and other professionals in sports medicine. Some of the college students I know began as student athletic trainers in junior high school.

How is the field of athletic training changing?

The big push is to have an athletic trainer at every high school in the United States. That will make school sports safer for all players.

Learn more about people who work as athletic trainers. Interview a trainer. Or write for information to the National Athletic Trainers Association, P.O. Drawer 1865, Greenville, NC 27834.

199

Main Ideas

- Your body needs regular exercise to stay healthy.
- Regular physical activities can help improve both your respiratory and circulatory systems and help you feel good about yourself.
- If you want to be physically fit, you must have a plan for regular physical activities and you must follow it.
- You can test yourself to find out how physically fit you are.
- Getting enough rest and sleep every day can help you become physically fit.

Key Words

Write the numbers 1 to 10 in your health notebook or on a separate sheet of paper. After each number, copy the sentence and fill in the missing term. Page numbers in ( ) tell you where to look in the chapter if you need help.

physical fitness (174)
endurance (175)
muscle strength (175)
flexibility (176)
blood pressure (178)

cardiorespiratory fitness (179)
aerobic exercise (179)
anaerobic exercise (180)
warm-up (182)
cool-down (183)

1. When your body works the best that it is able, you have ___?___ .

2. An exercise that prepares your body for hard exercise is called a ___?___ .

3. When your body is able to be active for a long time without getting too tired, you have ___?___ .

4. When you are able to move your body with ease, you have ___?___ .

5. People with healthy respiratory and circulatory systems are said to have ___?___ .

6. When your body is able to apply force with its muscles, you have ___?___ .

7. The force of blood against the walls of your arteries is ___?___ .

8. When you finish a hard physical activity, you should do a ___?___ .

9. Running a 50-yard (46-meter) dash is a form of ___?___ .

10. Exercise that helps you strengthen your heart and lungs is called ___?___ .

Remembering What You Learned

Page numbers in ( ) tell you where to look in the chapter if you need help.

1. How does exercise help you have good posture? (176)

2. What are four good exercises that can help improve your respiratory and circulatory systems? (179)

3. How does aerobic exercise help build endurance? (179)

4. What is one benefit each of doing aerobic and anaerobic exercises? (179–180)

5. Why do you need to prepare your body before you do hard physical activities? (182)

6. What should you do right after doing hard physical activities? (183)

7. How can you know if you are getting out of breath while jogging with someone? (184)

8. How far do you need to jog in 20 minutes to meet the endurance requirements for physical fitness? (190)

9. How many bent-knee curl-ups do you need to do in two minutes in order to meet the muscle-strength requirements for physical fitness? (191)

10. How many inches do you need to reach in the sit-and-reach test to meet the flexibility requirements for being physically fit? (192)

11. Why do you need 10 to 11 hours of sleep each night? (195–196)

Thinking About What You Learned

1. Why do aerobic exercises help improve your endurance, whereas anaerobic exercises do not?

2. How can you be responsible for having physical fitness?

3. How can people of different sizes and body builds all have physical fitness?

4. Why must you have a plan to help you build physical fitness?

5. How can performing certain tests help you in your effort to achieve physical fitness?

6. How might not being physically fit affect other parts of your life?

7. Predict how you might feel if you did not get enough sleep. How might the feeling affect your physical, mental, and social health while you are awake?

Writing About What You Learned

1. Interview six people of different ages. Find out what they know about physical fitness. Ask each person for a definition of physical fitness. Write three paragraphs about your findings.

2. Pretend you are preparing for a class debate about the usefulness of a certain sport in building and maintaining physical fitness. Choose any sport. Find out all you can about why the people who play that sport might be more fit than people who participate in other sports. Write your opinion in the form of an essay.

Applying What You Learned

SOCIAL STUDIES

Tell about some kinds of outdoor activities that are more likely to be done where you live than in other parts of the United States. Also, what are some outdoor activities done in other areas of the country that cannot be done in your area?

Modified True or False

Write the numbers 1 to 15 in your health notebook or on a separate sheet of paper. After each number, write *true* or *false* to describe the sentence. If the sentence is false, also write a term that replaces the underlined term and makes the sentence true.

1. <u>Physical fitness</u> helps you feel good.
2. You should warm up for at least <u>15</u> minutes before exercising.
3. If you can be active for long periods without getting tired, then you have good <u>muscle strength</u>.
4. Strong muscles in your <u>abdomen</u> can help you to have good posture.
5. A strong heart beats <u>more often</u> than a weak heart.
6. <u>Anaerobic</u> exercise builds muscle.
7. Too much <u>stress</u> can make you tired.
8. When you sleep, most of your body systems <u>speed up</u>.
9. Young people need <u>more</u> sleep because they are still growing.
10. <u>Endurance</u> is the force of blood against the walls of your arteries.
11. Balanced activity includes daily exercise, rest, and <u>sleep</u>.
12. <u>Cardiorespiratory fitness</u> is the ability to move your body with ease.
13. <u>Jogging</u> helps build strength.
14. Cool-down exercises should be done <u>fewer</u> times than warm-up exercises.
15. Any aerobic activity should be done for at least <u>20</u> minutes.

Short Answer

Write the numbers 16 to 23 on your paper. Write a complete sentence to answer each question.

16. Why is it a good idea to drink water before beginning aerobic exercise?
17. How are aerobic and anaerobic exercise different?
18. How does your body let you know it needs to rest?
19. Why is sleep important?
20. Why is cardiorespiratory fitness important to your health?
21. What test determines if you have endurance fitness?
22. Why do you need to exercise safely?
23. Why do you breathe more deeply when you exercise?

Essay

Write the numbers 24 and 25 on your paper. Write paragraphs with complete sentences to answer each question.

24. Write a plan for developing good physical fitness. Note the frequency and intensity of exercises and the length of time for each exercise.
25. Describe how the circulatory system benefits from regular aerobic exercise.

ACTIVITIES FOR HOME OR SCHOOL

Projects to Do

1. List as many different kinds of exercise as you can. Your list should have at least 15 different exercises. Put a green dot by each exercise that makes certain muscles work very hard. Those exercises build strength. Put a red dot by each exercise that includes a lot of bending and stretching. Those exercises give you greater flexibility. Put a yellow dot by each exercise that makes the whole body move. Those exercises help build endurance. Which exercises can help someone in all three ways?

2. Arrange a family discussion about fitness. Discuss physical activities two or more family members would like to do together. Select one activity that you can do with a family member for six weeks. Work together on ways to remind each other about the new plan.

Information to Find

1. Some people who jog or run regularly say they feel a "runner's high" after they have been running for a while. Some scientists believe that the feeling is caused by endorphins. *Endorphins* are substances made by the brain. Find out how endorphins affect the body. Ask your librarian to help you find magazine or newspaper articles about this topic.

2. Many dance exercises are designed to help increase flexibility. Learn

■ *Most dancers have excellent flexibility.*

some exercises that young dancers do. You might ask someone who takes dance lessons to show you. Or you might talk with a dance teacher. Demonstrate a few of the exercises to your class.

Books to Read

Here are some books you can look for in your school library or the public library to find more information about exercise and physical fitness.

Burstein, John. *The Force Inside You.* Putnam.

Cosgrove, Margaret. *Your Muscles and Ways to Exercise Them.* Dodd, Mead.

Trier, Carola. *Exercise: What It Is, What It Does.* Greenwillow.

203

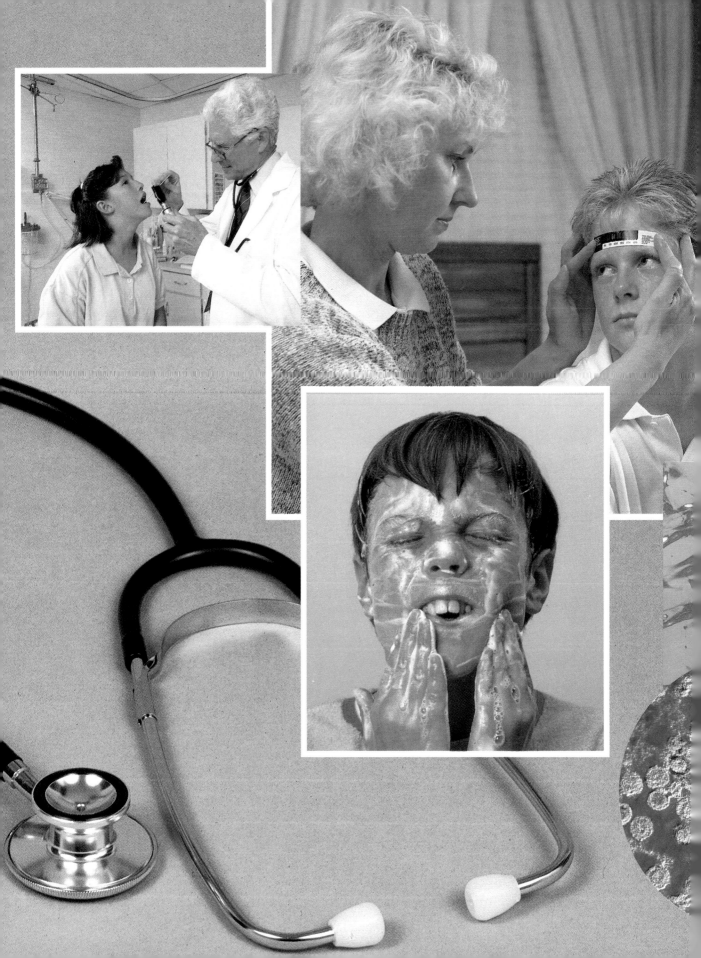

PROTECTING YOURSELF AGAINST DISEASE

Think of the people you see every day—your family, friends, neighbors, and people at school. They stay healthy most of the time. Their bodies work well more often than not. When the body does not work well, however, a person may feel ill. A person may have a disease.

Knowing what makes people ill can help you stay healthy. Caring for your health is your responsibility. If you follow good health habits, you may avoid getting diseases.

GETTING READY TO LEARN

Key Questions

- Why is it useful to learn about diseases and disorders?
- How much control do you have over diseases?
- What healthful habits can you practice to protect yourself from disease?
- What can you do to take responsibility for keeping disease from spreading?

Main Chapter Sections

1 Some Microbes Cause Communicable Diseases
2 How Your Body Fights Off Microbes
3 When Someone Gets Ill
4 The Challenge to Prevent Communicable Diseases
5 Noncommunicable Diseases

1 Some Microbes Cause Communicable Diseases

KEY WORDS

microbes
infection
disease
viruses
bacteria
fungi
protozoa
transmitted
communicable
   disease
toxins

When Ted woke up, he thought he was alone in his room. The door was closed, and the cat was outside. In fact, his room was filled with millions of living things. These things are called microbes. **Microbes** are living things so tiny that they can be seen only with a microscope.

Many kinds of microbes were in Ted's room. Some were floating in the air. Some microbes lived inside his potted plants. Some lived in the soil in which his plants were growing. Ted had microbes on his skin, even on his eyelashes. He also had some in his mouth, nose, and digestive system.

microbes (MY krohbz), living creatures so tiny that they can be seen only with a microscope.

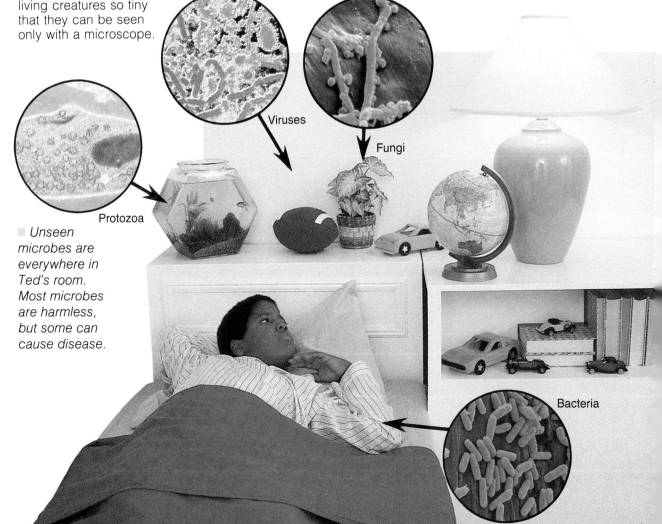

Viruses

Fungi

Protozoa

Bacteria

■ *Unseen microbes are everywhere in Ted's room. Most microbes are harmless, but some can cause disease.*

Most of the microbes in Ted's room cannot harm him. But some microbes could make Ted ill if too many of them got inside his body. They can cause an infection. An **infection** is the growth of disease microbes inside the body. When your body has an infection, you become ill with a disease. A **disease** is a breakdown in the way the body works. Part of the body is not working well.

infection (ihn FEHK shuhn), the growth of disease microbes somewhere inside the body.

disease (dihz EEZ), a breakdown in the way the body works.

What Kinds of Microbes Are There?

There are many kinds of microbes. They are as different from each other as different kinds of animals are. Most disease microbes, however, belong to one of four groups: viruses, bacteria, fungi, and protozoa. Look at the table "Some Diseases Caused by Microbes." Only a few of the diseases caused by microbes are included. Each of the groups of microbes can cause many different diseases.

SOME DISEASES CAUSED BY MICROBES

Microbes	Disease
Viruses	AIDS chicken pox cold infectious hepatitis influenza (flu) measles mumps polio rabies rubella (German measles)
Bacteria	pertussis (whooping cough) salmonella (food poisoning) strep throat tetanus tuberculosis
Fungi	athlete's foot ringworm
Protozoa	dysentery

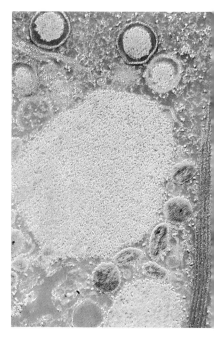

Viruses get inside living cells and make copies of themselves.

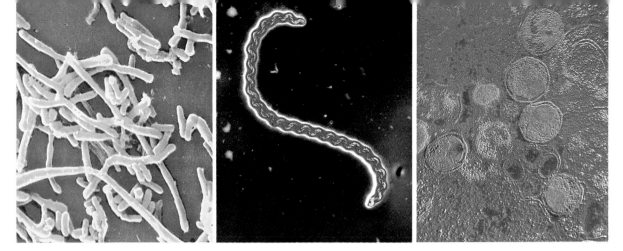

viruses (VY ruhs uhz), disease microbes; not much different from nonliving matter.

bacteria (bak TIHR ee uh), one-celled microbes; larger than viruses.

fungi (FUHN jy), organisms that live and grow like tiny plants.

protozoa (proht uh ZOH uh), one-celled microbes that can move without help.

Some fungi can cause disease.

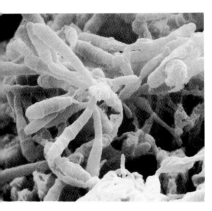

Viruses. The smallest microbes are **viruses.** Most viruses are almost like nonliving matter. But sometimes they get inside a living cell of a person, animal, or plant. Once inside they use the cell to make exact copies of themselves. They keep multiplying until the cell breaks open and dies. Then the viruses attack other, nearby cells. By attacking these cells, viruses can continue to multiply.

Bacteria. Larger than viruses, **bacteria** are one-celled microbes. They live in air, soil, water, plants, animals, and humans. Bacteria live almost everywhere. Bacteria are grouped by shape. They can be round, rod-shaped, or spiral. Bacteria depend on people, air, water, or food to move them from place to place.

Fungi. Another group of microbes is called fungi. **Fungi** are microbes that live and grow like plants. Different kinds of fungi have different shapes and sizes. If you look at most fungi under a microscope, you will see what looks like clumps of string. Most fungi grow best in dark, damp places. Fungi are moved from place to place in air, soil, and water and by plants, animals, and humans.

Protozoa. One-celled microbes that can move from place to place without help are **protozoa.** All protozoa are larger than bacteria. They live only in water or some other liquid. Some protozoa can live inside the human body.

How Do Microbes Spread?

Disease microbes are spread, or **transmitted,** to a person from someone or something that carries the microbes. When an illness caused by microbes is spread, it is called a **communicable disease.**

People. Contact between people spreads most communicable diseases. Often, diseases are spread by a person with a communicable disease who has not washed his or her hands. Microbes can then be spread to things that the person has touched. Microbes can also be released into the air when the person coughs or sneezes.

Clean hands can stop the spread of microbes to foods.

Always cover a sneeze or a cough.

People can keep from getting some diseases by staying away from people who are ill. People who are ill can be careful not to touch food, dishes, or utensils that are to be used by other people. Washing hands with soap and warm water is one way to keep from spreading microbes from one person to another. The most important times to wash hands are after using the toilet and before handling food. All people need to make sure to wash their hands before preparing and handling food. They should cover their mouths and noses with tissues when they cough or sneeze. Then they should throw away the tissues so that no one else handles them. They should then wash their hands. These health habits help stop the spread of microbes from one person to another.

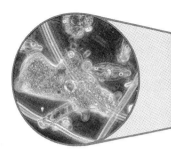
Standing water, even a puddle, contains microbes.

Water. Almost any standing water has microbes living in it. Standing water does not move or flow, as in a ditch or pond. The water is likely to have more microbes if it is warm, shallow, and dirty.

Water that has dangerous microbes living in it is called contaminated water. Drinking it will almost always make you ill. Some water is so contaminated that even swimming or standing in it can be dangerous. The microbes in the water can get into any break in your skin, no matter how small. They may get into your mouth or any other body opening. They may get on your hands and then later get into your food. Staying away from such water can help keep you safe from disease.

A clean swimming pool keeps microbes from growing.

Food. Microbes can grow in food. Microbes can get onto food from the hands of a person or from unwashed utensils and surfaces, such as cutting boards.

Wash food utensils in hot, soapy water.

Eating spoiled food can make you ill. Sometimes food spoils without looking or smelling bad. Bacteria in certain foods can grow and make poisons. This can happen to foods when they are left outside a refrigerator (at a temperature above 40 degrees Fahrenheit, or 4.5 degrees Celsius). Beef, pork, chicken, and fish can spoil in just a few hours. Eggs and milk and foods made from them, such as mayonnaise, can also spoil quickly. Potato salad, for example, needs to be kept refrigerated.

Canned foods can be kept longer than fresh foods. But sometimes foods are canned in the wrong way. Certain kinds of microbes then multiply inside the can. As they multiply, they make harmful chemicals called **toxins.** These toxins can cause one kind of *food poisoning.* Any bent, swollen, or badly damaged can could have these toxins inside it. Such cans should always be thrown away, and what is inside should never be eaten.

Certain foods must be kept cold to prevent them from spoiling.

toxins (TAHK suhnz), harmful chemicals made by microbes.

Insects and Animals. Microbes need food, water, and a warm, dark place in order to grow and multiply. They can get everything they need in garbage. Many microbes live and grow in garbage, dirt, and warm, standing water. Insects live and grow in these same places. The insects get microbes all over their bodies. When the insects walk or fly away, they carry microbes to other places.

Some insects get microbes inside their bodies. If such an insect bites a person, the microbes can pass right into the person's blood. Ticks can carry microbes that cause illnesses, such as Rocky Mountain spotted fever and Lyme disease.

Dirty places attract animals. Animals can spread many diseases. The microbes that cause these diseases grow inside the animals. Fleas pick up the microbes when they bite the animals. Later, these same fleas may jump onto people, bite them, and pass the microbes to them. This is one way that disease can pass from animals to people. Sometimes animals spread disease directly by biting humans. If garbage is stored in a closed container until it can be disposed of, it will not attract animals. This lowers the risk of spreading disease.

Animals can spread microbes from open garbage.

How Do Microbes Enter the Body?

Microbes enter the body in many different ways. Some microbes enter the body through the respiratory system. When people cough or sneeze, they release microbes into the air. Other people nearby could breathe the microbes in through their noses and mouths. Some viruses and bacteria can be transmitted in this way.

Some microbes enter the body through the circulatory system. Disease microbes can enter the body through cuts, scratches, and other breaks in a person's skin. Microbes may enter the circulatory system when a person is bitten by an insect or animal. Bites by people can also spread microbes. People who inject themselves with drugs from dirty or used needles may also allow disease microbes to enter their bodies. This is one way that the AIDS virus enters the circulatory system.

Disease microbes may enter the digestive system with the food you eat. Putting an unwashed hand or utensil into your mouth can also allow microbes to enter your digestive system.

Disease microbes may enter the body by sexual contact with another person. Infections that enter the body in this way are called *sexually transmitted diseases,* or STDs. AIDS is one example of an STD.

Knowing about microbes and how they spread to people can help you in three ways. First, you can stay away from places where microbes grow. Second, you can practice healthful habits that will keep microbes from getting into your body. Third, you can try to keep from spreading microbes to other persons even when you do not feel ill.

■ *Washing your hands after using the toilet helps stop the spread of microbes.*

REMEMBER?

1. What are three kinds of disease microbes?
2. What are four ways that disease microbes spread?
3. How do disease microbes enter the respiratory system? Circulatory system? Digestive system?

THINK!

4. Why is hand washing considered one of the most useful habits a person can form to avoid spreading most common illnesses?
5. What are some ways that you can protect yourself from becoming ill if someone in your family has a communicable disease?

Thinking About Your Health

Protecting Against Communicable Disease

How do you know if you are doing all you can to protect yourself and your friends from communicable diseases? If you say yes to each of the following sentences, you might be. If not, you should talk about this with your parent, guardian, school nurse, or teacher.

- You try to keep away from places where microbes grow.
- You stay home from school when you have a cold.

- You cover your mouth and nose with a tissue when you sneeze or cough, and then dispose of the tissue and wash your hands.
- You wash your hands before handling food.
- You follow good health habits, such as getting plenty of rest and sleep, exercising regularly, and eating a balanced diet.

213

2 How Your Body Fights Off Microbes

Thousands of microbes have reached Ted during the day. Yet Ted is still healthy. His body's strong defenses have fought off the microbes. Ted's defenses are fighting against microbes all the time. This fight is a natural function of Ted's body. Like Ted, you have a variety of defenses against microbes. Your skin is one. Other defenses are your eyes, ears, nose, mouth, and blood.

■ *Your body has defenses that fight microbes all the time.*

How Do Your Eyes and Ears Defend You?

Most microbes cannot enter your body through your eyes. The microbes are killed by tears, the liquid that makes your eyes moist. However, bacteria or viruses can cause an eye infection called *pinkeye*. It spreads easily from person to person. If you get pinkeye, you should see a physician, who will order medicine to treat the disease. Students with pinkeye should not touch their eyes. The

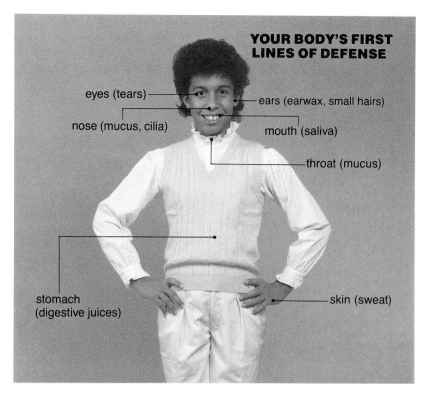

YOUR BODY'S FIRST LINES OF DEFENSE

eyes (tears)

ears (earwax, small hairs)

nose (mucus, cilia)

mouth (saliva)

throat (mucus)

stomach (digestive juices)

skin (sweat)

◾ *Most microbes are stopped by your skin, the mucus in your nasal passages, tears, earwax, saliva, and the digestive juices in your stomach.*

microbes that cause the disease could get on their hands and be spread to other people.

Microbes cannot get very far into your ears, either. Many microbes catch on the small hairs at the outer end of the ear canal. Or they stick to the earwax that lines the wall of the ear canal.

How Do Your Nose and Mouth Defend You?

Most microbes entering your nose are caught on the hairs in your nose. Many more are trapped in the mucus and cilia that line the nasal passages. Only a few microbes get as far as the trachea. There, still more of the microbes get stuck to mucus that lines the trachea. Mucus helps keep most microbes from entering your lungs.

Most of the microbes that enter the mouth are destroyed by saliva. The few microbes that reach the stomach are most often destroyed by digestive juices. Few microbes can live very long in a person's digestive system. However, some very dangerous microbes can get into the digestive system because of food poisoning. They can cause serious illnesses and sometimes death.

◾ *White blood cells kill microbes inside your body.*

Sarah had chicken pox, so now she is immune and cannot get it from her brother.

How Does Your Blood Fight Off Disease?

Not all microbes are stopped by the defenses of your eyes, ears, nose, and mouth. Some microbes may get past this first line of defense. Disease microbes may get into your blood and cause infection. When this happens, however, disease microbes face your body's second line of defense, which is in the blood itself.

White blood cells and other parts of the blood sense that disease microbes are present. They move quickly to the microbes. The white blood cells kill the microbes, stopping the spread of infection.

White blood cells can change their shape. This helps them surround the microbes and destroy them. At the same time, white blood cells make substances called antibodies. **Antibodies** help white blood cells destroy microbes. The antibodies stick to the surfaces of the microbes. This makes it easy for the white blood cells to destroy the microbes.

Each kind of antibody works against only one kind of microbe. Your white blood cells make a different antibody for each different microbe.

Antibodies stay in your blood after the infection has been destroyed. Some antibodies protect you from getting the same disease again. This protection is called **immunity.** Some antibodies stay in your blood for the rest of your life. Other antibodies stay for only a short time.

antibodies (ANT ih bahd eez), substances in the body that help fight disease.

immunity (ihm YOO nuht ee), the condition in which antibodies stay in your blood to protect you from getting a disease again.

216

How Do Vaccines and Antibiotics Help Defend You?

You can have immunity to certain diseases without actually getting them. **Vaccines** give you immunity. A vaccine against a certain disease is made of the same kind of microbe that causes the disease. But the microbes in the vaccine are weakened or even dead. They cannot multiply and make you sick. Your body, however, makes antibodies to fight against them. Once you have enough antibodies in your blood, you have immunity to that disease. If disease microbes of that kind enter your body, the antibodies are ready. They destroy the microbes before they can make you ill.

Certain microbes that enter your body are not stopped or killed by your natural immunity. Your body may need some extra help. A physician may order an antibiotic for you. An **antibiotic** is a medicine that can kill certain kinds of harmful bacteria. Antibiotics break down cell walls. Since bacteria have cell walls and body cells do not, only bacteria are affected. Antibiotics do not function like antibodies.

What Can You Do to Defend Your Body from Disease?

When your defenses against microbes are working well, your resistance is strong. **Resistance** is your body's ability to fight off disease on its own. You can keep your resistance strong by practicing daily health habits. Make sure you get the rest and sleep you need to feel full of energy. Eat a balanced diet. Get 20 to 30 minutes of hard exercise at least three times a week. Talk with family members about feelings or situations that worry you.

Washing helps keep your resistance to microbes strong. Make sure you wash your hands after using the toilet, after covering a cough, and before handling food or eating.

vaccines (vak SEENZ), substances that give you immunity to a disease without your getting the disease.

antibiotic (ant ih by AHT ihk), a medicine that can kill certain kinds of harmful bacteria.

resistance (rih ZIHS tuhns), the body's ability to fight off disease on its own.

Eating nutritious meals helps increase your resistance to some diseases.

Washing with soap and warm water removes many disease microbes from your skin. You should be responsible for washing every day. You need to wash your face, hands, feet, underarms, and the area covered by your underwear. Drying your skin after washing or bathing also reduces the chances of fungus growing on your body.

STOP REVIEW
SECTION 2

REMEMBER?

1. What is immunity?
2. How does a vaccine help you stay healthy?
3. What is resistance to a disease?

THINK!

4. How do you think a person can get pinkeye even though tears kill most microbes?
5. Apply what you know about the respiratory system. Draw a path of a disease microbe as it travels in the air to the lungs.

Making Wellness Choices

Rebecca has stayed home from school for two days because she has pinkeye. She is getting bored and watches from her window for her best friend Ginny to come home from school. Rebecca yells to Ginny when she sees her. She asks Ginny to come over after she changes into her play clothes.

 What should Ginny say? Explain your wellness choice.

218

3 When Someone Gets Ill

Have you ever gone to bed feeling fine only to wake up in the morning feeling ill? Communicable diseases often seem to begin suddenly. Disease microbes that enter the body multiply very fast. Because of this, the illness that the microbes cause can start with little warning.

What Are the Signs of Communicable Disease?

When Roger woke up one morning, his throat felt sore. His nose was a little stuffed, too. He did not seem to have much energy. Roger had a disease. The signs and feelings of a disease are its **symptoms.** Every disease has its own symptoms. Roger had the symptoms of a cold or influenza.

A headache, muscle aches, a sore throat, and tiredness are all symptoms of some communicable diseases. Another symptom is **fever,** or body temperature that is higher than normal. Most healthy people have a body temperature of 98.6 degrees Fahrenheit (37 degrees Celsius). A slight fever most often means that a person's body is very busy fighting an infection. Fever is one way the body fights a disease. Fever slows the increase of many kinds of microbes.

KEY WORDS

symptoms
fever
treatment
lymph nodes

symptoms (SIHMP tuhmz), signs and feelings of a disease.

fever (FEE vuhr), a body temperature that is higher than normal.

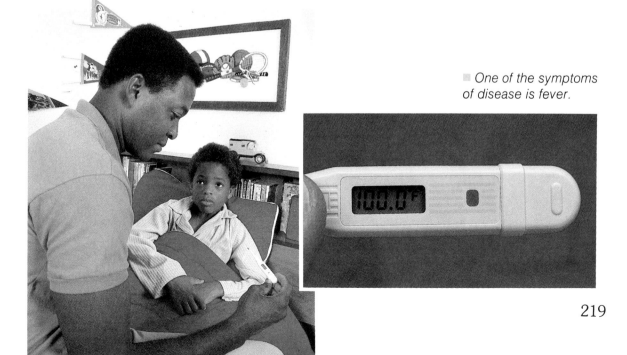

■ One of the symptoms of disease is fever.

219

A very high fever, however, can harm the body if the person loses water and does not or cannot replace it. High fever that lasts for three or more days can make a person less able to fight the infection. A high fever may be a symptom of a serious illness.

Communicable diseases sometimes change your body in ways you can see and touch. Rashes or spots on the skin are some of these changes. Red, swollen skin is also a sign of an infection.

How Does a Physician Decide on Treatment?

When you have symptoms of a disease, you may need **treatment,** or care for the disease. A parent or other family member might help care for you at home. You might also need to see a physician for medical treatment. A physician can tell your parent or guardian how to treat your disease. You might need to take medicine. Or your body might be strong enough to get well by itself in a short time if you get extra rest and drink a lot of water.

To decide what is causing the symptoms, a physician may do some tests. Asking questions and doing an examination also help a physician find the cause of the illness and decide what treatment is best.

A physician may begin by asking about the history, or story, of your illness. It is important to know when your body started to feel different. The way you describe how body parts feel is also very useful.

The last time Larry was ill, he went to see his family physician, Dr. Barker. She measured Larry's blood pressure. Blood pressure gives clues about the general condition of the body. A *sphygmomanometer* is the tool used to measure blood pressure.

Dr. Barker listened to Larry's heart and lungs using a tool called a *stethoscope*. This tool makes it easier to hear the soft sounds made by the heart and lungs. Dr. Barker knows how these organs should sound.

Next, Dr. Barker looked into Larry's eyes with a tool called an *ophthalmoscope*. She looked very carefully through Larry's pupil at his retina. The nerves and blood

treatment (TREET muhnt), care given to a person who shows symptoms of a disease.

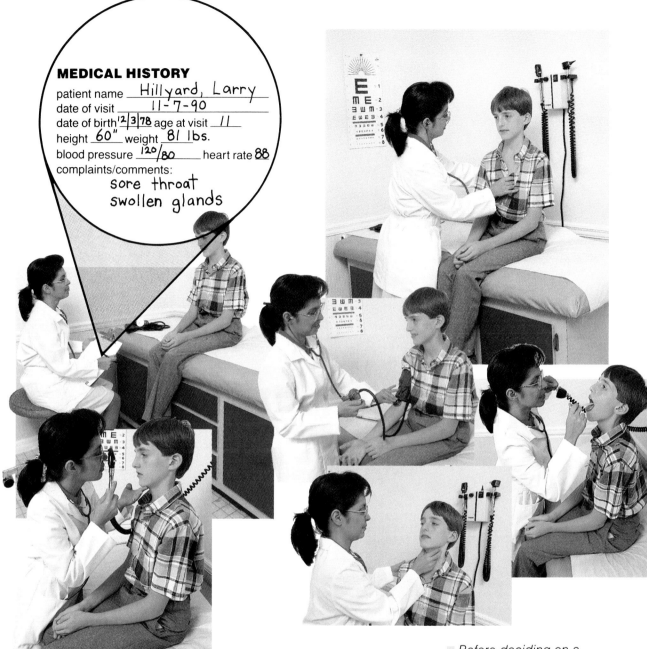

MEDICAL HISTORY
patient name ___Hillyard, Larry___
date of visit _____11-7-90_____
date of birth ¹²|³|⁷⁸ age at visit __11__
height _60"_ weight _81 lbs._
blood pressure ¹²⁰/₈₀ heart rate 88
complaints/comments:
____sore throat____
____swollen glands____

Before deciding on a treatment, a physician may ask you about your symptoms and check many parts of your body.

vessels there are not covered by skin or muscle. They are the only nerves and blood vessels in the body that can be easily seen. Some diseases such as diabetes can cause changes that can be seen in the nerves and blood vessels.

Dr. Barker then looked into Larry's mouth. She pushed Larry's tongue down with a flat piece of wood so she could see his throat. Dr. Barker could tell that Larry had an infection in his throat because it was red and swollen.

221

To find out more about Larry's illness, Dr. Barker checked Larry's lymph nodes. **Lymph nodes** are small glands where certain kinds of white blood cells are made. Lymph nodes help destroy harmful microbes and other matter that has entered the body. When a person has an infection, the lymph nodes often swell. Dr. Barker checked Larry's lymph nodes by feeling both sides of his neck. She also checked lymph nodes under Larry's arms and in his lower abdomen. Larry's lymph nodes were a little swollen.

Finally, Dr. Barker took samples of two liquids from Larry's body. One of her assistants got a little bit of his blood. The assistant also had Larry leave a small sample of his urine. The blood and urine were sent to a laboratory. There, both were checked using a microscope. Medical technologists looked for clues about Larry's illness, and they reported what they found to Dr. Barker.

The medical technologists counted the number of white blood cells in the blood sample. This told Dr. Barker about the infection in Larry's body. The medical technologists also studied the urine to see where Larry's infection might be. There were no white blood cells or bacteria in it. This told Dr. Barker that Larry's infection was not in the excretory system.

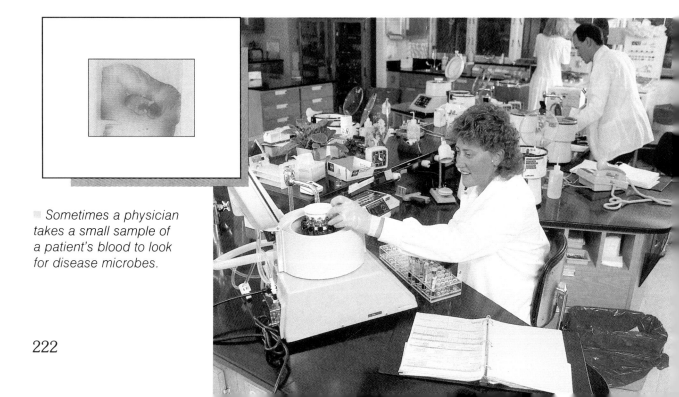

◼ Sometimes a physician takes a small sample of a patient's blood to look for disease microbes.

Larry was well enough to play soccer two weeks after his illness.

What Is the Physician's Advice?

When Dr. Barker finished all the tests, she decided Larry had influenza, which is caused by a virus. She was also certain that Larry was not fighting any other infections. There is no medicine that can fight influenza viruses. But Larry is generally very healthy, so Dr. Barker knew his body's own defenses could make him well. What he needed was rest so that his defenses could have a chance to work. Dr. Barker told Larry's parents that he should drink a lot of water or juice and stay in bed for a few days. She told Larry to then build up to his usual activity gradually. Dr. Barker also warned the family not to give Larry aspirin for his fever. Using aspirin for some viral illnesses, especially influenza, can cause dangerous health problems for young people. Dr. Barker told them about other medicines to use if Larry's fever stayed high.

Larry followed Dr. Barker's advice. A day later, the fever began to drop. A week later, he felt well enough to go back to school. Two weeks later, he felt as if he had never been ill.

**REVIEW
SECTION 3**

REMEMBER?

1. What is a symptom of a disease?
2. What are three things a physician may do to gather information about an illness?
3. Why does a physician take a person's blood pressure?

THINK!

4. Why is fever a useful reaction for your body?
5. Why is rest important for a person who has an illness caused by a virus?

Modern Technology "Sees" Inside the Body

Physicians have always used tools to help them check the health of their patients. A stethoscope, for example, is used to make the sound of a heartbeat loud enough for a physician to hear it clearly. A thermometer is used to measure a person's body temperature.

New tools are being developed. Old tools are being improved to help physicians learn more about what goes on inside the body.

One kind of X-ray machine, for example, makes pictures of the inside of the body. Another kind of X ray shows movement inside the body. A physician may want to use this kind of X ray to see how well a person digests food. When this kind of X ray is taken, the person drinks a certain liquid. As the person drinks, a camera films the drink moving through the person's body.

There is another kind of X ray that is set up with a computer. It is called a *CAT scan*. With it a physician can see a person's body layer by layer, from front to back or from head to foot. A CAT scan produces images of the body by rotating a part of the machine around the body.

An ultrasound machine is another tool helpful to physicians. Ultrasound uses sound waves to "see" the shape and size of an organ inside the body. Sound waves are directed at a particular organ. The sound waves bounce off the organ and are recorded on film as an image. A series of ultrasound pictures taken over time can show changes in the size and shape of a body organ.

There are many other tools used by physicians and other health workers. These tools give very accurate information about such things as heart rate and blood content. Because of new inventions such as these, health workers can learn more than ever about their patients. This makes health care today better than it has ever been.

■ *This person is having a CAT scan.*

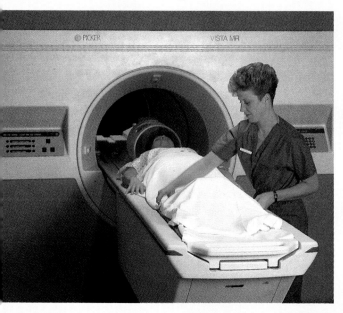

Thinking Beyond

1. How does the development of new medical tools help people maintain good health?
2. What kind of new inventions can you imagine that would make health care even better than it is today?

4 The Challenge to Prevent Communicable Diseases

The tiny microbes that cause communicable diseases are all around us every day. Most of the time, healthy people do not get infections. Their bodies can most often fight the disease microbes that enter them. There are times, however, when people get ill. The kinds of communicable diseases people may get are as different as the microbes that cause them. Vaccines prevent some diseases. For other diseases, work goes on to discover ways to prevent and cure them.

KEY WORD

contagious

How Can Childhood Diseases Be Prevented?

Mumps, measles, and chicken pox are caused by viruses. A person who has mumps has swollen glands in the face. A person who has measles develops small red spots. A person who has chicken pox gets a different kind of rash.

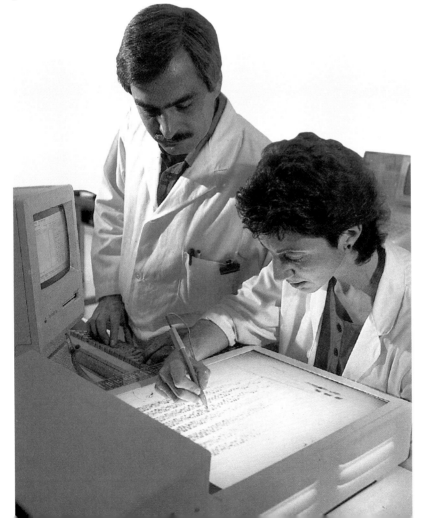

Scientists are always searching for ways to prevent disease.

The red spots become blisters and turn into crusty bumps. All three diseases cause a sore throat, muscle aches, fever, and discomfort that last about a week.

Mumps, measles, and chicken pox are often called childhood diseases. In the past, almost all children caught them. These diseases are very **contagious.** That means it is easy for them to spread among people. They are spread most often in the spray from coughs and sneezes.

Because people form immunity to these diseases, they usually get the disease only once. That is why adults do not often get mumps, measles, or chicken pox. When adults do get one of these diseases, they can become very ill.

Today, there are vaccines for mumps and measles. There is also a chicken pox vaccine, but it is not widely used. Scientists know a lot about how to keep these diseases from spreading. Today, fewer young people get mumps or measles. However, most young people still get chicken pox.

What Is AIDS?

Scientists have been able to control most childhood diseases. However, scientists do not know how to cure some new diseases, such as AIDS.

AIDS stands for "acquired immunodeficiency syndrome." It is an infection caused by a virus. The virus that causes AIDS weakens the body's immunity to certain other diseases.

contagious (kuhn TAY juhs), easily spread among people.

■ *The virus that causes AIDS gets into a cell, below. When the cell has made more viruses, some leave, right, and invade other cells.*

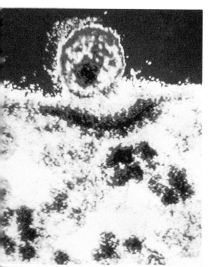

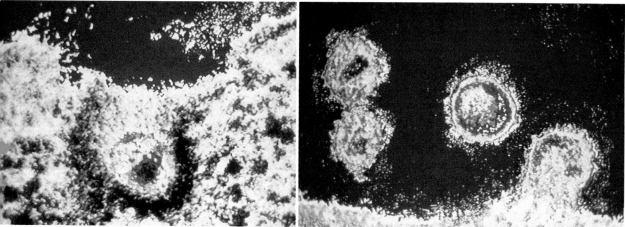

People who have AIDS are not able to fight off other diseases. These other diseases can be very strong and may cause death.

AIDS is not very contagious. The AIDS virus cannot be spread by touching a person who has it. You also cannot get AIDS by being in the same room with a person who has the disease. Healthy people can work, play sports, and go to school with a person who has the AIDS virus without fear of getting the disease.

The AIDS virus is most often transmitted in one of three ways. First, it can be transmitted from one person to another by sexual contact. AIDS is a sexually transmitted disease. Second, AIDS can be spread from one drug abuser to another when injection needles carrying the virus are shared. Third, AIDS can be transmitted from a mother to her baby before or during birth. In rare cases, a person can be infected if blood with the AIDS virus in it enters his or her blood through a cut in the skin. A small number of physicians and other health workers have been infected with AIDS in this way.

It is not easy to get AIDS. But anyone who takes a chance can get it. AIDS can be prevented when people do not take chances with their health.

REVIEW
SECTION 4

REMEMBER?

1. Why is it important to follow your physician's advice if you have a communicable disease?
2. Why do few adults get measles?
3. How does AIDS affect the body?

THINK!

4. What should you do if your friend has a communicable disease, such as mumps, measles, or chicken pox?
5. Why is AIDS very dangerous?

5 Noncommunicable Diseases

**noncommunicable
disease** (nahn kuh MYOO
nih kuh buhl • dihz EEZ),
an illness that cannot
spread among people

chronic (KRAHN ihk),
long-lasting health
problem.

Not all diseases are caused by microbes. A disease that does not spread among people is called a **noncommunicable disease.** Noncommunicable diseases can affect any organ or body system.

People may live with a noncommunicable disease for many years. Such long-lasting health problems are called **chronic.** With good health habits and proper treatment, people who have chronic diseases can enjoy long lives and loving relationships with family and friends.

■ *Bill's grandmother has a chronic disease that makes it difficult for her to get around without a metal walker for support.*

What Causes Noncommunicable Diseases?

Physicians do not know the causes of certain noncommunicable diseases and disorders. Some, however, are passed from parents to children. Others occur mainly in older people because certain body parts become worn.

The things around you can also cause or trigger a noncommunicable disease. Getting too much sun can cause diseases of the skin, including some kinds of skin cancer.

228

A broad-brimmed hat can protect a person from the sun's harmful rays.

Air pollution from motor vehicles, tobacco, and asbestos building materials can cause diseases of the respiratory system. Certain jobs expose workers to chemicals that can cause diseases. Some of the dangers of disease were not known when the chemicals were invented.

Getting a noncommunicable disease can depend on your choices about how you live. Smoking cigarettes causes many health problems. Smoking may affect the mouth, heart, lungs, and blood vessels. Drinking alcohol can damage your stomach, liver, heart, and brain. Not getting enough exercise and eating a diet high in fat, sugar, and salt can harm the circulatory, respiratory, and digestive systems. You can lower the chances of getting many diseases by practicing good health habits.

What Are Some Noncommunicable Diseases?

There are many kinds of noncommunicable diseases. They are not infections. A person cannot pass these kinds of diseases to other people.

Cancer. There are many different kinds of cancer. *Skin cancer* happens when cancer cells form and grow in the skin. *Lung cancer* happens when cancer cells grow in the lungs. *Leukemia* is a kind of white blood cell cancer of the circulatory system.

Spots on this X ray of the lungs show that the person has lung cancer.

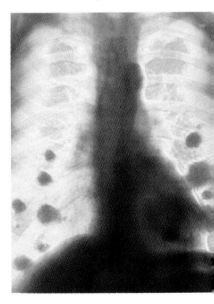

229

Many kinds of cancer can be treated if they are caught soon enough. The list below gives the seven early warning signs of cancer. Notice that the first letter of each of the seven early warning signs spells CAUTION. Having one or more of the signs does not mean a person has cancer. Only a physician can tell for sure.

WARNING SIGNS OF CANCER IN ADULTS

- **C**hanged bowel or bladder habits
- **A**ny kind of sore that does not heal
- **U**nusual bleeding or discharge
- **T**hickening or lump in any part of the body
- **I**ndigestion or difficulty in swallowing
- **O**bvious change in a wart, mole, or birthmark
- **N**agging cough or hoarseness in the throat

This health worker is protected from any harmful effects of the patient's radiation treatment for cancer.

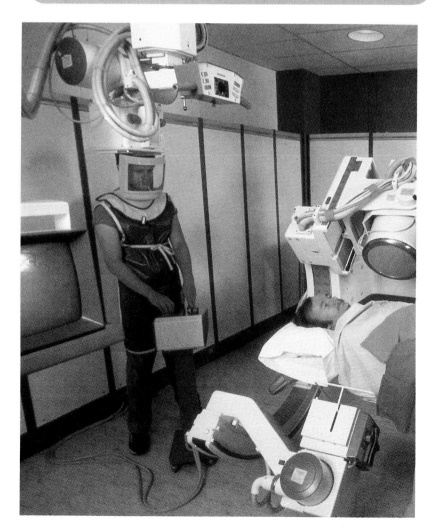

Early treatment of cancer can keep the disease from spreading to other parts of the body. Three kinds of treatment for cancer are used often. They are operations, medicines, and the use of certain powerful X rays. With these kinds of treatment, cancer cells can often be destroyed before they cause much damage. If cancer is treated early, the person with the disease has a much better chance of controlling it.

Heart Disease. More adults in the United States die each year of heart disease than of any other disease. Heart disease can weaken the heart muscle and cause it to stop working as it should.

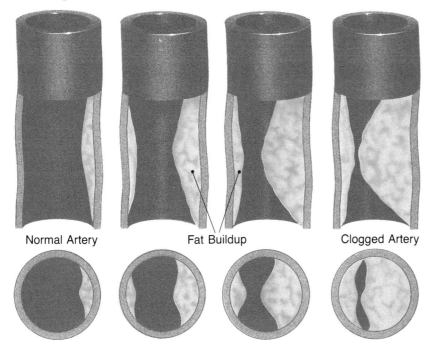

Normal Artery   Fat Buildup   Clogged Artery

When too much fat builds up in the arteries, a person can have a heart attack.

High blood pressure and too much fat in the blood can lead to one kind of heart disease. Fats in the blood stick to the inside walls of arteries. The artery openings become clogged, blocking the flow of blood to the heart muscle. The result may be a heart attack. A *heart attack* means that the blood supply to a part of the heart has stopped. The loss of blood damages the muscle in that part of the heart. Although the heart can still pump blood, it is much weaker. A heart attack is very dangerous. It calls for immediate and proper medical care.

People's health habits can make them likely to develop heart disease. People who smoke cigarettes, for example, are more likely to get heart disease than those who do not smoke. People who eat foods high in fat and people who do not exercise enough are also more likely to get heart disease.

Diabetes. Your digestive system turns the food you eat into a sugar called glucose. Your blood carries it to all the cells of your body. The cells then turn the glucose into energy for all your body's needs. Your body uses a hormone called **insulin** to carry glucose into the cells. Sometimes a person's body does not make enough insulin. This causes a disease called *diabetes*.

Without enough insulin, glucose stays in the blood and does not enter the cells. This causes a person to become thirsty, hungry, and weak.

Scientists are still looking for a cure for diabetes. However, it can be treated and controlled. People who have diabetes need a balanced amount of sugar in the blood at all times. To get this, they need to eat foods low in sugar and fat. They also need to get regular exercise and rest. They need to be very careful not to become overweight. Sometimes, though, certain treatment is needed. Some people who have diabetes need to give themselves injections of insulin each day. They have much responsibility for controlling their health problem.

insulin (IHN suh luhn), a hormone that carries glucose into the cells.

Some people who have diabetes must inject themselves with insulin each day.

Epilepsy. What if your brain sent orders to muscles in your arm without your wanting it to do so? Your arm might shake without your control. Such a moving of body parts without your control is called a **seizure.** A seizure can make any group of muscles move. This most often lasts for only a few minutes. The seizure finally stops by itself. Often a person is not awake during a seizure and later cannot remember what happened. Seizures can happen in both children and adults. People who have repeated seizures may have a disorder called *epilepsy.*

There are many causes of epilepsy. Some people are born with nervous system problems that may cause seizures. Sometimes head injuries cause epilepsy. Anyone with epilepsy needs a physician to order the right medicines to keep seizures from happening.

■ *Tags alert health workers about special medical conditions.*

seizure (SEE zhuhr), the moving of body parts without control.

**STOP REVIEW
SECTION 5**

REMEMBER?

1. What are three causes of noncommunicable health problems?
2. Why is the early treatment of cancer so important?
3. What is the problem that diabetes causes for the body?

THINK!

4. How might the way a person lives his or her life be a cause of health problems?
5. What is a responsible thing to do if you notice a sore that does not heal?

People in Health

An Interview with a Medical Technologist

James I. Stephens knows that diseases can be mysteries. He is a medical laboratory technologist in Fridley, Minnesota.

What does a medical laboratory technologist do?

A medical laboratory technologist performs laboratory tests that help a physician decide if a patient has a disease. The technologist most often performs these tests with samples of blood or other body liquids from the patient. Then he or she examines or tests the sample. The technologist gives the

■ *As a medical technologist, Mr. Stephens performs certain tests on blood and other body fluids.*

results of the test to the physician. The physician uses the test results in deciding how to treat the patient's problem.

For what kinds of diseases do you test?

Checking for the number of red blood cells and white blood cells helps identify certain diseases. Too few red blood cells may be a sign of anemia. A person with anemia might be weak enough to become ill. Too many white blood cells may be a sign of an infection already in the body. Another test is done for the level of glucose, or sugar, in the blood. A high sugar level may mean the patient has diabetes. There is no cure for diabetes at this time. A person with diabetes may need to be treated throughout his or her life.

How do you use computers in the laboratory?

Computers are being used more and more to help the technologist do the tests. For example, the technologist uses a computer to keep records and to add and subtract numbers. He or she also uses a computer to receive test orders and send test results. A physician orders a test for a particular patient. The technologist receives the order, takes blood or another liquid from the patient, and does the test. Then the technologist types the results into a computer and sends them to the physician.

■ *Medical technologists work in hospitals and laboratories.*

What kind of training did you need to become a medical laboratory technologist?

I studied medical technology for four years at the University of Minnesota and got a college degree. Most technologists need the same kind of training. Besides that, they need to complete one year of training in a medical laboratory. They also must pass a national test. However, there are closely related careers that require less training time. A medical laboratory technician helps the technologist. A technician needs only two years of training after high school.

What do you like most about being a medical laboratory technologist?

I enjoy always having something new and different to do or learn. The tests that I do are always changing. Also, it is satisfying to know that the work I do is important to medicine. Medicine today cannot be practiced well without the tests done by the technologist.

In what way, if any, does a technologist work directly with patients?

The major way is in taking blood or other sample liquids from a patient. It is very important that the person who takes a sample from a patient be as caring as possible. Sometimes a patient is afraid of having a blood sample taken. That person must be made to feel comfortable so he or she can relax.

Learn more about people who work as medical laboratory technologists. Interview a medical laboratory technologist. Or write for information to the American Society for Medical Technology, 330 Meadowfern Drive, Houston, TX 77067.

Main Ideas

- Different kinds of microbes cause different kinds of diseases.
- Microbes can be spread in a variety of ways.
- Most microbes that cause disease can enter the body in a variety of ways.
- Diseases cause changes in the body that can warn you that you have an illness.
- Good health habits and substances such as vaccines help prevent the spread of communicable diseases.
- Some people develop or are born with diseases that are not caused by microbes.
- Some diseases may be caused by the health choices you make.

Key Words

Write the numbers 1 to 11 in your health notebook or on a separate sheet of paper. After each number, copy the sentence and fill in the missing term. Page numbers in ( ) tell you where to look in the chapter if you need help.

microbes (206)　　protozoa (208)
infection (207)　　transmitted (209)
disease (207)　　toxins (211)
viruses (208)　　resistance (217)
bacteria (208)　　chronic (228)
fungi (208)

1. Harmful chemicals made by certain microbes are called ___?___ .

2. The body's ability to fight off disease on its own is called ___?___ .

3. One-celled microbes that can move by themselves are ___?___ .

4. Very small living things that can cause disease are called ___?___ .

5. The growth of microbes somewhere inside your body is an ___?___ .

6. Microbes can be ___?___ to a person from someone carrying them.

7. The smallest microbes are ___?___ .

8. Long-lasting diseases or disorders are called ___?___

9. One-celled microbes that live almost everywhere are called ___?___ .

10. Microbes that live and grow like plants are ___?___ .

11. A ___?___ is a breakdown in the way the body works.

Write the numbers 12 to 24 on your paper. After each number, write a sentence that defines the term. Page numbers in ( ) tell you where to look in the chapter if you need help.

12. communicable disease (209)
13. antibodies (216)
14. immunity (216)
15. vaccines (217)
16. antibiotic (217)
17. symptoms (219)
18. fever (219)
19. treatment (220)
20. lymph nodes (222)
21. contagious (226)
22. noncommunicable disease (228)
23. insulin (232)
24. seizure (233)

Remembering What You Learned

Page numbers in ( ) tell you where to look in the chapter if you need help.

1. What are four ways that harmful microbes spread? (209–211)

2. What are three ways that your body prevents disease microbes from entering it? (214–216)

3. What do white blood cells do to keep you healthy? (216)

4. How do antibodies help you if you get ill? (216)

5. How can you become immune to some diseases without getting ill? (217)

6. What are four ways to help your body have strong resistance? (217–218)

7. How might a fever be helpful in fighting an infection? (219)

8. What do lymph nodes do when the body has an infection? (222)

9. What is meant by the term *childhood diseases*? (225–226)

10. How does a disease like AIDS challenge scientists? (226–227)

11. What causes a noncommunicable disease? (228–229)

12. List four noncommunicable diseases or disorders. (229–233)

13. List the seven warning signs of cancer. (230)

Thinking About What You Learned

1. Why should you keep the space between your toes dry?

2. Is a cold a chronic disease? Explain your answer.

3. Why is it important to see a physician about an early warning sign of cancer?

4. Why might using someone else's towel be unhealthful?

5. Why is wearing a hat in bright sunlight a good health habit?

Writing About What You Learned

1. Write a story describing how you will prepare foods for a picnic to keep people safe from food poisoning. Describe when you need to wash your hands and the utensils you use.

2. Invite a physician or school nurse to your class. Ask the physician or nurse to tell what can be done by people to stop the spread of a specific communicable disease. After the talk, write a summary report comparing what you read in the chapter with what you heard in the talk.

Applying What You Learned

ART

Create hand-washing reminders for all the people in the school. Plan some for the gym, rest rooms, classroom sinks, cafeteria, and teachers' lounge. Ask your teacher where they may be posted.

Modified True or False

Write the numbers 1 to 15 in your health notebook or on a separate sheet of paper. After each number, write *true* or *false* to describe the sentence. If the sentence is false, also write a term that replaces the underlined term and makes the sentence true.

1. Washing your hands can prevent the spreading of <u>communicable</u> disease.

2. One-celled microbes that can move by themselves are <u>fungi</u>.

3. <u>Mumps</u> is a communicable disease.

4. Covering your nose and mouth with a tissue when you <u>sneeze</u> is one way to avoid spreading a disease.

5. Harmful chemicals that can cause food poisoning are called <u>antibodies</u>.

6. Infections due to close body contact are <u>noncommunicable diseases</u>.

7. <u>Saliva</u> destroys microbes.

8. <u>White blood cells</u> will kill microbes in the bloodstream.

9. If you receive a vaccine, then you will have <u>an infection</u>.

10. Eating a balanced diet will help your <u>resistance</u>.

11. Muscle aches may be a <u>symptom</u> of a disease.

12. Lymph nodes are small glands where <u>fungi</u> are made.

13. A physician measures your blood pressure using <u>an ophthalmoscope</u>.

14. Many <u>microbes</u> live and grow in garbage and standing water.

15. You should not use unwashed <u>utensils</u> used by someone who is ill.

Short Answer

Write the numbers 16 to 23 on your paper. Write a complete sentence to answer each question.

16. What are two ways you can get immunity to a disease?

17. Describe how a responsible person should wash daily.

18. How are fungi and protozoa the same? How are they different?

19. How are communicable diseases spread?

20. Describe what you can do to prevent food from spoiling.

21. Name three ways microbes can enter the body.

22. How does your blood protect you from an infection?

23. How is the AIDS virus transmitted?

Essay

Write the numbers 24 and 25 on your paper. Write paragraphs with complete sentences to answer each question.

24. Describe how people might check themselves for cancer.

25. Write an essay about daily health habits that keep your body healthy.

ACTIVITIES FOR HOME OR SCHOOL

Projects to Do

1. Keep a chart for three days on which you mark each time you wash your hands. Also write down why you washed your hands each time. For example, you should always wash your hands before eating. You also should wash your hands after using the rest room. At the end of the three days, review when you washed your hands. Does your chart show that you are practicing good health habits?

2. Ask a parent or guardian to help you create a family health problem "tree" like the one shown here. On one line, write in your name and those of your brothers and sisters. Mark a second line with the names of your parents and their brothers and sisters. In each person's box, write the names of

■ Study this family "tree."

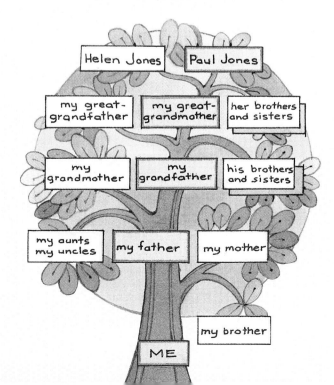

all known noncommunicable health problems that person has. Problems could also be the results of serious communicable diseases.

Information to Find

1. Much is changing in the area of arthritis care. Do you have a family member with arthritis? Find out about current treatments for different kinds of arthritis. Find out about treatments people have tried in the past, such as copper bracelets or DMSO. Contact the local chapter of the Arthritis Foundation or a physical therapist.

2. A communicable disease called *smallpox* is caused by a virus. It was once a very common and dangerous disease. Through a special vaccination program and good health habits, not one person in the world now has smallpox. Find out when the last known case of smallpox occurred. Also find out what factors helped eliminate this disease from people around the world.

Books to Read

Here are some books you can look for in your school library or the public library to find more information about the prevention and treatment of diseases.

Burns, Sheila L. *Allergies and You.* Messner.

Haines, Gail Kay. *Cancer.* Franklin Watts.

Nourse, Alan E. *AIDS.* Franklin Watts.

239

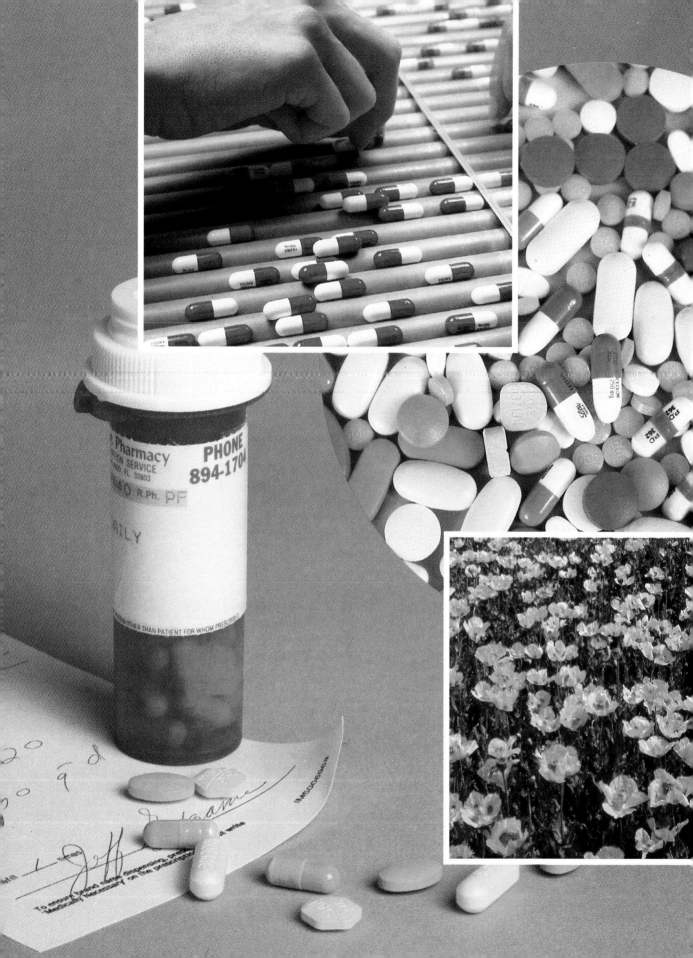

CHAPTER 8

MEDICINES AND ILLEGAL DRUGS

"Drugs have saved many lives." "Drugs have destroyed many lives." Which of these statements is true? They both are. Some drugs are medicines that can be very useful in fighting disease. But all drugs can be harmful. Medicines used the wrong way are dangerous. Some drugs are so dangerous that it is against the law for anyone to use them.

Illegal drugs are not found in stores. These drugs are sold by people who do not care about other people's health and happiness. Knowing the dangers of these drugs can help you choose never to use them. Illegal drugs can destroy a person's health for the rest of his or her life. They can even be deadly!

GETTING READY TO LEARN

Key Questions

- Why is it important to learn about medicines and drugs?
- How can you learn to be safe with medicines?
- How can you learn to refuse drugs?
- How can you take responsibility for your health when it comes to medicines and drugs?

Main Chapter Sections

1 How Medicines Can Help You
2 Medicine Use, Misuse, and Abuse
3 Illegal Drugs
4 Refusing Illegal Drugs

241

1 How Medicines Can Help You

medicine
drug
side effects
prescription
OTC medicines

medicine (MEHD uh suhn), a drug used to treat or cure a certain health problem.

drug (DRUHG), any substance other than food that causes changes in the body.

Donna stayed home from school one day last week because she had a cold. Donna's cold symptoms made her feel bad. She had a runny nose, and she felt weak. Her mother decided that Donna did not need to see their family physician. What did Donna do to feel well again? She stayed in bed for a day and rested. Donna's mother made sure that Donna drank plenty of water and fruit juices. Since Donna did not have an upset stomach, she was able to eat healthful foods. She felt much better after a few days. These health practices helped Donna get over her cold and feel well again.

For a mild illness, some people may choose to follow simple health practices like those that Donna followed. Other people, however, may also choose to use medicines. A **medicine** is a drug used to treat or cure certain health problems. A **drug** is any substance other than food that causes changes in the body. All medicines are drugs. All drugs are *not* medicines!

■ *Rest, extra fluids, and medicines often help the body fight off minor illnesses.*

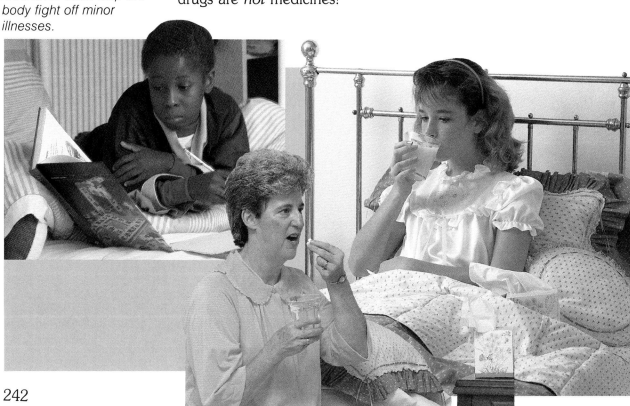

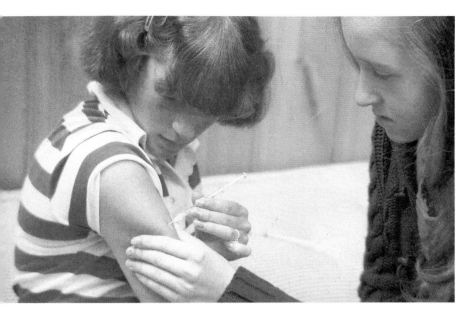

Medicines do not cure some diseases, such as diabetes. But medicines may allow people with these diseases to lead normal lives.

What Can Medicines Do to the Body?

There are many kinds of medicines. Each kind causes a certain change in the body. Cough syrup and allergy injections, for example, are medicines with certain purposes. Aspirin is another medicine with a purpose. Aspirin helps reduce fever, swelling, and pain.

Some medicines, such as those for diabetes, cannot cure a disorder or disease. They can help people who have health problems feel better and function normally for a while. Medicines of this kind lessen the symptoms of a health problem.

All medicines cause changes in the body. Most of these changes make people who are ill feel better, if only for a short while. However, some medicines have effects that are not wanted. These effects also may not be expected. Unnecessary or unwanted changes in the body caused by a medicine are called **side effects.**

The side effects that some people get from certain medicines are caused by allergies. People who have an allergy to penicillin may break out in a rash. *Penicillin* is used to treat infections caused by bacteria. Other medicines may cause side effects such as weakness or an upset stomach. If you get any of these side effects while you are taking a medicine, you need to tell a parent or other adult.

side effects, unnecessary or unwanted changes in the body that are caused by a medicine.

Tell a parent or other adult about any unexpected side effects from medicines you take.

243

The adult can then decide whether to check with your physician. A different medicine that results in fewer or no side effects might be used to treat the problem.

Taking the wrong medicines can harm a person's health. Knowing about medicines and using them safely can help you stay healthy.

What Are Prescription Medicines?

Some medicines cannot be bought without an order from a physician or some other qualified doctor. The order for a medicine is a **prescription.** A prescription is ordered for only one person. No one should use another person's prescription. A health worker called a *pharmacist* prepares the medicine for a prescription. Pharmacists work in hospitals and in many stores where medicines are sold. Pharmacists have been trained to prepare and package medicines safely.

prescription (prih SKRIHP shuhn), an order from a physician or other qualified doctor for a medicine.

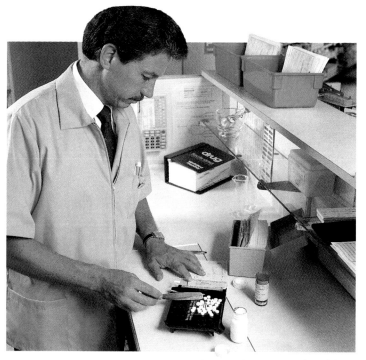

■ *A pharmacist prepares a prescription medicine that a physician has ordered for a patient.*

It is possible for two people to have the same health problem yet receive different prescriptions. The reason for the difference is that a physician orders medicine only after he or she considers the answers to many questions about a person. For example, what is the age of the person? Is the

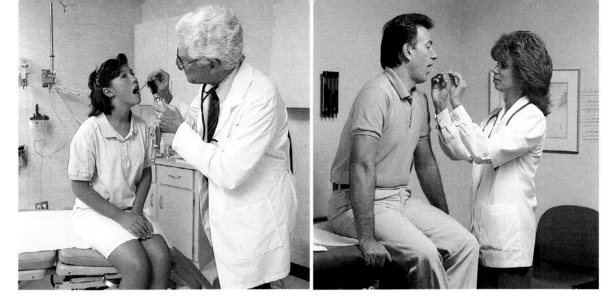

person taking any other medicine? Does the person have any allergies to medicines? Knowing all these things helps the physician order the right medicine for the person's health problem. Taking a prescription medicine ordered for another person is dangerous. It is an unwise and unsafe health choice.

These people may have similar health problems but may receive different prescriptions.

What Are Over-the-Counter Medicines?

Some medicines can be bought without a prescription. They can be bought in pharmacies and in most food stores. These medicines are called over-the-counter medicines, or **OTC medicines.** OTC medicines are generally not as strong as prescription medicines. But OTC medicines can have dangerous side effects if they are used too often, for the wrong reason, or incorrectly.

People need to read carefully the labels on OTC medicines before buying them. Many labels tell what symptoms the medicines are used to treat. Labels may also warn of dangers of taking the medicine. Some OTC medicines should not be taken if people have certain health conditions. For example, young people with fever from influenza or chicken pox should never take aspirin or medicines with aspirin in them. The aspirin may cause a serious health problem. Nonaspirin medicines for fever are available. They may be used in place of aspirin.

Some labels tell how long an OTC medicine should be used to treat a symptom. If the symptom does not stop in a certain amount of time, then a physician needs to be seen.

OTC medicines, over-the-counter medicines; can be bought without a prescription.

MYTH
AND
FACT

Myth: Aspirin is a safe medicine.

Fact: Aspirin is a medicine that can help most people when it is used safely. However, even when used safely, aspirin may cause side effects. Aspirin may irritate the lining of the stomach. It may also cause a ringing in the ears.

■ *Read the label on any OTC medicine to be sure you are getting the right medicine for your needs.*

J 1 6 6 8 6

Calamine Lotion

WARNING: Keep this and all drugs out of the reach of children. In case of accidental ingestion, seek professional assistance or contact a poison control center immediately.

OTC medicines are easy to get. However, that does not mean people should take them for every ache and pain. Think back to what Donna did when she was ill with a cold. She got over her illness by following some simple health practices. Donna's mother helped her see that not all symptoms need to be treated with a medicine for her to feel better.

STOP REVIEW
SECTION 1

REMEMBER?

1. What are two differences between prescription and OTC medicines?
2. What are three kinds of information given on an OTC medicine label?

THINK!

3. Why are medicines not needed for some illnesses?
4. Why is it dangerous for one person to use another person's prescription medicine?

2 Medicine Use, Misuse, and Abuse

People who choose to use medicines must use them in safe ways if the medicines are to be helpful. Some people use medicines without remembering to read the directions. Other people use medicines in ways that are dangerous. Any medicine can be dangerous when not used in the proper way. You can learn how to use medicines wisely and responsibly. Using medicines in the right way should become a life-long health habit.

KEY WORDS

dosage
self-medication
medicine abuse

How Can Medicines Be Used Safely?

A parent or guardian can show you how to use medicines safely.

Any medicine can be dangerous. Also, medicines can have side effects. Therefore, you should not decide on your own to take a medicine.

If you do not feel well, talk with a parent, a guardian, or a school nurse. Your parent may decide to take you to see a physician. You should take a medicine only when a responsible adult tells you to do so. Ask how to use the medicine properly. Make sure you know and understand all the directions for using the medicine.

Safety guidelines should be followed when using any medicine. The directions for using a medicine are always on the label. An OTC medicine comes with a label printed on the box, bottle, or tube. A prescription medicine has a label prepared by the pharmacist.

dosage (DOH sihj), the amount of medicine to take at one time.

The label tells the name of the medicine and how it should be taken. It tells the amount to be taken at one time by an adult and a child. This amount is called the **dosage.** The label tells how often to take the medicine. You need to follow all these directions exactly. The label may also tell about possible side effects and the date when the medicine is no longer safe to use.

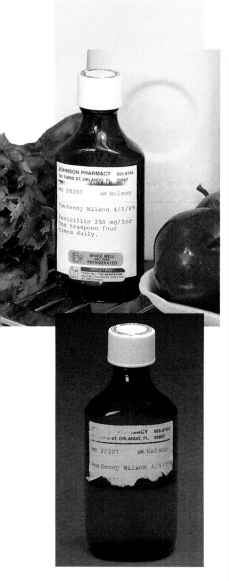

■ You should not use a medicine that is old or that has a missing label.

When using any medicine, follow these safety guidelines:

■ Always check with a parent, guardian, or school nurse *before* taking any medicine.

■ Do not use an OTC medicine unless a responsible adult decides you need one.

■ Do not use any prescription medicine unless your physician or another qualified doctor tells you to do so.

■ Read the directions on the label each time you use a medicine.

■ Always use medicines exactly the way the directions tell you to use them. Report troublesome side effects to a parent or other adult.

■ Do not take two or more medicines at the same time unless your physician tells you to do so. Two medicines together can affect the body in ways that neither medicine does by itself.

■ Do not take a medicine if you are not sure what it is for.

■ Throw out any old medicine. Read the *expiration date* on the label. You should not take medicine after this date.

■ Throw out any container of medicine that has no label.

■ Keep all medicines out of the reach of very young children.

How Can a Person Avoid Medicine Misuse?

Using a medicine without following the directions exactly is medicine misuse. Suppose the right dosage of a medicine is two pills every four hours. Taking three pills at one time would be misuse of the medicine. Taking two pills every three hours would also be misuse. Dangerous side effects may come from taking too many pills or taking pills too often. The body works best to fight off an illness or symptom when it has the proper amount of medicine. Putting too much medicine in the body at one time can be harmful.

Suppose a person has a headache and takes aspirin to ease the pain. This action is called self-medication. **Self-medication** is deciding on your own what medicine to take, instead of asking a physician. After three days, the headache still has not gone away. The person then tries another medicine. None of the OTC medicines helps. Before going to see a physician, however, the person tries yet another way to get rid of the headache. The person tries two different pain-relief medicines together. This is one example of medicine misuse.

▪ If you are not sure about the directions for taking a medicine, ask a parent or guardian.

self-medication (sehlf mehd uh KAY shuhn), deciding on your own what medicine to take, instead of asking a physician; can be a form of medicine misuse.

249

medicine abuse (MEHD uh suhn • uh BYOOS), taking any medicine on purpose in a way that harms one's health.

Self-medication can be dangerous to your health. People are often wrong when they think they know what to take for an illness just by observing the symptoms. Many different illnesses have the same symptoms. Each illness may require a different medicine. Only with the help of proper tests can a physician identify a person's illness. Then the physician can decide what kind of medicine should be used.

What Are the Dangers of Medicine Abuse?

A medicine may not help a person at all when it is misused. Instead, it may harm a person's health. Taking any medicine on purpose in a way that harms one's health is **medicine abuse.**

Medicine abuse can make people ill. It can even cause death. Few people start out intending to harm themselves with medicine. They may just use medicines carelessly. They may think a few mistakes cannot do any harm. But regular medicine misuse can lead to medicine abuse.

Some people form habits of medicine abuse because they think that all medicines are safe. Medicines are safe only when they are used according to directions. You must know how to use medicines safely in order to avoid medicine abuse.

STOP REVIEW
SECTION 2

REMEMBER?

1. Describe three guidelines for using medicines safely.
2. What is medicine misuse?
3. Why could self-medication be a form of medicine misuse?

THINK!

4. Why would using a medicine without knowing the directions be medicine misuse?
5. How might it be harmful to think that all medicines are safe?

Keeping Safe from Harmful Substances

Glues, paints, cleaning products, and insect sprays are all chemicals. Chemicals help people do many kinds of jobs, but many chemicals are poisons. This means they can cause illness or death if they come into contact with the human body. People can get poisons into their bodies by breathing, touching, eating, or drinking them. You can use household chemicals safely if you follow these safety rules:

- Always follow label directions about how to use a chemical. The label will tell you how to protect yourself. It may tell you to keep the windows open for fresh air, or to wear gloves and goggles.
- Always keep a chemical in its original container. The label on a container names the chemical and tells you what to do if the chemical poisons someone.
- Always keep all chemicals where young children cannot reach them. Remember that small children cannot read. They may think an orange chemical is an orange soft drink. Store dangerous chemicals on high shelves, or lock them up.
- Always follow label directions for storing and mixing chemicals. Some chemicals become more dangerous if they become too hot or too damp, or if they are mixed with other chemicals. Never use two chemicals at one time unless the labels say you can do so.

You need to protect yourself from harmful substances.

- Keep near your phone the telephone number of the poison control center. If a person is poisoned, you must call for help right away. Have the container with you so you can read its label to the worker at the center. Then do what the worker tells you to do.

Thinking Beyond

1. Why might you tell a friend to use certain glues and spray paints outside?
2. Why might it be dangerous for someone to use two chemicals at the same time?

251

3 Illegal Drugs

illegal drugs
drug dependence
tolerance
overdose
marijuana
cocaine
crack

illegal drugs (ihl EE guhl
• DRUHGZ), drugs that it is
against the law to sell,
buy, have, or use.

When some people talk about drugs, they may mean medicines. However, there are many drugs that are not medicines, and these drugs are very dangerous. It is against the law to sell, buy, have, or use these drugs. These are **illegal drugs.** People who use illegal drugs harm their bodies. They may also hurt other people. And they can get into trouble by breaking laws.

How Can Illegal Drugs Harm the Body?

Illegal drugs harm many parts of the body. The part that is harmed most is the brain. Illegal drugs change the way the brain works. They disturb the way the brain takes in information and sorts through it. The things that a drug user sees, hears, and feels run together in the brain. This causes the person to be confused. Some illegal drugs can also destroy brain cells.

Talking with others about illegal drugs can help people decide not to use them.

People who start to use illegal drugs want to change how they feel. After a time, the drug abusers need the drugs. This is called **drug dependence.** There are two kinds of drug dependence. Sometimes a drug abuser believes he or she needs a certain drug to feel all right, even when this is not true. This is called *emotional dependence*. Sometimes a drug abuser comes to need a certain drug to prevent unpleasant physical symptoms. This is called *physical dependence*. Drug dependence of either kind makes it very hard for a drug abuser to stop taking the drug without the help of special health workers.

People who abuse illegal drugs build tolerance to the drugs that they take over a long time. **Tolerance** is the adjustment the body has made to the effects of a drug. Because of tolerance, a drug abuser must take larger amounts of a drug in order to have the same feeling that smaller amounts once caused. The person's body may then build tolerance to the new, even larger amount. In this way, tolerance leads drug abusers to keep adding to the amounts of illegal drugs they take. The amounts can become very dangerous.

A drug abuser always risks taking an overdose. An **overdose** is an amount of a drug large enough to cause great harm to the body. An overdose of some illegal drugs causes death. A person can have an overdose even the first time he or she takes an illegal drug. First-time drug users do not know how much of the drug could result in an overdose. Many people die from overdoses.

What Is Marijuana?

An illegal drug made from a plant called hemp is known as **marijuana.** People who use marijuana usually smoke it. Like tobacco, marijuana has many harmful substances in it. In fact, marijuana contains more than 400 harmful substances. Most of them are dangerous. One of the most dangerous is a substance known as THC.

Shortly after a person breathes in marijuana smoke, THC causes changes in certain cells deep inside the brain. The marijuana smoker feels confused and cannot concentrate.

drug dependence (DRUHG • dih PEHN duhns), a need for a drug or a belief that a drug is needed for feeling all right.

tolerance (TAHL uh ruhns), ability of the body to adjust to the effects of a drug.

overdose (OH vuhr dohs), an amount of a drug large enough to cause great harm to the body or even death.

marijuana (mair uh WAHN uh), an illegal drug made from the hemp plant.

253

Marijuana interferes with acting in safe ways.

Scientific tests have shown that marijuana contains many harmful substances.

The person has trouble remembering names or what he or she reads. The person may suffer a loss of balance as well. This can cause the marijuana smoker to have trouble doing even simple things, such as riding a bicycle or walking.

THC and other harmful substances in marijuana do more than just change cells in the brain. When marijuana is smoked, THC and other substances damage the lungs. Marijuana has substances in it that can cause lung cancer. Scientists have found that marijuana smoke has even more cancer-causing substances than tobacco smoke.

Drug abusers who use marijuana can form an emotional dependence on it. They think they need to use marijuana to feel all right. The drug becomes an important part of their lives. Because of this, their personalities change in bad ways. They act as if they do not care about themselves. They may not remember simple facts. They seem to forget their responsibilities.

Young users of marijuana face a bigger problem than adult users because their personalities are still forming. Marijuana can keep young people from thinking, learning, and acting in ways that will help their self-esteem. Self-esteem is important for handling problems. Some young people use marijuana to escape from problems. What they really need is a positive self-concept and caring from others.

Marijuana is illegal in all states. Because of its health dangers, there are laws against growing, selling, using, or having any amount of marijuana. People involved with marijuana can be arrested for breaking these laws.

The penalty may be a fine, a jail sentence, or both. Because of these penalties, adult drug dealers try to get young people to sell marijuana for them.

What Are Cocaine and Crack?

Cocaine is an illegal drug made from the leaves of the coca plant. People use this drug to change the way they feel. Cocaine can cause harm to the body. Cocaine can dangerously speed up the nervous system so much that it may cause a seizure. Cocaine also affects the heart rate and may cause irregular heart rhythms. The result may be death. In people who survive, cocaine can cause physical and emotional dependence.

Crack is an illegal drug made from cocaine. Crack is made by treating cocaine powder and turning it into a solid block. This block is broken up into small pieces called crack or *rock*. Drug abusers most often smoke crack in pipes.

When crack is smoked, the drug is inhaled. It reaches the brain in seconds. Crack quickly changes the way drug abusers feel and act. One minute, it makes them feel happy. The next minute, they feel terrible. The chemicals in crack cause these sudden changes in personality. Crack can also cause heart attacks and death in young people who are otherwise healthy.

Using or possessing marijuana is illegal in every state.

cocaine (koh KAYN), an illegal drug made from the leaves of the coca plant.

crack, an illegal drug made from cocaine.

Crack is a very dangerous drug. It kills!

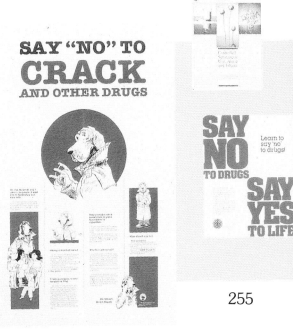

SAY "NO" TO
CRACK
AND OTHER DRUGS

SAY NO TO DRUGS

Learn to say no to drugs!

SAY YES TO LIFE

More than any other illegal drug, crack changes the electrical activity and chemistry of the brain.

Many people who use crack cannot tell the difference between what is real and what is not. They see things that are not there. They may become very afraid for no reason. Like cocaine, crack causes physical and emotional dependence. It is not easy for those who use crack or cocaine to stop using it unless they have help.

Crack is one of the most dangerous illegal drugs. It causes harm to the body and the personality. It quickly causes drug dependence. Punishment for selling, using, or having crack is usually a jail sentence.

STOP **REVIEW**
SECTION 3

REMEMBER?

1. Why do some people abuse drugs?
2. How is marijuana dangerous to a person's physical and emotional health?
3. How does tolerance to an illegal drug develop?

THINK!

4. How might the way people do simple things be affected by using marijuana?
5. How might a physical dependence on marijuana or cocaine affect an abuser's relationships with others?

Making Wellness Choices

While Mary and Ellen are walking to school one morning, a high school boy stops his car beside them. He asks the girls if they want something for free. Mary asks, "What do you mean?" The boy holds out a small plastic bag. Mary looks at the bag. It has tiny rocks of white powder in it. The boy offers the bag to Mary and tells her to take a rock.

 What should Mary and Ellen do? Explain your wellness choice.

4 Refusing Illegal Drugs

People who do not feel good about themselves or their lives are less able to refuse drugs offered by their peers. They make the mistake of thinking that illegal drugs will make them feel better. Soon they find out that using illegal drugs becomes a need that can cause new problems. Using illegal drugs keeps a young person from growing properly— physically, emotionally, intellectually, and socially. This is partly because the person pulls away from family, school, and other groups. These groups help people learn skills and ways to handle feelings.

Why Are There Laws Against Dangerous Drugs?

Anyone who uses an illegal drug is breaking the law and could be caught and punished. The laws against illegal drugs are meant to protect your health, your family, and your community. They are made to help keep your community a safe and pleasant place in which to live. The use of illegal drugs has caused many family problems and breakups.

MYTH AND **FACT**

Myth: Trying illegal drugs is a brave and grown-up thing to do.

Fact: People who think they are brave and grown-up because they use illegal drugs are wrong. They are just risking their lives. Acting grown-up and being grown-up are different. The difference lies in being responsible. Being grown-up means you are responsible for your actions.

■ *Most people do not use or support the use of illegal drugs.*

257

It has caused a great deal of violence and crime, especially theft to get money for drugs. People who sell or use illegal drugs can make a community an unsafe place to live.

Why Should You Refuse Illegal Drugs?

There may be times when you need to use the facts you have learned about illegal drugs. Some people may ask you to try drugs. They may give you illegal drugs and tell you that the drugs will not hurt you. A stranger, a classmate, or even a friend or relative may offer you drugs. Someone you admire may dare you to take an illegal drug or some substance you cannot identify.

You need to refuse illegal drugs or any substance that can harm your health. You *never* need to use illegal drugs, not

Knowing the harm that illegal drugs can cause, many young people refuse to take them.

even once. By refusing what can harm you, you are showing others that you are a strong-willed person. Refusing drugs is a health choice that will help you form self-confidence. By refusing to use drugs you are showing that you are a responsible individual.

Certain things are helpful to think about even before anyone offers you illegal drugs. Thinking about these things will help you focus on your priorities, the parts of your life that are really important. You will know and understand why drugs are not for you. You will be better prepared to turn down illegal drugs with confidence.

People do not need drugs to enjoy life and to feel good about themselves.

1. *Think about yourself.* You might think this sounds silly, but if people offer you drugs, they are offering them to *you!* Think about how *you* will be harmed by the drugs. Ask yourself, "How could using drugs hurt *me?*"

2. *Think about your family and other people who care for you.* Other people want to help you grow in many good ways. They give you love, and you share your love with them. You share experiences with them. Ask yourself, "How could drugs destroy the things I share with the people who love me?"

3. *Think about your responsibilities.* Other people count on you and need you. You probably have chores to do at home. You may be a member of a sports team or youth group. You need to give full attention to your schoolwork so you can do as well as you can. Ask yourself, "How might drugs keep me from being a responsible person?"

4. *Think about the things you like to do.* You most likely have at least one favorite thing that you enjoy doing. Maybe you enjoy playing a musical instrument or playing a computer game. These things require close attention to what you are doing. To be the best you can be at any activity calls for practice. Practice helps improve your skills and your self-concept. Ask yourself, "How could drugs destroy my chances of becoming the best I can be in activities I already enjoy?"

5. *Think about the law.* If a person uses, sells, has, or buys illegal drugs, that person is breaking the law. When a person is arrested, he or she gets a court record. Some records remain with a person for life. A person who has been arrested may not be able to get certain jobs, such as those in medicine or law.

Taking time to think about these parts of your life is important. Thinking about them *now* and having answers to the questions *now* can help you refuse drugs later.

■ *You have responsibilities to your family and to yourself. Saying no to drugs lets you meet your responsibilities.*

260

If you have trouble with any of the questions, talk with a parent or other trusted adult right away. You can think about the consequences of using drugs, and you can be ready to make a positive health choice. If someone asks you to try drugs, you can feel good about yourself when you say, "No!"

REVIEW
SECTION 4

REMEMBER?

1. Why are there laws against dangerous drugs?
2. What five things can you think about to prepare yourself to refuse illegal drugs?

THINK!

3. How might using illegal drugs cause a person to lose friends?
4. Why is it important to be thinking now about reasons for refusing drugs later?

Thinking About Your Health

Am I Prepared to Refuse Illegal Drugs?

Read the following questions. Think about each one and answer yes, no, or maybe.

1. Do I feel good about myself?

2. Am I willing to act for what I know is important to me?

3. Do I feel good about myself for refusing something that I know will harm me? Do I feel proud when I do refuse?

4. Am I someone who does not let my friends tell me what to do?

5. Can I talk to my parents or other trusted adults about any serious problems?

Think about why you answered the questions the way you did. If you answered no or maybe to any of the questions, list two things you can do to change your behavior or feelings so that all of your answers will be yes.

An Interview with a Pharmaceutical Chemist

Patricia B. Fleming makes sure medicines are safe for people to use. She is a pharmaceutical chemist in Richmond, Virginia.

What does a pharmaceutical chemist do?

A pharmaceutical chemist tests medicines as they are being made. The word *pharmaceutical* means "having to do with medicine." I make sure that medicines meet standards for safety. I check the ingredients in the medicines. I make sure the ingredients do what they are supposed to do in the body.

■ *Ms. Fleming is testing one kind of medicine to make sure it meets safety requirements.*

How exactly do you test medicines?

Since the company I work for makes millions of tablets and other forms of medicines at one time, I test only samples from each batch of medicine being made. The tests imitate what happens to a medicine as it passes through the body. To test medicine tablets, I set up a tablet "bath." I use six cups of six different liquids. Each cup has a certain liquid that is like a liquid in the human body. I put pieces of the tablets in each cup. At the end of four hours, I check the cups. I make sure the correct amount of medicine has been released in each cup. If it has, the batch of tablets has passed the test.

Who sets the standards that tell you the correct amount of medicine for each tablet?

Standards for medicines are set up by the Food and Drug Administration (FDA) of the United States government. The FDA sends inspectors to laboratories where the medicines are made. Their inspectors make sure that standards are being met.

With all the different kinds of medicines being made at your laboratory, how do you keep from confusing them?

Every medicine must have its own identity. Every kind of tablet has its own shape, color, name, and identification number. Besides that, different batches of prescription tablets must have different national drug-control numbers printed on them. If you look in a physician's desk-reference book, you can find the correct name, number, and description of every medicine. If a person accidentally takes an overdose of a prescribed medicine, a physician can quickly identify the medicine. He or she can do this by looking at just one tablet. This helps the physician find a fast way to treat that person.

How important is the label on a medicine?

The label on every medicine is very important. The label names the medicine and tells how to take that medicine. Also, the label shows the expiration date, the date when the medicine is no longer good. It is very important to read the label on a medicine. It is important to look for and read any warnings. Sometimes certain foods should not be eaten when a medicine is being taken.

Pharmaceutical chemists work with new chemicals that someday may be used as medicines.

The chemicals in medicine are very powerful. They can be dangerous if not taken properly.

What education does a person need in order to test medicines?

A person needs to study chemistry for at least four years in college. I studied chemistry and am called a chemist. But the title for this job is different in different companies. People who test medicines in other companies might be called laboratory technicians.

What other subjects are important to know for this career?

A person who wants to work in this field should study mathematics as well as chemistry. That person should also study at least one foreign language. In particular, German and French are good to know. The reason is that new facts about medicines appear all the time. This information is the result of research done in many different countries. To keep up with this knowledge, a person must be able to read foreign languages.

Learn more about medicine safety and the people who make sure medicines are safe. Interview a pharmaceutical chemist. Or write for information to the Food and Drug Administration, Office of Consumer Affairs Public Inquiries, 5600 Fishers Lane (HFE-88), Rockville, MD 20857.

CHAPTER REVIEW

Main Ideas

- Knowing about medicines and using them safely can help you stay healthy.
- Any medicine can be dangerous when used unwisely.
- Medicine misuse can be avoided by following the directions on the label.
- People who abuse drugs can harm their bodies, harm other people, and get into trouble by breaking laws.
- When you obey the laws against illegal drugs, you help protect your own health and the health of others in your community.
- Thinking *now* about yourself, your family, your responsibilities, the things you like to do, and the law can help prepare you to refuse illegal drugs.

Key Words

Write the numbers 1 to 9 in your health notebook or on a separate sheet of paper. After each number, copy the sentence and fill in the missing term. Page numbers in ( ) tell you where to look in the chapter if you need help.

side effects (243)   medicine abuse
prescription (244)   (250)
OTC medicines   illegal drugs (252)
   (245)   tolerance (253)
dosage (248)   overdose (253)
self-medication (249)

1. The unwanted effects of a medicine are called ___?___ .

2. It is against the law to sell, buy, have, or use ___?___ .

3. Using medicine on purpose in a way that harms one's health is called ___?___ .

4. The adjustment the body has made to the effects of a drug is called ___?___ .

5. Medicines called ___?___ can be bought in many food stores.

6. The ___?___ is the proper amount of a medicine to be taken.

7. An ___?___ is an amount of a drug large enough to cause serious harm to the body or death.

8. An order for medicine from a physician or a dentist is called a ___?___ .

9. Taking OTC medicines on your own is called ___?___ .

Write the numbers 10 to 15 on your paper. After each number, write a sentence that defines the term. Page numbers in ( ) tell you where to look in the chapter if you need help.

10. medicine (242)
11. drug (242)
12. drug dependence (253)
13. marijuana (253)
14. cocaine (255)
15. crack (255)

Remembering What You Learned

Page numbers in ( ) tell you where to look in the chapter if you need help.

1. How are medicines helpful? (243)

2. What is the difference between an OTC medicine and a prescription

medicine? How are they similar? (244–245)

3. What are three things a physician or other qualified doctor considers about a person before ordering a medicine? (244–245)

4. What are two warnings that may appear on OTC medicine labels? (245)

5. List five guidelines to follow for using medicines wisely. (248)

6. What are two examples of medicine misuse? (249)

7. Why is medicine abuse dangerous? (250)

8. How do some illegal drugs affect the brain? (252)

9. How does THC in marijuana harm the body? (253–254)

10. What body part is most seriously affected by cocaine? (255)

11. How does cocaine affect a drug abuser physically? (255–256)

12. Name two reasons why young people might use illegal drugs. (257)

Thinking About What You Learned

1. How might avoiding OTC medicines for a mild illness be a safer choice than using OTC medicines?

2. Why is it important for medicine labels to have warnings on them?

3. Why should a parent, guardian, or nurse help you take medicines?

4. Why should a person see a physician if an OTC medicine does not help?

5. Why is using illegal drugs a dangerous decision for people who do not feel good about themselves?

6. How is a "friend" who offers you drugs not a real friend?

Writing About What You Learned

1. Interview five adults to find out their definitions of *proper medicine use, medicine misuse,* and *medicine abuse.* Ask each person to give you an example of each. In a paragraph or two, write what you learned.

2. Write a short story about a person who is pressured to try something he or she thought was wrong. Describe what happened and what he or she thought about before deciding what to do. Use the questions in Section 4, "Refusing Illegal Drugs," to organize your ideas. What else did the person think about? How did he or she feel about the decision?

Applying What You Learned

LANGUAGE ARTS

Social health and emotional health are parts of your total wellness. Prepare a speech on this topic: "Using illegal drugs affects a person's social and emotional health. Illegal drugs can keep a person from enjoying wellness."

Modified True or False

Write the numbers 1 to 15 in your health notebook or on a separate sheet of paper. After each number, write *true* or *false* to describe the sentence. If the sentence is false, also write a term that replaces the underlined term and makes the sentence true.

1. <u>Side effects</u> are unwanted changes in the body caused by a medicine.

2. Any <u>medicine</u> can be dangerous when used unwisely.

3. OTC medicines are generally <u>stonger</u> than most prescription medicines.

4. Deciding on your own what medicine to take is <u>medicine abuse</u>.

5. Marijuana is illegal in <u>most</u> states.

6. <u>Cocaine</u> can dangerously speed up the working of the nervous system.

7. Saying no to illegal drugs shows you are a <u>strong-willed</u> person.

8. The amount of medicine taken at one time is the <u>prescription</u>.

9. Medicine misuse can be avoided by following the directions on the <u>label</u>.

10. The <u>dosage</u> will tell you when a medicine is no longer good.

11. There are <u>two</u> kinds of drug dependence.

12. Someone who must take more and more of a drug to get an effect has built up <u>tolerance</u>.

13. An <u>overdose</u> can happen the first time an illegal drug is taken.

14. The order for a medicine is a <u>side effect</u>.

15. When marijuana is smoked, <u>THC</u> harms the lungs.

Short Answer

Write the numbers 16 to 23 on your paper. Write a complete sentence to answer each question.

16. What is the difference between crack and cocaine?

17. How is smoking marijuana like smoking tobacco?

18. How can you make a responsible decision when someone offers you an illegal drug?

19. What should you do if an OTC medicine has an old expiration date?

20. Why is it important to follow the dosage on any medicine label?

21. How are emotional and physical dependence on drugs different?

22. How does crack damage the body?

23. Why should you never use another person's prescription medicine?

Essay

Write the numbers 24 and 25 on your paper. Write paragraphs with complete sentences to answer each question.

24. Explain what you would do if a friend of the best soccer player on your team offered you marijuana?

25. Describe what steps you might take to relieve a headache.

ACTIVITIES FOR HOME OR SCHOOL

Projects to Do

1. Design a book cover that says you have made a decision not to use drugs. Make several of your book covers. Use them as covers for your textbooks.

■ *Tell your friends why illegal drugs are dangerous.*

2. Work with a partner to make a poster. The poster should list ways you have fun without using drugs. Ask your teacher or principal to place your class's posters in the hallway, library, or main office of your school.

Information to Find

1. Medicines come from three main sources. Some are made from parts of plants and animals. Some are made from certain minerals. Many medicines are made by chemists in the laboratories of drug companies. Find out what kinds of medicines come from these three sources. You might ask your librarian for books about how medicines are made.

2. The discoveries of some medicines have affected people's lives greatly. The discovery of penicillin had a great effect. Find out who discovered penicillin and what effect it had on people of that time.

3. Many OTC medicines are sealed in tamper-resistant packages. Find out the reasons for this kind of packaging. You might ask your librarian for magazine and newspaper articles about this topic.

4. Talk with a police officer in your community. Ask what kinds of problems are caused by illegal drugs in your area. Find out what is being done to solve these problems. Ask the officer if there are ways you can help in solving the problems.

Books to Read

Here are some books you can look for in your school library or the public library to find more information about medicines and illegal drugs.

Lambert, Mark. *Medicine in the Future.* Franklin Watts.

Leahy, Barbara H. *Marijuana: A Dangerous "High" Way.* B. Leahy.

Madison, Arnold. *Drugs & You.* Messner.

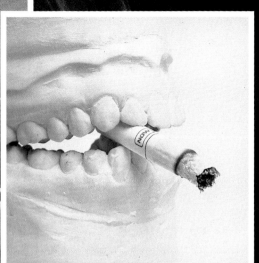

ALCOHOL AND TOBACCO

Two drugs you may have heard about or seen people using are alcohol and nicotine. Nicotine is a drug found in tobacco. Do you know what alcohol and nicotine can do to the body? Do you know what they can do to a person's health?

Most young people your age will have to make choices about these and other drugs someday. Knowing the facts about alcohol and tobacco can help you make wise choices. Deciding not to drink alcohol and not to use tobacco are wise choices for young people. These choices can help you be and stay healthy. Knowing how to say no can also help you feel strong and good about yourself.

GETTING READY TO LEARN

Key Questions

- Why is it important to learn about the dangers of alcohol and tobacco?
- Why is it important to know how you feel about the use of alcohol and tobacco?
- How can you learn to turn down alcohol and tobacco?
- How can you take responsibility for your health when it comes to alcohol and tobacco?

Main Chapter Sections

1 About Alcohol
2 About Tobacco
3 Refusing to Use Alcohol and Tobacco

269

1 About Alcohol

alcohol
depressant
intoxicated
problem drinking
alcohol
    dependence
withdrawal

Winnie and her friends want to try something new. They are trying to think of something new to do. Winnie's friend Karen says she knows where she can get some alcohol. She says it might be fun to try drinking it and see what happens. Some of the others agree. Winnie does not like the idea, but she feels worried about saying so. She is afraid her friends will think she is being a coward. How can Winnie say no to the idea of drinking alcohol? What can she tell her friends to make them think about the problems alcohol can cause? Knowing about alcohol can help Winnie and her friends say no.

The healthful choice is not to drink alcoholic beverages.

What Are the Short-term Effects of Alcohol?

Alcohol is a drug found in drinks such as beer, wine, and whiskey. Because alcohol is a drug, any drink with alcohol can cause changes in people who drink it. The more alcohol people drink, the more the drug changes them. Each of the changes is harmful.

The first physical changes that take place in a person who drinks alcohol are called *short-term effects*. Short-term effects wear off after a day or two. They can happen to anyone who drinks alcohol.

Alcohol passes through the stomach wall very quickly. Most of the alcohol goes directly from the stomach and the small intestine into the circulatory system. The alcohol mixes with the blood and is carried to all parts of the body. As more alcohol goes into the blood, it causes more harm to the body. Alcohol also harms the stomach. It can irritate the stomach so much that it can cause a person who has been drinking to vomit.

Many people wrongly think that alcohol makes someone more alert because the drinker may seem more active. But alcohol is a depressant. A **depressant** slows down the whole body, especially the nervous system.

■ *Alcohol slows down the nervous system.*

alcohol (AL kuh hawl), a drug found in drinks such as beer, wine, and whiskey.

depressant (dih PREHS uhnt), a substance that slows down the whole body, especially the nervous system.

271

Alcohol affects the part of the brain that controls speech, judgment, attention, and personality. Some people who drink do not speak clearly when they talk. Some people talk loudly or get very quiet. Some people tell personal secrets to strangers. Alcohol can make people do things they would not normally do.

Alcohol can weaken a person's ability to judge what is dangerous or harmful. Alcohol can lead people to do things they may later regret. For example, when some people drink, they insult their friends or start fights. They may feel bad when other people tell them about their behavior.

Alcohol harms the part of the brain that controls muscle movement. People who have been drinking have trouble keeping their balance. They may not be able to focus their eyes or control other body movements. They may bump into things when they try to walk.

intoxicated (ihn TAHK suh kayt uhd), strongly affected by alcohol.

As alcohol collects in their bodies, people become intoxicated. Being **intoxicated** means being strongly affected by alcohol. Breathing and heart rates slow in people who are intoxicated. Because the body slows down, an intoxicated person may "pass out."

These changes happen to anyone who drinks enough alcohol. However, it takes less alcohol to cause these changes in the body of a smaller and younger person. Therefore, the effects can be more dangerous in young people. Since young people have small bodies, even a little alcohol can cause the changes that a larger drink would cause in an older

■ Alcohol causes a loss of balance. A person may even stumble or fall.

person. Also, a younger person's cells are more likely to be harmed by alcohol than an adult's cells because the young person's cells are still growing.

What Are the Long-term Effects of Alcohol?

The habit of drinking several drinks every week can harm any drinker's body. It causes *long-term effects.* Alcohol can damage the brain and other parts of the nervous system. It can cause people to be unable to remember or to think clearly. Such people may not be able to make wise decisions.

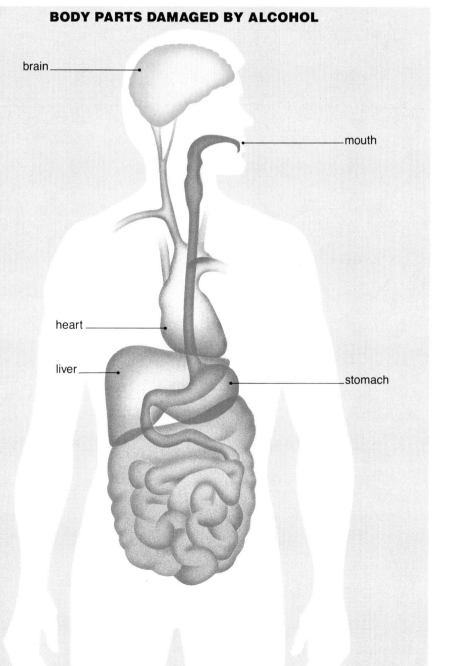

BODY PARTS DAMAGED BY ALCOHOL

brain

mouth

heart

liver

stomach

■ *Long-term use of alcohol can harm many body parts.*

273

They may often act as if they are angry at others. In fact, they are really upset with themselves. They may be less able to make their muscles work properly. Their hands may shake so much that they have trouble using them.

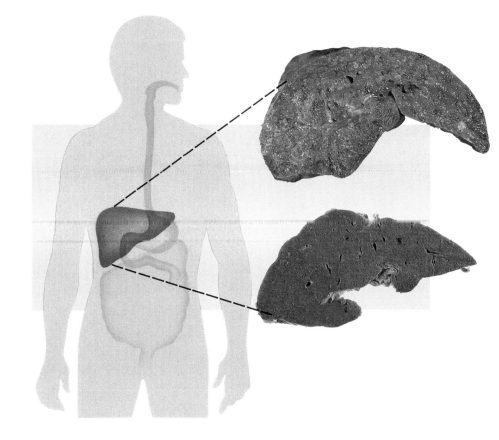

The liver disease cirrhosis is caused by drinking alcohol. A healthy liver is at the bottom right, and a diseased liver at the top right.

Alcohol can harm the liver. The liver is an organ that does many different jobs. One of the liver's jobs is to make chemicals that help stop bleeding. The liver also stores some nutrients needed by the body. It controls the use of iron in the body. The liver also helps clean the blood. Alcohol is one of the substances the liver cleans out of a person's circulatory system. Having too much alcohol in the blood can cause the liver to work too hard. Alcohol changes how the liver breaks down nutrients. Alcohol can even damage tissue in the liver. The damage is called *cirrhosis*. Cirrhosis of the liver cannot be cured. The only thing a person can do about cirrhosis is to protect the liver from further damage by not drinking any more alcohol. A person can die of cirrhosis.

What Are the Problems with Drinking Alcohol?

Using alcohol in ways that cause physical, social, or legal problems is **problem drinking.** People who drink can harm their bodies, harm their relationships with others, and get into trouble with the law.

Problem drinkers often cause trouble for themselves when they act mean or foolish. They may start fights or damage property. They may embarrass themselves, their families, and their friends. Sometimes they cause accidents in which other people are harmed. For these reasons, most communities have laws against being intoxicated in public places.

Problem drinkers become less able to make wise decisions. They cannot think clearly enough to study their choices. They do not think about the consequences of their behavior. They may try to avoid taking responsibility for the problems they cause.

problem drinking, the use of alcohol in ways that cause physical, social, or legal problems.

A police officer can test a person who may have broken a law against driving after drinking alcohol, left. Other laws prohibit the drinking of alcohol in public places, such as parks.

■ *Driving while intoxicated is the number one cause of traffic deaths in the United States.*

Some people injure themselves or others in accidents while they are drinking or when they are already intoxicated. The alcohol harms their ability to control their bodies. For example, good swimmers who have been drinking can accidentally drown. Intoxicated persons standing near pools or in boats can fall into the water and drown.

The greatest danger is for people who have been drinking to drive cars, motorcycles, or boats. People who drink cause more than half of the serious motor vehicle accidents in the United States. The accidents often result in death or permanent injury to the driver, passengers, or people nearby.

What Happens When a Drinker Loses Control?

Many adults drink alcohol in a way that does not cause problems. They do not drink very much at one time. They do not drink alcohol very often. However, some people who drink alcohol cannot stop drinking. They become intoxicated whenever they can. They find it hard or impossible to stop using alcohol. After a time, they need alcohol or believe they need it to feel all right. Their condition is called **alcohol dependence.** Alcohol dependence makes it very hard for a person to stop drinking without the help of special health workers.

Misusing alcohol is another form of drug abuse. Not being able to stop using alcohol is considered a disease, called *alcoholism.* People who have the disease are called *alcoholics.*

alcohol dependence
(AL kuh hawl • dih PEHN duhns), a condition in which a person needs alcohol or believes he or she needs it to feel all right.

▪ *Some people are so dependent on alcohol that they even drink at work and risk losing their jobs.*

Anyone who drinks alcohol can suffer from alcohol dependence. An alcoholic can be young or old, male or female. Young people who drink alcohol take a chance of becoming problem drinkers and possibly alcoholics. Physical size and incomplete emotional growth make it hard for young people to handle the changes alcohol may cause. Alcohol has very strong effects on all people.

Alcoholism can keep people from doing things well. Alcohol can cause problems at home, work, or school. It makes an alcoholic act in ways that may hurt the feelings of people who love him or her. Most alcoholics do not mean to hurt people. Alcohol can interfere with making decisions.

withdrawal (wihth DRAWL), process in which an alcoholic stops drinking or a drug user stops taking drugs; usually causes painful physical symptoms.

When alcoholics stop drinking, they go through **withdrawal.** During withdrawal, their bodies adjust to not having alcohol. Withdrawal can cause painful symptoms that can last for days or weeks. Alcoholics going through withdrawal need help. Most communities have groups or centers that help alcoholics get through withdrawal. Many alcoholics must go to the hospital when they go through withdrawal. Alcoholics can become healthy again only if they stop drinking. Even one drink can make the person lose control again.

Where Can Problem Drinkers and Their Families Find Help?

Most problem drinkers need help and the care of others to stop abusing alcohol. They need to talk with people who can understand their problem. They can find such help and care at a meeting of a special group called *Alcoholics Anonymous,* or AA.

Alcoholics Anonymous brings together people with alcohol problems. It gives present and recovering alcohol-dependent people a chance to talk with one another. Discovering and sharing their feelings often helps them understand how they can stop abusing alcohol. Alcoholics Anonymous has helped many people stop drinking.

■ *Some people who have drinking problems join support groups to help themselves overcome alcohol dependence.*

Alcoholics Anonymous also offers a program called *Al-Anon.* It is for families of alcoholics. Another program, called *Alateen,* is for the teenage children of alcoholics. *Pre-Alateen* is a program for young people ages 8 to 12 who are children of alcoholics. Alcoholics Anonymous has branches all over the United States.

Why Do Some People Use Alcohol?

People who drink alcohol do so for different reasons. Some families and religious groups have certain times when it is proper to drink a little alcohol. Some people drink because they think alcohol helps them relax. They think alcohol helps them forget their problems or troubled feelings. Some people drink to be part of a group, as at a party.

Young people also start drinking for a lot of different reasons. Many start drinking alcohol because their friends drink it. They do not want to feel left out when the drinking starts. Their friends may use peer pressure, trying to make them believe that drinking is fun and not dangerous. Other young people start drinking because they want to find out what alcohol is like. A few young people think drinking is a daring or grown-up thing to do. That idea leads them to drinking.

■ Peers often pressure one another to drink alcohol. You need to refuse.

No one who starts drinking intends to become a problem drinker or an alcoholic. Most people believe they will always be able to control their drinking. That belief helps them decide that it is safe to take their first drink. Some of them turn out to be wrong in their belief. That is why there are more than 13 million problem drinkers and alcoholics in the United States.

STOP REVIEW
SECTION 1

REMEMBER?

1. What body system is most affected by alcohol?
2. What two major organs in the body are harmed by alcohol?
3. List three ways in which problem drinkers may harm other people.

THINK!

4. Suppose you were in a situation like Winnie, the girl whose story you read in this section. What would you tell your friends to make them think about the dangers of alcohol?
5. Why should a person with alcohol dependence try to get special help instead of trying to quit drinking on his or her own?

Making Wellness Choices

Vanessa and four other girls are sleeping over at Jodi's house tonight. All the girls are in Jodi's room. Jodi's parents are in the family room. Jodi has a pint of whiskey. She passes it around to the other girls. One by one they take a drink. The bottle then reaches Vanessa.

She is very sure she does not want to drink. But she feels that she will ruin the party if she does not take some alcohol.

 What should Vanessa do? Explain your wellness choice.

2 About Tobacco

Tobacco is a plant that looks something like spinach, except that it is bigger. The dried leaves of the plant are used in many forms. Some people use smokeless tobacco products, such as snuff and chewing tobacco. Others smoke shredded tobacco leaves in pipes and cigars. But of the people who use tobacco, most smoke it in the form of cigarettes.

KEY WORDS

carbon monoxide
stimulant
carcinogens
tumors
sidestream
    smoke

▬ Tobacco is smoked in cigarettes, pipes, and cigars. Tobacco is also sniffed or chewed.

Tobacco in any form can harm people's health. Cigarettes are thought to be the most dangerous because people breathe in cigarette smoke. Drugs and gases in the smoke then enter the circulatory system and are carried to all the cells in the body. The drugs in tobacco are the most abused drugs in the United States.

What Is in Tobacco?

So far, scientists have found more than 3,000 different substances in cigarette smoke. Of those, 200 are known to be poisons.

One of the harmful substances in cigarette smoke is a gas called **carbon monoxide.** When carbon monoxide is inhaled, it takes the place of some of the oxygen in the blood. The more carbon monoxide there is in the blood,

carbon monoxide (KAHR buhn • muh NAHK syd), a harmful gas in cigarette smoke.

281

stimulant (STIHM yuh luhnt), a drug that speeds up the heart and makes certain nerves work harder.

the less oxygen there is for the cells to use. Enough carbon monoxide can cause body cells to die.

Nicotine is another harmful substance in cigarette smoke. *Nicotine* is a stimulant. A **stimulant** is a drug that speeds up the heart and makes certain nerves work harder. Nicotine makes the blood vessels smaller. Then the heart must work harder to pump blood through the circulatory system. Nicotine is the habit-forming drug in tobacco. It makes it hard for most people who smoke to stop.

Cigarette smoke also has in it a sticky substance called *tar.* Tar looks something like dark brown glue. People who smoke one pack of cigarettes a day put about a quart (one liter) of tar into their lungs every year.

The bottle, right, contains tar from burned cigarettes. Tar builds up in a smoker's lungs. Harmful substances in smokeless tobacco damage the gums, left.

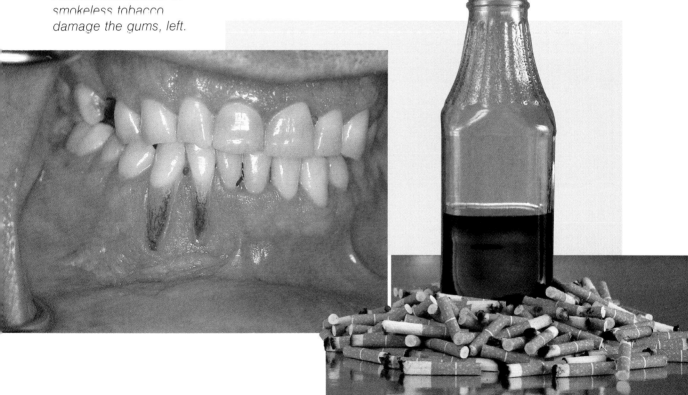

People who use smokeless tobacco are also affected by the chemicals found in all tobacco products. Each time they use tobacco, they take a little bit of each of those drugs into their bodies. The harmful substances are absorbed through the lips or gums. The longer people use tobacco, the more harm they do to their bodies.

What Are the Short-term Harmful Effects of Tobacco?

Seconds after entering a person's body, the drugs and other harmful substances in tobacco cause many changes. Nicotine makes the heart beat faster. A faster heartbeat may cause the person to feel restless and tense. At the same time, tar and carbon monoxide may make the person feel tired and faint because the body is getting less oxygen. Every puff from a cigarette causes all these changes.

Tobacco can dull a person's sense of taste and sense of smell. Using tobacco of any kind gives a person bad breath. Tobacco can also color the teeth dark yellow or brown. The high amount of sugar in most smokeless tobaccos can cause cavities in teeth. Cigarette smoke can make a person's clothes smell bad. It can make a person's eyes water. All these are only the immediate harmful effects of using tobacco.

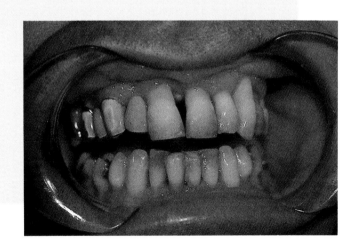

Tobacco can stain teeth yellow or brown.

Smoking cigarettes can also cost people more than their health. The price of cigarettes is high, so smokers have less money for other things. People who smoke cause many fires. Some of the fires they cause are deadly. Also, most adults who smoke pay more money for their insurance than those who do not smoke.

283

What Are the Long-term Harmful Effects of Tobacco?

As people keep using tobacco, their cells and their body systems are harmed. Many of the substances in tobacco are carcinogens. **Carcinogens** are substances that cause cancer. *Cancer* is a noncommunicable disease in which harmful cells begin to grow fast and take the place of healthy cells.

Certain substances in smokeless tobacco change the way cells grow in the mouth. Harmful cells may grow on the gums, the tongue, and the inside of the cheeks and lips. The cells form white patches. The patches in the mouth are signs of a noncommunicable disease called *leukoplakia,* which may become oral cancer. Scientists have found that oral cancer develops more rapidly in young people who use smokeless tobacco than in adults who do.

carcinogens (kahr SIHN uh juhnz), substances that cause cancer.

■ *People who use smokeless tobaco may develop white patches in the mouth, right, that lead to cancer. The tar from tobacco can damage healthy cilia, below, which keep the respiratory system clean.*

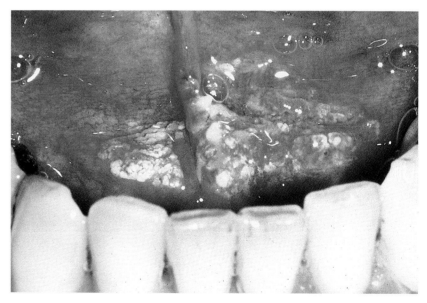

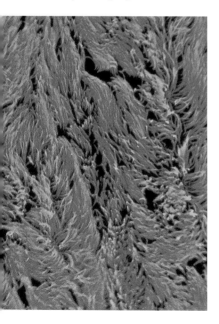

Cigarette smoke does its worst damage to the respiratory system. People who smoke cannot exercise very long before they have trouble breathing. Many people who smoke a lot cough hard much of the time. They may suffer from *chronic bronchitis,* caused mostly by tar. The tar builds up in the bronchial tubes and destroys the cilia. The lining of the bronchial tubes also swells up and produces more mucus. Then the tubes cannot clean themselves or get rid of mucus. The smoker with chronic bronchitis coughs almost constantly to get rid of the mucus.

Once the cilia stop working, more tar can get into the lungs. The tar coats the tissues that line the alveoli. Then oxygen cannot pass into the circulatory system very well. The result is a noncommunicable disease that is called *emphysema.* The disease causes shortness of breath. Emphysema can lead to death.

■ *Some people with emphysema must breathe pure oxygen to prevent shortness of breath.*

Tar in cigarette smoke has carcinogens in it. They may cause **tumors,** or lumps, to grow in a smoker's lungs. Tumors can make the lungs stop working as they should. When that happens, a person can become very ill with lung cancer. The American Cancer Society reports that many of the people who get lung cancer are heavy smokers. People often do not know they are getting lung cancer when it begins.

Cigarette smoking makes it more likely for someone to get heart disease. The combination of nicotine and carbon monoxide creates strain for the heart muscle. If heart disease develops, the heart cannot circulate enough oxygen and nutrients to the body cells.

tumors (TOO muhrz), lumps that grow in the body.

Even nonsmokers sometimes breathe cigarette smoke.

sidestream smoke (SYD streem • SMOHK), tobacco smoke breathed in by a person other than the smoker.

Nonsmoking areas are available in many public places.

When people smoke cigarettes indoors, the smoke can build up in the air. Everyone nearby breathes the smoke and is harmed by it. Smoke from burning tobacco is called **sidestream smoke.** Studies show that sidestream smoke has even more of certain harmful substances than what a smoker inhales.

People who breathe sidestream smoke risk some of the same long-term harmful effects as smokers. People who are allergic to smoke may have troublesome reactions, such as an asthma attack. Tissues in the respiratory systems of children are very sensitive to irritating smoke. For these reasons, some communities do not allow smoking in certain places, such as elevators, schools, and other public buildings.

NO SMOKING PLEASE
SMOKING IS PERMITTED ONLY IN DESIGNATED AREAS.

Why Do Some People Use Tobacco?

Every day some people decide to use tobacco for the first time. They may decide to smoke their first cigarette or to dip their first snuff. After that they may decide to use tobacco again and again. Many people who use tobacco for the first time are young people. They begin using tobacco before they know that the nicotine in it is habit-forming. They use tobacco before they understand the dangers of tobacco.

There are many reasons that some people start using tobacco. Some people try their first cigarette just to see what it is like. They are curious. Some try their first snuff because they think it is safer than cigarettes. They see sports stars using snuff. Many young people start using tobacco because they admire others who use it. Often a parent, an older brother or sister, or a friend uses tobacco. Other people start because they want to belong to a group of people who use tobacco. They hope that using tobacco will help them make friends. Some young people start using tobacco because they think it will make them look grown-up. That idea can come from other people. It can come from movies, television shows, and advertising.

Take a careful look at some advertising for cigarettes. The people in the advertisements often look young, happy, and popular. They may be having fun in exciting places. They may be doing things you would like to do. Advertising often makes tobacco seem to go with having fun and being well liked. Many people believe that idea without really thinking about it.

Advertisements never tell how hard it is to stop using tobacco once a person starts. Some people form a strong dependence on tobacoo. They need, or they believe they need, tobacco to feel all right. People who smoke a lot have a hard time going without cigarettes. Many of them feel they need a cigarette every one or two hours, or even more often. When they try not to smoke, they feel restless and grumpy. For that reason, many people keep smoking once they have started the habit.

■ People who use smokeless tobacco harm their health and spoil their appearance.

People who smoke a lot can become healthy again only if they stop using tobacco. People often need help to stop smoking. Many communities have programs or classes to help people who want to quit smoking. Many people learn about the programs from their physicians or from one of three major groups worried about the harm caused by smoking. The three groups are the American Cancer Society, the American Heart Association, and the American Lung Association. Each of the groups has offices in every state in the United States.

■ The American Cancer Society has help for people who want to stop using tobacco.

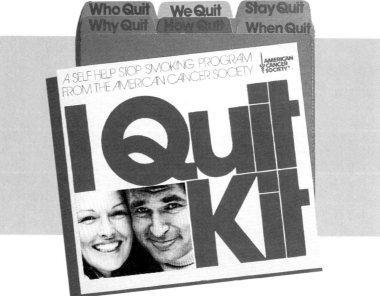

REVIEW

SECTION 2

REMEMBER?

1. What are three harmful substances in cigarette smoke?
2. How does using tobacco affect a person's appearance?
3. What are three reasons young people give for starting to smoke?

THINK!

4. "One puff from a cigarette has never killed anyone." Explain how that idea could make the difference between good health and poor health.
5. Some tobacco advertising attempts to persuade young people to use tobacco if offered. How do such advertisements present tobacco?

Thinking About Your Health

Promising Yourself Not to Use Alcohol and Tobacco

A contract is a written promise. In your health notebook or on a separate sheet of paper, write a self-contract. This is a promise to yourself. Use the example shown at the right when you write your contract. It describes what you promise yourself to do the next time someone offers you snuff, a cigarette, or a drink that contains alcohol.

I, _____, will say
   (Write your name.)
no to using alcohol and tobacco because

_____.
   (Explain your reason or reasons for this action.)

_____
   (Sign your name.)

_____
   (Write today's date.)

289

Smokeless Tobacco

Many people who smoke cigarettes are worried about what tobacco smoke does to their lungs. Some think using smokeless tobacco instead is a good answer to their problem, but smokeless tobacco is dangerous, too.

Smokeless tobacco comes in two main forms: chewing tobacco and snuff. Both are used in the mouth, where saliva makes the tobacco wet. The moisture releases nicotine and other dangerous chemicals from the tobacco leaves. The chemicals irritate the tissues of the cheeks, gums, tongue, and throat. The juice from smokeless tobacco colors the teeth, causes bad breath, and causes gum problems. Gum disease can make the teeth loosen and fall out. Using smokeless tobacco can also cause cancer of the mouth.

Most people who use smokeless tobacco spit out the juice. But a little bit of juice is always being swallowed. The nicotine and other dangerous chemicals in the swallowed juice travel to the digestive system. The juice can harm the lining of the digestive system and cause sores to form in the stomach or intestine. These sores are called ulcers.

The chemicals in smokeless tobacco enter the blood through the mouth and stomach tissues, and the blood carries the poisons to all parts of the body. The effects of nicotine and other chemicals on the body are the same for all kinds of tobacco. The only dangerous substance not present in smokeless tobacco is the tar produced when tobacco is burned.

Thinking Beyond

1. Why do some people use smokeless tobacco?
2. Are those good reasons? Explain your answer.

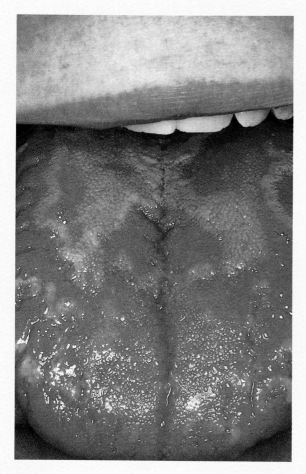

■ *This tongue disease can be caused by using smokeless tobacco.*

3 Refusing to Use Alcohol and Tobacco

What is the most important decision you have made so far today? Maybe it was deciding what clothes to wear to school. Maybe it was deciding what to eat for breakfast.

Some decisions you make each day are simple to make. Other decisions might take some serious thinking. Would you choose to do something or use something if you *knew* your life would be at risk? Right now, you might say, "Of course not!" In the future, however, you will be faced with some very hard decisions. Some will involve your health and safety. Many young people are preparing now to refuse activities and substances that are dangerous to their health. You can be responsible for preparing yourself, too.

FOR THE
CURIOUS

According to one survey, 93 of every 100 children in grades four through six believe cocaine or crack is a drug. But only 45 in 100 call beer, wine, or liquor a drug.

Many young people have decided to say no to alcohol and tobacco.

Young people can work together to help stop alcohol abuse.

Why Do Some People Choose Not to Use Alcohol?

Some people do not drink alcohol. Many of them, young and old, know about the health problems caused by drinking alcohol. A few people react to alcohol as if they were allergic to it. Some people follow family or religious rules against using alcohol. They refuse to drink. Some people say they have no reason to drink. They are comfortable not drinking, even in social groups where others drink.

Concerned parents have become involved in trying to stop alcohol-related traffic injuries and deaths.

State laws do not allow young people to have, drink, or sell alcohol. Making laws against drinking is one way, a community shows it cares about its young members. Many families have rules against the drinking of alcohol by their young people. People's concerns about safety and health and staying in control of their bodies are also good reasons not to drink alcohol.

Why Do Many People Choose Not to Use Tobacco?

Today the dangers of tobacco are becoming widely known. People can no longer ignore the health and safety dangers. By law, cigarette packages must now carry one of the following warning labels:

SURGEON GENERAL'S WARNING: Quitting Smoking Now Greatly Reduces Serious Risks to Your Health.

SURGEON GENERAL'S WARNING: Smoking By Pregnant Women May Result in Fetal Injury, Premature Birth, And Low Birth Weight.

SURGEON GENERAL'S WARNING: Cigarette Smoke Contains Carbon Monoxide.

SURGEON GENERAL'S WARNING: Smoking Causes Lung Cancer, Heart Disease, Emphysema, And May Complicate Pregnancy.

Many people who have used tobacco for a long time are trying to stop. When they started to use tobacco regularly, they did not know about all the health problems. Most of them want to protect their health. They want to be better able to taste food. They are tired from coughing all the time.

Every day, many people decide that smoking is not worth the health risks.

They would like to be able to enjoy exercise again. They know tobacco costs a lot of money. These are a few reasons that many people are trying to give up tobacco.

Each year, many people succeed in giving up cigarettes. People try many different ways to stop smoking. Some people stop smoking all at once. Some try to stop smoking little by little. They smoke fewer cigarettes each day until they are smoking none at all.

Many people choose never to start smoking or using smokeless tobacco. They know about the dangers of tobacco. They take responsibility for helping protect their health by not using tobacco in any form.

What Steps Can Help You Say No to Alcohol and Tobacco?

People need to refuse things that can harm them. By refusing to use alcohol and tobacco, people choose to stay healthy and safe. They make a health choice that can reduce risks that are within their control. Knowing that you can refuse risky actions and practicing ways to refuse can help your self-concept. You show yourself that you are in control.

You can follow some steps that can help you stay healthy and safe. By following these steps, you can refuse offers to try alcohol or tobacco.

1. If someone asks you to try alcohol or tobacco, say "No, thank you." Always try to be polite. If a person keeps asking you, you can say "no way" in a convincing way.
2. Another way to say no is to tell a person you have something else to do. You can tell the person you are going to ride your bicycle, play with your friends, or work on your hobby.
3. Knowing the facts about alcohol and tobacco can really help you say no. If someone asks you to try alcohol or tobacco, you can say, "No thanks. I know that tobacco and alcohol can make a person my age very sick."
4. Sometimes the pressure from peers to try alcohol or tobacco can be strong. When this happens, you can walk away.

5. Another way to say no to alcohol or tobacco is to change the subject. For example, if someone asks you to smoke, you might suggest, "Let's go ride skateboards." Or ask, "Did you meet the new kid in the neighborhood?"

 *If someone offers you cigarettes or alcohol, say no.*

STOP REVIEW SECTION 3

REMEMBER?

1. Why do some people choose not to drink?
2. Why do some people choose not to smoke?
3. What steps can you follow to refuse an offer to try alcohol or tobacco?

THINK!

4. Why are some people comfortable not drinking in a group? What role does self-esteem play in helping people make decisions?
5. What are some ways you can have fun and feel good without using alcohol or tobacco?

An Interview with an Alateen Sponsor

Dan knows the effects that alcoholism can have on family and friends. He is an Alateen sponsor in San Francisco, California.

What is Alateen?

Alateen is a fellowship, or group, of young people whose lives have been affected by a friend's or a relative's alcoholism. Very often the young person has a parent who is an alcoholic. Alateen provides a safe, private place where young people can go and talk about their problems. At Alateen meetings, young people help each other by sharing experiences and encouraging each other.

What does an Alateen sponsor do?

As a sponsor of an Alateen group, I try to provide guidance and share my experiences with the group. However, I am not a counselor. I do not provide professional help. My main responsibility is to help keep the meetings on track.

For this interview, why would you not allow your face to be photographed or your last name to be used?

One of the traditions of this program is that it offers privacy. At the meetings, no one keeps records and no one writes down any names. When people's backgrounds are not questioned, many young people will speak freely about how they feel. To keep this idea of privacy, I felt I could not give my full name here.

What are some of the ways young people are affected by another person's alcoholism?

Young people often feel ashamed and blame themselves for the alcoholic's problem. In a case where a parent is the alcoholic, the young person may wrongly believe that if he or she were a better child, the parent would not drink. Also, a young person may find that he or she worries all the time about the alcoholic. The young person may waste a lot of energy trying to figure out ways to make the alcoholic stop drinking. Many kids are ashamed. They try to keep the alcoholism a secret. These young people suffer greatly. For all these reasons, Alateen can be useful. Young

▪ *Alateen helps young people whose lives are affected by someone with a drinking problem.*

people have a place to go to say what is in their hearts. Just telling someone that there is a problem can be a tremendous help.

What is an Alateen meeting like?

A group that meets may vary in size from two or three members to more than sixty. Group size is different from city to city. Basically, the young people who attend run their own meetings, which last about an hour. Each meeting has different things going on. For example, at the beginning of most meetings, brochures are passed out, and someone reads the basic steps of the Alateen program. Then new people introduce themselves by their first names only. Then there might be one person who talks about a certain topic, such as anger or fear. That person will talk about his or her experiences and open up discussion to the group. Finally, the other young people will begin to share their experiences.

In some places, there are groups for young people under 12 years old. These groups are called Pre-Alateen.

How is Alateen different from Alcoholics Anonymous?

Alateen is not a group for young people who have drinking problems themselves. Young people who have such problems can get help through Alcoholics Anonymous. Alateen is a support group for young people who are friends or relatives of alcoholics. Alateen is actually part of a larger group called Al-Anon, which is the adult version of Alateen.

Learn more about Alateen and Pre-Alateen. Contact your local Al-Anon office. Or write for information to Al-Anon Family Groups, 1372 Broadway, New York, NY 10018-6106. You can also call 1-800-356-9996.

Main Ideas

- Alcohol harms the body in many ways.
- People who abuse alcohol may harm themselves and other people.
- Alcohol interferes with a user's ability to make decisions.
- Tobacco in any form is harmful to health.
- Many people begin using tobacco before they fully understand its dangers.
- Many people choose not to drink alcohol or use tobacco because they are concerned for their health and safety.
- There are simple steps you can follow to help you refuse things that can harm you.

Key Words

Write the numbers 1 to 11 in your health notebook or on a separate sheet of paper. After each number, copy the sentence and fill in the missing term. Page numbers in ( ) tell you where to look in the chapter if you need help.

alcohol (271)
depressant (271)
intoxicated (272)
problem drinking (275)
alcohol dependence (277)
withdrawal (278)

carbon monoxide (281)
stimulant (282)
carcinogens (284)
tumors (285)
sidestream smoke (286)

1. Cigarette smoke contains a gas called ___?___ .

2. Harmful substances that cause cancer are called ___?___ .

3. A drug found in drinks such as beer, wine, and whiskey is called ___?___ .

4. Harmful substances in cigarette smoke can cause lumps, or ___?___ , to grow in a smoker's lungs.

5. People who are experiencing strong effects of alcohol are ___?___ .

6. Any drug that speeds up the heartbeat rate is a ___?___ .

7. Any drug that slows down the whole body is called a ___?___ .

8. Smoke breathed in by a person other than the smoker is called ___?___ .

9. People who are alcoholics go through ___?___ when they stop drinking.

10. Using alcohol in ways that cause physical, social, or legal problems is ___?___ .

11. When people come to need, or believe they need, alcohol to feel all right, they are said to have an ___?___ .

Remembering What You Learned

Page numbers in ( ) tell you where to look in the chapter if you need help.

1. What kind of drug is alcohol? (271)

2. What are some effects of being intoxicated? (272)

3. What parts of the body are harmed by using alcohol for a long time? (273–274)

4. What is alcoholism? (277)

5. Why do young people who drink face a greater danger of becoming problem drinkers? (277)

6. What are three reasons that some people start drinking alcohol? (279)

7. Why are cigarettes the most harmful form of tobacco? (281)

8. What are the short-term harmful effects of tobacco? (283)

9. Which part of cigarette smoke is the main cause of emphysema? (285)

10. How does smoking play a role in causing lung cancer? (285)

11. What do advertisements for tobacco seldom tell you? (287)

12. Why do some people not drink alcohol at all? (292–293)

Thinking About What You Learned

1. How might using alcohol affect a person's personality?

2. Why do most communities have laws against being intoxicated in a public place?

3. Suppose a person stops smoking cigarettes after having smoked for ten years. How might the person's health be affected for the rest of his or her life?

Writing About What You Learned

1. Interview five adults who are nonsmokers. Write in your health notebook or on a sheet of paper the following questions to ask them. After the interviews, write what you have learned from them.
   - How do you feel about being around people who smoke?
   - What do you dislike most about smoking?
   - Do you know how smoking can harm a smoker's health?
   - Do you think that smoking should be allowed in public places? Why?

2. The reasons that young people give for smoking include the following:
   - My friends do.
   - It looks grown-up.
   - My parents smoke.
   - I'm curious about it.

   Choose one of the reasons, and write a letter to an imaginary friend who is using the reason as an excuse to begin smoking. Tell the friend why smoking is harmful.

Applying What You Learned

SOCIAL STUDIES

Look for No Smoking signs in your community. When you see some, ask the owner or manager of the business why No Smoking signs are placed there. Report your findings to the class.

Modified True or False

Write the numbers 1 to 15 in your health notebook or on a separate sheet of paper. After each number, write *true* or *false* to describe the sentence. If the sentence is false, also write a term that replaces the underlined term and makes the sentence true.

1. <u>Alcohol</u> is a drug found in drinks such as beer, wine, and whiskey.

2. Nicotine is a <u>depressant</u>.

3. A <u>short-term</u> effect of drinking alcohol is cirrhosis.

4. The <u>tar</u> in cigarette smoke is a carcinogen.

5. People who smoke <u>prevent</u> fires.

6. A person who is <u>intoxicated</u> by alcohol may pass out.

7. People who drink alcohol do things they normally <u>would not</u> do.

8. <u>Carbon dioxide</u> is a harmful gas found in cigarette smoke.

9. If a problem drinker feels sick when trying to stop drinking, he or she may be going through <u>withdrawal</u>.

10. <u>Al-Anon</u> helps alcoholics.

11. Snuff is a form of <u>tobacco</u>.

12. Nicotine makes blood vessels <u>larger</u>.

13. The high amount of sugar in <u>alcohol</u> can cause cavities.

14. <u>Leukoplakia</u> is a disease caused by smokeless tobacco.

15. Drinking alcohol slows down the <u>nervous system</u>.

Short Answer

Write the numbers 16 to 23 on your paper. Write a complete sentence to answer each question.

16. Name three diseases caused by tobacco.

17. Give two health reasons for not wanting to drink alcohol.

18. How are alcohol and tobacco alike?

19. Describe why some people begin smoking tobacco.

20. How is smokeless tobacco different from cigarettes? How is it similar to cigarettes?

21. What are the short-term effects of drinking alcohol?

22. How does alcohol interfere with the user's ability to make decisions?

23. What are five ways you can refuse an offer of alcohol or tobacco?

Essay

Write the numbers 24 and 25 on your paper. Write paragraphs with complete sentences to answer each question.

24. Create a story in which someone your age is asked to drink alcohol. Describe how the person acts and write what he or she says.

25. Discuss how self-esteem is a part of saying no to alcohol and tobacco.

ACTIVITIES FOR HOME OR SCHOOL

Projects to Do

1. Think of a saying or slogan that might help someone decide not to begin smoking cigarettes. For example, your slogan might be "Don't start. Not starting is easier than stopping!" Draw a picture to illustrate your slogan. Put your slogan and picture on a poster.

■ *Make posters about not smoking.*

2. The United States government's surgeon general has set a goal of a "Smoke-Free Young America by the Year 2000." One project is to help the kindergarten class of 1987 keep from beginning to smoke through their high school graduation in the year 2000. Find a way your class can help in your school or neighborhood. You may want to ask to give younger students a lesson about not smoking. You are models for younger students, so they will respect what you say and do about smoking.

Information To Find

1. Some people think smokeless tobacco is safer than cigarettes. Find out how smokeless tobacco can threaten a person's wellness. Use newspapers, pamphlets, and books to find information about the dangers of smokeless tobacco. Look for information in your school library or public library. Prepare a written or oral report for your class.

2. Look in a telephone book for a nearby branch of the American Cancer Society. Write or call the organization. Ask for facts about the Great American Smokeout. Ask for information about other antismoking programs organized by the American Cancer Society and other organizations.

Books to Read

Here are some books you can look for in your school library or the public library to find more information about the dangers to young people of alcohol and tobacco.

DeVault, Christine, and Bryan Strong. *Danny's Dilemma.* Network Publications.

DiGiovanni, Kathe. *My House Is Different.* Hazelden.

Hyde, Margaret O. *Know About Smoking.* McGraw-Hill.

Odor, Ruth S. *What's a Body to Do?* Child's World.

YOUR SAFETY

Accidents are one of the greatest threats to your health and safety. If you know how to be safe, you can prevent most accidents. As you grow older, you and your peers earn privileges, such as riding bicycles without an adult watching you. With those privileges comes the responsibility of acting in a safe manner.

Being safety-minded should always be an important part of the way you think. Acting safely is your responsibility. Knowing how to stay safe and how to help if someone is injured can make you feel good about yourself.

GETTING READY TO LEARN

Key Questions

- Why is it important to learn about safety and first aid?
- Why is it important to know how you feel about keeping yourself and others safe?
- How can you learn to make choices that will help keep you safe?
- How can you take more responsibility for your own safety?

Main Chapter Sections

1 Planning for Safety
2 Practicing Safety and First Aid
3 Bicycle Safety
4 Fire Safety
5 Water Safety

1 Planning for Safety

accident (AK suhd uhnt), an unexpected event that can cause someone harm.

Accidents can happen anywhere at any time. An **accident** is an unexpected event that can cause someone harm. Accidents can happen when you are at home or while you are traveling. Many accidents, however, do not have to happen at all.

You can play and work without having accidents. One way to help keep yourself from having accidents is to know what causes them. Planning for your safety also means being prepared in case an accident happens. You may need to help someone. You may need to help yourself.

■ *The best plan for safety is to prevent accidents from happening.*

What Causes Accidents?

Forgetting to follow safety rules is one cause of accidents. Being careless is a second cause. Some people forget safety rules and act carelessly because they feel they will always be safe. Sometimes showing off by not following the

directions of the safety patrol or crossing guards causes serious injuries to someone going to or from school. Many of the activities that people do may seem simple and safe. A person who is responsible for his or her own safety must think about safety all the time.

Hazards often can be found in many young people's activities. A **hazard** is something that can cause you harm. Some hazards are things in your environment. Others are the result of actions of people. You need to keep away from hazards to remain safe.

Hazards can be found at home, at school, and in neighborhoods. A broken swing on a playground is a hazard if someone tries to swing on it. Broken glass in a place where you play is also a hazard. Someone might step on it. You can keep away from such hazards by checking an area before you begin playing. You can help keep an accident from happening to someone else if you tell an adult about any hazards you find. Doing so shows you are responsible. Preventing accidents can help keep people from getting injured.

By taking unnecessary risks, people create hazards. Some people try new equipment without reading directions. Others take a dare to try something for which they do not yet have the skills. You can prevent the kinds

■ *Some hazards are clearly marked with warnings. However, you must rely on your own judgment to avoid most hazards.*

hazard (HAZ uhrd), something in the environment or an action of a person that can cause you harm.

305

■ *Many hazards of electrical appliances can be avoided if you carefully read the operating instructions.*

of accidents that come from such hazards. Before you do something, you must learn enough about it to reduce the risk of injury to yourself or others.

What Can You Do When a Serious Accident Happens?

emergency (ih MUR juhn see), a situation that calls for quick action, as when someone is injured in an accident.

When an accident causes an injury and help is needed right away, there is an **emergency.** Some emergencies are more serious than others. Car accidents and building fires are two kinds of very serious emergencies. If you see a serious accident, you need to stay calm. Staying calm can help you remember what you need to do in an emergency.

■ *Know who to call in an emergency.*

In an emergency, you need an adult to help you. You can get help by using the telephone. Call 911 or 0 (zero) to reach the police, the sheriff, the fire department, or an ambulance or other emergency medical service (EMS). You can use 911 or 0 (zero) when there is an accident or when there is an emergency of some other kind. You can call one of the numbers when someone hurts you or threatens to hurt you or others.

When you call 911 or 0 (zero), tell the operator that you want to report an emergency. Say exactly where the emergency is. Be sure to let the operator hang up before you do. Then you will know that he or she has all the facts that are needed about the emergency.

When helping with any emergency, you should not try to do something for which you are not trained. You could cause further harm to someone who is hurt.

The American Red Cross offers first-aid courses for everyone.

Act in a responsible way by learning skills for caring for people, including yourself, after different kinds of accidents. Immediate care for someone who has been injured is called **first aid.** You can learn first aid by taking courses offered by such groups as the American Red Cross.

first aid, the immediate care given to someone who has been injured.

REVIEW
SECTION 1

REMEMBER?

1. What are the causes of most accidents?
2. What should you do in a serious emergency?
3. What is a responsible action if you see a hazard, such as a broken swing at a playground?

THINK!

4. How might being careless while doing a simple activity be dangerous?
5. What makes some accidents more serious than others?

Thinking About Your Health

Do You Know How to Be Safe?

Do you know all you need to know to be safe? If you cannot agree with all the following statements, you might need to know more. You may want to talk about safety with a parent, your guardian, your school nurse, or a teacher.

■ You can identify a hazard.

■ You know how to avoid injury in a dangerous situation.
■ You know an accident if you see one.
■ You know what to do if you come upon an accident.
■ You know what to do for yourself if you have an accident.

308

2 Practicing Safety and First Aid

Falls are accidents that happen often to young people. Falls happen often because young people are active. They are often busy working and playing. Safe practices can help you avoid falls and injury. Knowing what to do when an accident happens can help you and others in an emergency.

How Can You Prevent Trips, Slips, and Falls?

People often trip and fall because they are not watching where they are going. You can keep from tripping by paying attention to things around you. Watch out for chairs, toys, and other people that might be in your path. Never carry something so big that it blocks your view of the way ahead.

At school, do not run in the halls, even when you are in a hurry. Walk on the right-hand side of the hall to keep out of other people's way. This keeps you from bumping others.

■ *You can avoid accidents if you play carefully and watch what you are doing on stairs and other hazardous places.*

To avoid falls at school, you need to be careful on stairs and walk, not run, in the halls.

Take stairs one at a time. Always hold the handrail to keep from falling if you should slip. Stay alert for hazards.

People your age often slip when they are active and moving fast. Shoes with rubber soles are safer when you play an active game. Rubber soles grip the ground better than other kinds of soles. They help keep you from slipping.

You can also keep from having an accident by being careful in slippery places. Any icy surface can be slippery.

Pay attention to signs that warn of danger in public places.

The wet pavement around a swimming pool can be slippery. Smooth concrete that is wet from rain or damp air can be very slick. A waxed floor is another slippery surface. Try to stay away from slippery places, or walk across them very slowly and carefully.

Kitchen and bathroom floors get wet and slippery from spilled water. You can help your family by being careful not to spill liquids and by quickly wiping up any spills that happen. Bath mats and rugs keep you from slipping when getting into and out of the tub or shower. Some families add grab handles to showers and tubs for members who need extra help to bathe safely.

People can fall when they are reaching for something on a high shelf. They may stretch too high by standing on their toes. Some people take foolish chances by standing on something weak or wobbly. A chair could tip over or break if you stand on it. A stepladder or a step stool has a wider base to prevent tipping. Use one when you need to reach for something on a shelf above your head.

■ Use a safe stepladder when putting things on high shelves.

311

How Can You Be Safe at Play?

Bumps or falls can happen if you play in a place where you have not been before. Check the place to make sure it is safe before you play there. Look for holes that may be hidden by grass. Search for metal and broken glass that might be on the ground. Check for tree roots or stumps that you could trip over while running. Look for steep hills or drop-offs from which you could fall. Make sure that motor vehicles are not used in the area.

Jim and his friends want to play baseball in a big, empty field. They know they will be safe from cars there, but they also want to be safe from bumps and falls. So the children check the field carefully for stumps, holes, and other dangers. They do this every time they play somewhere new. Their habit helps keep them safe.

■ *Before you play on a strange field, check for hidden dangers.*

What Injuries Are Caused by Trips, Slips, and Falls?

Trips, slips, and falls can cause scrapes and bruises. They can also cause deep cuts and broken bones.

Gerald loves to read. He used to read even when he was walking. But now Gerald pays attention to where he is walking because he tripped once while reading. He not only tore pages from a library book but also scraped his hands

312

on the sidewalk. A **scrape** is an injury in which the top layers of skin are torn. Now Gerald carries his book closed and watches where he is walking.

Bruises happen often to young people who are playing. A **bruise** is an injury in which the skin is not damaged but blood vessels break under the skin. Bruises cause a black-and-blue mark on the skin. A bruise can happen when you fall or even when you bump into someone while playing.

All scrapes, bruises, deep cuts, and broken bones need first aid. The kind of first aid needed depends on the kind of injury.

scrape (SKRAYP), an injury in which the top layers of skin are torn.

bruise (BROOZ), an injury in which the skin is not damaged but blood vessels break under the skin.

What Emergency Procedures Can You Follow When Minor Injuries Happen?

Sometime you may have to care for an injury in a minor, or less serious, emergency. You may even have to help yourself.

If you have a nosebleed, there is a simple emergency procedure you can use on yourself. You first need to stay calm. This will help you think about what you need to do. Then you should sit and lean your head forward so that you do not swallow blood. Hold the whole lower half of your nose between your thumb and fingers. Breathe through your mouth. Squeeze both sides of your nose. Hold your nose that way for about ten minutes. Doing so will help the blood clot, or become thick. When this happens, your nose will stop bleeding. While you squeeze your nose, try to sit quietly. Too much activity may keep your nose bleeding. Do not blow your nose for a day after it has stopped bleeding. Leaving your nose alone will help the clot stay in place.

If you have a nosebleed, sit quietly while you squeeze your nose.

Some scrapes need only simple first aid. Other scrapes may need to be treated by a physician. A scrape in which there is very little bleeding is a shallow scrape. Only the top layer of skin is rubbed off. First wash your hands. Then wash the scrape gently with soap and water. Rinse the wound and dab it dry with a clean cloth. Cover the scrape with a **sterile,** or germfree, bandage. Keep the scrape covered to protect it from microbes. Keep it protected until it starts to heal. Remove the bandage at bedtime to allow air to help the scab dry.

sterile (STEHR uhl), germfree.

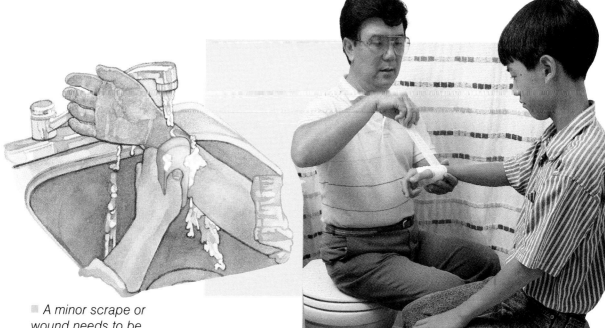

A minor scrape or wound needs to be cleaned and covered with a sterile bandage.

Scrapes that are deep usually bleed. Such scrapes need to be cleaned in the same way as shallow scrapes. However, some deep scrapes have dirt that is not easy to remove. Do not try to remove this dirt. Ask an adult for help. A physician may pour an antiseptic over the injured area. An **antiseptic** is a medicine that helps kill microbes. The medicine may help keep an infection from starting.

First aid for bruises is very simple. You need to put a cold-pack over the bruise as soon as you can. A cold-pack can be made by wrapping ice cubes in a towel. Or you can use a package of frozen food wrapped in a towel or cloth.

antiseptic (ant uh SEHP tihk), a medicine that helps kill microbes.

314

A bruise needs to be treated with a cold-pack, such as this one using a package of frozen food. Putting a cold-pack over a bruise prevents bleeding under the skin.

A cold-pack will slow the bleeding under the skin. In that way, it will keep the bruise from getting larger. After about two days, you can take a warm bath or soak the bruise in warm water. After that, you may use heat on a bruise for about 15 minutes three times each day for the next two or three days. Heat will help the circulatory system absorb the blood that made the bruise.

REVIEW
SECTION 2

REMEMBER?

1. Name four activities that may cause falls.
2. Why should you use a stepladder when trying to reach something over your head?
3. What kinds of injuries can be caused by trips, slips, and falls?
4. What should you do as first aid for a scrape?

THINK!

5. How might you prevent an accident when reaching for something over your head without the use of a stepladder?
6. How might staying calm during an emergency help you and an injured person?

MYTH
AND
FACT

Myth: Do not wash a wound because you may wash germs into the wound.

Fact: There are a few wounds that should not be washed, such as scalp and neck wounds. All minor wounds, however, should be washed with soap and water.

Wearing Safety Gear

Football players are big, but not as big as they look. They use a lot of padding to help protect their bodies from injuries. Other people at work and at play help protect their bodies with special equipment. Using the right safety gear to reduce the dangers of an activity is a smart habit. It is part of being responsible for your own protection. Here are some of the things people wear to protect themselves:

Helmets. These hard, round shells protect the skull and brain. They have padding on the inside. Wear a helmet for contact games like football. It is also smart to wear a helmet when riding a bicycle, a skateboard, a moped, or a motorcycle.

Earplugs and Earmuffs. Earplugs are soft rubber stoppers made to fit inside the ear canal. Earmuffs fit over the outer part of the ear. People of all ages need to wear earplugs or earmuffs to protect against hearing loss when doing noisy work, such as mowing grass or running power tools.

Goggles. Wearing goggles in a factory or a laboratory is a safety habit that is often a rule for the people who work in such a place. Some people make the wise decision to wear goggles while playing sports. Wear goggles to protect your eyes in games in which a ball or another player could injure you by a sudden hit.

Seat Belts. This safety equipment in a motor vehicle holds a person in place during a sudden stop. Wearing a seat belt reduces the chance of serious injury if there is a car accident. Wear a seat belt whenever one is available in the motor vehicle in which you are riding. In most states, wearing a seat belt is the law.

■ *Buckle your seat belt when riding in a car.*

There are many more kinds of safety gear for work and play. There are special shoes, gloves, and masks. Sometimes there is a rule or law requiring safety gear to be worn. But often the choice is yours to wear the equipment or not.

Thinking Beyond

1. How might a helmet protect a bicycle rider who fell?
2. Suppose you are in charge of making safety gear for students in an activity of your choice. What will the safety gear be like?

3 Bicycle Safety

When you have the skill and are given permission to ride a bicycle with other traffic, you are responsible for staying away from hazards. If you follow safe bicycle riding rules, you will be less likely to have an accident. You can have fun while riding a bicycle and still be a safe rider.

What Are Some Bicycle Safety Rules?

Bicycles often share the road with motor vehicles. Bicycle riders must follow the same rules as motor vehicle drivers. Bicycle riders also have to follow rules of their own. In most communities, bicycles are not allowed to be ridden on the sidewalks. This rule helps protect the safety of **pedestrians,** or people who are walking. One traffic rule is that pedestrians have the right-of-way.

Here are some other rules to remember and follow when you ride your bicycle:

- Ride on the right-hand side of the street, or in a bicycle lane if there is one.
- Always move in the same direction as cars in your lane.
- When you ride with someone, ride single file, not side by side.
- Stop at all street crossings and look for other vehicles, even if you have a green light.
- Walk your bicycle across busy streets.
- Follow directions of crossing guards and traffic police officers.

KEY WORD

pedestrians

pedestrians (puh DEHS tree uhnz), people who are walking.

■ You need to understand and obey traffic signs.

■ Safe bicycling means learning how to operate your bicycle and following safety rules while riding.

317

What Road Signs and Signals Do You Need to Know?

Bicycle riders have to obey the same road signs that car drivers obey. Car drivers must stop at red lights and stop signs. Bicycle riders must do the same. The signs shown below are some common traffic signs that bicycle riders and car drivers must understand and obey.

Both bicycle riders and car drivers should signal that they plan to stop or make a turn. By giving the proper signal, you let other riders and drivers know what you plan to do. Use hand signals when you ride your bicycle. Before you turn, look carefully and quickly behind you to make sure that you are not cutting in front of a car, a pedestrian, or another bicycle.

■ Following the directions on these signs can help you stay safe while riding your bicycle.

How Can You Keep Your Bicycle Working Properly?

Your bicycle safety depends on having a bicycle in good working order. Your responsibility for that is the same that a motor vehicle owner has for a car or motorcycle. Check your bicycle from time to time to make sure it works properly. If you find anything wrong with your bicycle, repair it before riding it again.

1. Clean the wheel reflectors, and make sure they are firmly attached to the spokes.
2. Clean the back reflector. Make sure it can be seen from at least 300 feet (91 meters) away at night.
3. Adjust the brakes so that they catch quickly, firmly, and evenly all the way around the rim.
4. Clean and oil the chain.
5. Adjust the seat to your height, and make sure the nut that holds it in place is tight.
6. Clean and oil the cranks for each pedal.
7. Adjust the handlebars to your height, and tighten the nut.
8. Make sure the headlight works and can be seen from at least 500 feet (152 meters) away at night.
9. Make sure the horn works and can be heard from at least 100 feet (30 meters) away.
10. Tighten the nuts that hold the wheels in place.
11. Replace any bent or broken spokes.
12. Make sure the tires have enough air. Replace them if the treads are worn.

The picture shows some places that need to be checked on a bicycle. Have a parent or another adult help you check your bicycle for safety.

Make sure that your bicycle has the proper safety equipment and is in good working condition.

How Can You Be Safe Riding at Night?

Riding a bicycle at night calls for certain safety equipment. Your bicycle must have a headlight that works. It must also have reflectors on the fenders, pedals, and spokes. The front reflectors should be yellow or white, and the ones in back should be red. Those colors are the same as the colors of the headlights and taillights on cars. They show car drivers which direction you are going.

You should always wear light-colored clothing when you ride after dark. Light-colored clothing reflects car lights. This makes it easier for drivers to see you. Even during the day, you should wear at least one piece of bright-colored clothing.

■ *Extra safety features are necessary for riding your bicycle at night.*

What Are More Bicycle Safety Tips?

Carl knows that it is dangerous to zigzag in traffic. So he rides in a straight line, except when he is turning a corner. He is careful not to ride too fast. If he rode too fast, he might not be able to stop safely. He never applies his brakes too suddenly. A sudden stop could flip the bicycle over or send Carl flying over the handlebars.

Carl follows other good safety rules. He always stops and looks for cars before entering a street from a driveway or another street. He keeps both hands on the handlebars,

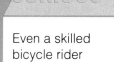 *To carry objects while riding a bicycle, you need to place them in a basket. Your hands must be free for signaling and steering.*

except when he is signaling. He has a basket on his bicycle for carrying books and packages.

Following bicycle safety rules helps Carl keep from having an accident. These rules can help you, too. Having safe habits will help protect you when you ride your bicycle.

FOR THE
CURIOUS

Even a skilled bicycle rider should walk a bicycle across a busy street.

 **REVIEW**
SECTION 3

REMEMBER?

1. On which side of the street should people ride bicycles?
2. Why should you use hand signals when riding your bicycle?
3. What do you need to do if you find something wrong with your bicycle?

THINK!

4. How might you be a hazard if you were to ride your bicycle facing traffic?
5. How might riding side by side on a busy street be dangerous?

4 Fire Safety

Every year, many people are hurt in fires. Some people even die. Most fires are started by people who are careless. Responsible and safe practices can help you avoid causing accidental fires. They can also help you save yourself if you ever get caught in a fire.

■ *Many home fires are caused each year by the improper storage of flammable materials.*

flammable (FLAM uh buhl), capable of burning.

How Can You Prevent Fires?

Think about what causes fires. There must be something very hot to start a fire. It could be a burning match, a lit cigarette, or hot sparks from a fireplace. Electric heaters and stoves can cause fires, too. Damaged electrical wires can make hot sparks. They could start a fire.

Something else is needed to start a fire. There must be materials that will burn. These materials are said to be **flammable.** Paper, wood, and cloth are flammable. Most things made of plastic will also burn. Keep things that make sparks or heat away from things that are flammable.

Burning matches, lit cigarettes, and cigarette lighters are often found near flammable objects. You can prevent fires by being careful near matches, cigarettes, and lighters. Put matches and lighters where young children cannot see or reach them. Before throwing out a used match, make sure it is really out. Dip the hot end in water. If you hear a sizzling sound, you know the match is out. Then touch the end carefully to make sure it is cold.

Many fires start near heaters, wood-burning stoves, or home furnaces. Those things may not look hot enough to start a fire. But the heat builds up over time inside their walls. To prevent fires, keep furniture, clothing, newspapers, and rugs away from all heaters.

Some liquids, such as paint thinner, are flammable because they give off gases that can burn very fast. Flammable liquids should be stored in metal or plastic containers with tight lids. The containers should be marked FLAMMABLE. Keep all flammable liquids away from heat, such as a water heater or furnace.

Sparks from damaged electrical wires sometimes start fires. Ask an adult to show you how to check the cords of all appliances in your home to see if they are damaged. Look closely at the place where the cord leaves the appliance and at the base of the plug. If you find a damaged wire, unplug it at once. Do not touch the damaged part.

A good way to prevent home fires is to inspect electrical cords and replace any that are damaged.

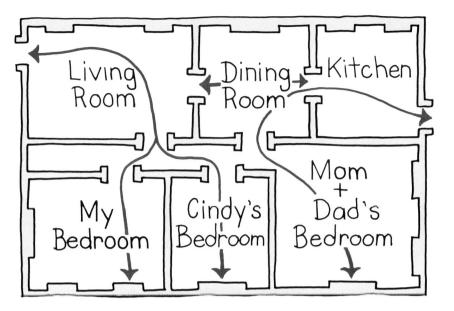

Meet here ✗

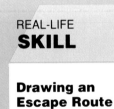

▪ Marla's floor plan includes two escape routes from each room.

How Can You Escape a Fire?

How well do you know the inside of your home? If your home were filled with smoke from a fire, could you escape? Many people die inside their homes in a fire because they become afraid. They get lost in their own homes because they do not have a plan for escaping. If a fire starts in your home, you must know how to get out quickly.

Marla's family drew up a plan for getting out of their home in case of fire. On a map of the inside of the home, Marla's mother marked two ways to leave the home from each room. She also marked a place outside where the family would meet after escaping. Once a month the whole family practices the escape routes. Now everyone knows the escape routes. If a fire ever starts in Marla's home, the family will know how to escape quickly and safely.

If you wake up at night and smell smoke, or if you hear the smoke alarm, get on the floor. You need to stay near the floor. This is because smoke rises toward the ceiling and leaves usable air near the floor. Breathing smoke can keep you from getting air into your lungs. You need to stay calm and think about your escape plan.

Crawl on your knees to the door, but do not open it right away. Test the door by putting your hand on it as high as you can reach. If the door feels cool, open it just a little and check for smoke in the hallway. Then stay low as you crawl carefully to an outside door. As you go, shout to the rest of your family to alert them to the fire.

If your bedroom door is warm when you test it, do not open it. The fire is right outside. Your escape plan should also have a way to leave your room if the door is blocked by fire.

■ *Following certain procedures will help you get out of a fire safely.*

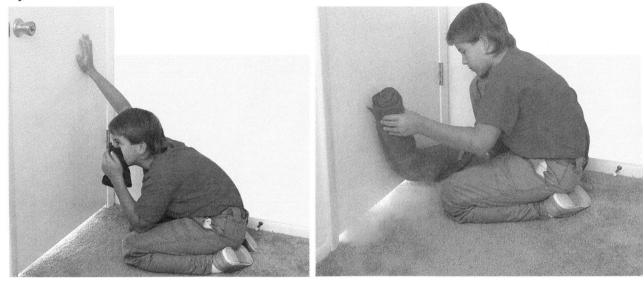

What Should You Do After You Escape?

Once you are out of your house or apartment building, never go back in to try to save anything. Go to the place where your family has arranged to meet. Then call the fire department right away.

If there is a fire alarm box near your house, use it to call the fire department. If you cannot find a fire alarm box, use a neighbor's telephone to call 911 or 0 (zero). Tell the operator that you want to report a fire. The operator will send the fire department. Be sure to say exactly where the fire is. Let the operator hang up before you do. Then you will know that the operator has all the facts about the fire.

■ *You can use a fire alarm to call the fire department for help.*

How Can You Stay Safe During a Home Fire?

Sometimes when a house or an apartment building catches fire, people get trapped inside. Even if they have an escape plan, they may not be able to escape. Their escape routes may be blocked.

325

If you cannot find a safe way out of your home, wait for the fire department to save you. Shut all the doors of the room you are in. To keep out smoke, block the cracks under the doors with sheets, blankets, towels, or clothing. If possible, wet the cloth first. A wet cloth helps to block out smoke.

Go to a window so that the fire fighters can reach you. Open the window just a little. Stay near the fresh air and shout for help. You can also hang a large cloth or sheet out the window as a signal. It will let the fire fighters know where you are. If there is smoke in the room, keep your nose and mouth covered with a cloth, a towel, or a handkerchief. Wet the cloth if you can. Breathing through the cloth will help protect you from the smoke. Stay low and stay close to the window.

REVIEW
SECTION 4

REMEMBER?

1. What two things are needed for a fire to start?
2. Why is it important for each home to have a fire escape plan?
3. In a fire, what should you do before you open a door?

THINK!

4. Why should matches and lighters be kept out of the reach of young children?
5. Why should a fire escape plan have two ways for leaving each room?

5 Water Safety

By knowing and following rules of water safety, you can protect yourself from injury and help others who are in danger. Following the rules can also make swimming and boating more fun.

How Can You Be Safe While Swimming?

The most common swimming emergency is drowning. Many people who cannot swim well drown when they suddenly find themselves in deep water. People who swim well drown by swimming too far and becoming tired. Other causes of drowning are sudden cramps, panic, and injuries. Injuries often result from diving into water that is too shallow or that contains hidden rocks. Most drownings happen within 3 to 6 feet (1 to 2 meters) of safety.

You can lessen the risk of drowning by following some rules of swimming safety:

- If you cannot swim, float, and tread water, take a swimming class from your school or from a group such as the American Red Cross, the YMCA, or the YWCA.
- Read and follow the directions on all signs posted near swimming areas. The signs often warn of hazards, such as strong currents, shallow water, and sudden drop-offs.

Taking swimming lessons and life-saving classes can help you be safe near the water.

- Swim only where a lifeguard is on duty.
- Never swim alone. Swim with friends so that someone will be there to help you in case of an accident.
- If you cannot swim well, do not trust an inner tube or an air mattress to keep you safe. You could float into deep water and fall off.
- If you swim long distances, ask someone to follow you in a boat. He or she can pick you up if you begin to tire.
- Leave the water as soon as you begin to feel tired or chilled so that you will not get a cramp.
- Leave the water if you notice any signs of a storm. Swimming during an electrical storm is very dangerous.
- Never dive into water without knowing how deep it is.
- Never swim at night in an unlighted body of water.

How Can You Prevent a Water Accident?

Even when people follow safety rules, they sometimes could drown. If you ever find yourself in such situations, you can avoid drowning by following some basic rules.

- Stay calm.
- Do not waste energy by moving a lot.
- Float on your back or tread water, and call out for help.
- If possible, wave an arm so that someone can see you.

Sometimes a muscle cramp can put you in danger of drowning. Remain calm. The cramp may go away if you

Rubbing the muscles can help stop a leg cramp.

swim a different way. You may also be able to make the muscle feel better by rubbing it. If repeated rubbing does not help, float on your back and call out for help.

If you see someone else drowning, you must act fast. Do not swim out to the drowning person unless you are a strong swimmer and have been trained in lifesaving. Many other drownings happen when swimmers who are not trained lifesavers try to carry in other swimmers who are in trouble. The following list tells you how to help someone who is drowning.

- If the person is close to a dock or near the side of a pool, lie down and reach out your hand or something for the person to grab.
- If the drowning person is too far away to be reached, push out a piece of wood or throw out a life preserver. The person can hold on to the object and float while you go for help.
- If the person is far from shore, take a boat out to save him or her. Be sure that you know how to run the boat safely.

Throw a life preserver to someone beyond your reach who is having trouble in the water.

Everyone should wear a U.S. Coast Guard - approved flotation device while boating.

Extend an oar to someone who falls out of a boat. The others in the boat can help by using their weight to keep the boat balanced.

How Can You Be Safe While Boating?

You need special knowledge to be safe in a boat. The U.S. Coast Guard, the American Red Cross, and some community groups hold classes to teach people how to handle boats safely. In those classes, you will learn rules of boating safety. You will also learn what to do in a boating emergency.

If you ask yourself the following questions each time you are in a boat, you will be better able to keep yourself and others safe.

- Is everyone in the boat wearing a U.S. Coast Guard-approved personal flotation device?
- Do all those who do not swim know that they must wear their life jackets at all times?
- Does everyone in the boat know what to do in a boating emergency?
- Is the boat big enough to hold all the passengers safely?
- If the boat is small, do the passengers know that they should not stand up?

What Should You Do in a Boating Emergency?

If someone falls out of the boat, reach out and grab the person if you can. If you cannot, hold out a paddle or a life preserver for the person to grab. Stay low and hang on to the boat when pulling the person in so that you do not tip the boat or fall out of it yourself.

If your boat has a leak, stay calm. Make sure all passengers are wearing life jackets. Check the boat for damage. If you find a hole, stuff it with blankets or rags. Use a paddle to push the material into the hole. Scoop out the water, and head for shore. If you cannot find any damage, start scooping out water at once. Call and wave both arms over your head for help, and move the boat toward shore.

If your boat turns over, hold on to the boat, and wave or call for help. Stay calm. An overturned boat will float and is much easier for a rescuer to see than a swimmer is. If you try to swim for shore, you may become too tired to reach it.

STOP REVIEW SECTION 5

REMEMBER?

1. What is the most common swimming emergency?
2. What do you need to do if you are in danger of drowning?
3. What are three ways to keep safe while boating?

THINK!

4. Why should you swim with a friend?
5. Why is standing in a small boat a hazard?

Making Wellness Choices

Kenny takes chances, even though he knows he might be harmed. When he is dared to do something, he does not have the courage to say no. Susan and her friends see Kenny at the community swimming pool. They yell to him and dare him to jump off the diving board.

They know that Kenny is afraid of deep water.

? What could you say to Kenny? What could you say to Susan and her friends? Explain your wellness choice.

331

An Interview with a Police Officer

> *Sergeant Phil Gainey helps young people learn about safety. He is a police officer in Tacoma, Washington.*

As a police officer, how do you help young people learn about safety?

I am in charge of a team of police officers who visit schools and give talks about safety. The members of the team visit elementary and middle schools. Besides teaching safety, the team tries to establish a healthy relationship between young people and the police department.

What safety rules do you discuss with young people?

Young people need to know about many kinds of safety, such as pedestrian safety, home safety, and personal safety.

■ *Sergeant Gainey teaches about safety.*

For pedestrian safety, young people need to know to watch where they are going. Before they cross a street, they should *stop, look* both ways, and *listen.* Listening is important because cars can often be heard before they can be seen. Tips for home safety might be to keep away from medicines, chemicals, and cleaning supplies that could be harmful. Personal safety tips might include not answering the door when home alone and not telling anyone on the telephone that you are home alone.

What is the most important safety tip you can offer young people?

I think that young people should be responsible for their own safety. One of the most important ways they can do so is by thinking over what they are about to do. After giving certain situations more thought, they might see that there are safer ways to do things. For example, if a child has been asked by a friend to go out after dark, they might decide it would be safer to meet earlier in the evening when it is still light and to stay at one of their houses.

What special ways do you use to teach safety?

· The officers who go to the elementary schools use a motorcycle to help them with their classes. The motorcycle is named Harvey. Harvey "speaks" and gives tips on safety. If a police officer is talking about pedestrian safety, Harvey offers the safety tip that it is important to

Harvey the talking motorcycle gives safety tips.

stop, look, and listen before crossing a street. The talking motorcycle was first used many years ago when the police department decided it wanted a fun way to teach safety. Another fun way to teach safety is to have bicycle rodeos.

What is a bicycle rodeo?

A bicycle rodeo is a safety event that includes a bicycle inspection and a test of children's bicycling skills. The rodeo is a fun way for children to learn about bicycle safety. In addition, it helps children learn how much skill they need to control their bicycles.

What do the bicycle riders do in the rodeo?

The riders take part in different kinds of road tests that check how well they handle their bicycles. One test is called the speed tunnel. This is a test in which

the young people must use great control while riding their bicycles as slowly as they can. To pass the test, the young people must have not only the correct equipment on their bicycles but also control in steering their bicycles. If they go through the test too fast, they must do it again.

What do you like best about your job?

I enjoy being around people and working with young people. I like knowing that I am able to influence young people in a positive way. Police work is exciting. I enjoy all kinds of police work and cannot think of anything I would rather do.

Why did you decide to work with young people?

I have always been interested in working with young people. I think that we must always give young people information and guidance. The young people of today will be our future leaders.

Learn more about traffic safety. Interview a police officer or a school crossing guard. Or write for information to the American Automobile Association (AAA) Foundation for Traffic Safety. 1000 AAA Drive, Heathrow, FL 32746–5064

Main Ideas

- One way to help prevent accidents is to know what causes them.
- Trips, slips, and falls are accidents that happen often to young people.
- If you are responsible and follow safe bicycle-riding practices, you will be less likely to have an accident.
- By being responsible and following safe practices, you can help prevent accidental fires.
- Every family should have a fire escape plan and practice it regularly.
- By following safety rules, you can prevent accidents in and around water.

Key Words

Write the numbers 1 to 10 in your health notebook or on a separate sheet of paper. After each number, copy the sentence and fill in the missing term. Page numbers in ( ) tell you where to look in the chapter if you need help.

accident (304)   bruise (313)
hazard (305)   sterile (314)
emergency (306)   antiseptic (314)
first aid (308)   pedestrians (317)
scrape (313)   flammable (322)

1. When an accident causes injury to someone and help is needed immediately, there is an ___?___ .

2. An unexpected event that can cause someone to be hurt is called an ___?___ .

3. Something that can cause an accident to happen is called a ___?___ .

4. A ___?___ is an injury in which top layers of skin are torn.

5. Materials that can burn, such as paper, are said to be ___?___ .

6. The immediate care you give to someone who has been injured is ___?___ .

7. An ___?___ is a medicine that helps kill microbes.

8. A ___?___ is an injury in which the skin is not damaged but blood vessels under the skin are broken.

9. People who are walking are called ___?___ .

10. A germfree bandage is one that is ___?___ .

Remembering What You Learned

Page numbers in ( ) tell you where to look in the chapter if you need help.

1. What are two things that can cause an accident? (304)

2. What should you do first when a serious accident happens? (306–307)

3. What are some hazards that can cause people to trip and fall? (309)

4. Name three places where falls are likely to happen. (310–311)

5. What are three hazards that are likely to be found on a playground? (312)

6. What are the steps for stopping a nosebleed? (313)

7. What do you need to do for a scrape? (314)

8. List four safety rules for riding your bicycle in traffic. (317)

9. What should be done to a used match before it is thrown away? (323)

10. How should a flammable liquid be stored? (323)

11. What should you do to help a drowning person who is far from shore? (329)

Thinking About What You Learned

1. Why do accidents happen so often to young people?

2. How might playing an active game close to a busy street be a careless thing to do?

3. How can you be helpful when an emergency happens but you do not know what to do?

4. Why do you think showing off might be a hazard?

5. Suppose a person has two injuries, a deep cut and a deep scrape. Which injury needs first aid first? Why?

6. How might having a basket on a bicycle help you ride safely?

7. Why is it important to have a meeting place as part of a plan for escaping a fire?

8. Give an example of an accident that can happen when a water safety rule is forgotten.

Writing About What You Learned

1. As a class, prepare a safety bulletin for your families. Your bulletin should include information about safety practices, hazards, emergencies, and first aid. You may want to include as a special feature a list of safety tips.

2. Write the letters of the word SAFETY, one letter to a line, in your health notebook or on a sheet of paper as shown below. Then use each letter of the word as the first letter of a safety tip or safety practice. Here is an example:

   Staying calm is an important part of first aid.

   Always keep matches out of the reach of young children.

   Falls can often be prevented by watching where you are walking.

   Everyone should think and act safely.

   Take stairs one at a time.

   Yell to warn family members of a fire in your home.

Applying What You Learned

LANGUAGE ARTS

Prepare a speech that tells how certain actions by people can lead to accidents. Your speech could be about show-offs, daredevils, or daydreamers, for example.

Modified True or False

Write the numbers 1 to 15 in your health notebook or on a separate sheet of paper. After each number, write *true* or *false* to describe the sentence. If the sentence is false, also write a term that replaces the underlined term and makes the sentence true.

1. Something that is capable of burning is <u>flammable</u>.
2. Every family should have a <u>fire escape</u> plan.
3. Hang up <u>before</u> the operator when making an emergency phone call.
4. A <u>bruise</u> is an injury in which the top layers of the skin are torn.
5. You should wear <u>goggles</u> to protect your eyes in a dangerous situation.
6. Always ride a bicycle in the <u>opposite</u> direction as cars in your lane.
7. If you smell smoke in your house, you should <u>walk</u> to the nearest exit.
8. Breathing through a wet cloth will help protect you from <u>smoke</u>.
9. Never <u>dive</u> into water without knowing how deep it is.
10. Something that is germfree is <u>antiseptic</u>.
11. <u>Pedestrians</u> walk.
12. Putting ice on a <u>bruise</u> will help slow the bleeding under the skin.
13. A slippery, wet floor is <u>an accident</u>.
14. A physician may put an antiseptic on a <u>scrape</u> that is deep.
15. Shoes with <u>leather soles</u> grip the ground better than shoes with other kinds of soles.

Short Answer

Write the numbers 16 to 23 on your paper. Write a complete sentence to answer each question.

16. How is a scrape different from a bruise?
17. Why do young people have more trips, slips, and falls?
18. If you think there is a fire in your house, why should you test doors before opening them?
19. How can you care for a small scrape?
20. What are four things you can do to avoid drowning?
21. Why is it important to leave the water as soon as you begin to feel tired?
22. What safety gear should you wear when riding a bicycle?
23. What first-aid procedures should you follow if you have a nosebleed?

Essay

Write the numbers 24 and 25 on your paper. Write paragraphs with complete sentences to answer each question.

24. Write an essay describing what safety rules you would tell a friend to follow when swimming.
25. Describe how good self-esteem is related to responsible behavior when riding a bicycle.

ACTIVITIES FOR HOME OR SCHOOL

Projects to Do

1. Make a "Wrong-Right" safety poster. Draw a person doing something unsafe, and label the picture Wrong. Then draw the same person doing the action in a safe way, and label the picture Right. Think of a safety slogan for your poster.

2. For one week, keep a journal of things you have done that will make your home, school, or neighborhood safer. You might clean up a grease spill in your kitchen, for example. You might sweep up some broken glass on a playground. Write down each thing you do. Compare your list with those of two classmates. The lists can help remind you of the many ways you can help protect the safety of yourself and others.

3. Make a map of your neighborhood. If your community has bicycle lanes, mark them on the map. If it does not, mark the streets that you think should have bicycle lanes.

■ A neighborhood map can help you plan bicycle lanes.

4. Draw a map of each floor in your school building. Show on the map where each fire alarm box is located. Show fire extinguishers, too. Show the path you would take from your classroom to the outside of the building during a fire drill.

Information to Find

1. Garrett Morgan made the first traffic signal. Find out more about Garrett Morgan and his work. Use an encyclopedia, or find library books on the contributions of American inventors to making people safe.

2. Visit two stores in your community that sell smoke alarms. Find out if certain types of smoke alarms are meant to be used for special purposes. What other differences are there among types of smoke alarms? Share what you learn with your family and classmates.

Books to Read

Here are some books you can look for in your school library or the public library to find more information about safety and first aid.

Chlad, Dorothy. *Bicycles Are Fun to Ride*. Children's Press.

McGee, Eddie. *The Emergency Handbook*. Wanderer Books.

Schlachter, Rita. *Good Luck, Bad Luck*. Troll Associates.

337

GUARDING THE COMMUNITY'S HEALTH

The people of a community may live in a few houses in the country, or they may live in a town or large city. Whatever its size, a community provides certain services for all its members and works to help make its surroundings pleasant, safe, and clean.

Your community's services protect people's lives and health. Your community also gives you health messages to help you learn more about ways to stay healthy. Your community works to guard your health.

GETTING READY TO LEARN

Key Questions

- Why is it important to know how your community can help you stay healthy?
- Why is it important to know the way you feel about keeping your community healthy and safe?
- How can you learn to make healthful choices about protecting your environment?
- What can you do to become more responsible for protecting your community's environment?

Main Chapter Sections

1 Community Health Needs
2 Private Health Agencies
3 The Community's Environment

1 Community Health Needs

agency (AY juhn see), a group of people who carry on business or services for others.

health department, a government agency concerned with meeting specific kinds of health needs in the community.

You and your family can meet some of your health needs on your own. However, you and your family cannot take care of all of them. For example, you cannot test all your own food and water to make sure they are safe. You cannot stop the spread of all diseases.

In many communities, agencies provide several kinds of services for the members of the community. An **agency** is a group of people who carry on business or services for others. Communities have many kinds of public and private agencies. An agency can be part of government, or it can be a private business.

One kind of government agency is a health department. A public **health department** is made up of health workers who meet certain kinds of health needs in the community. It may be run by a city, a county, or a state. People in a community pay for the health department's services through taxes.

■ *Getting health information*

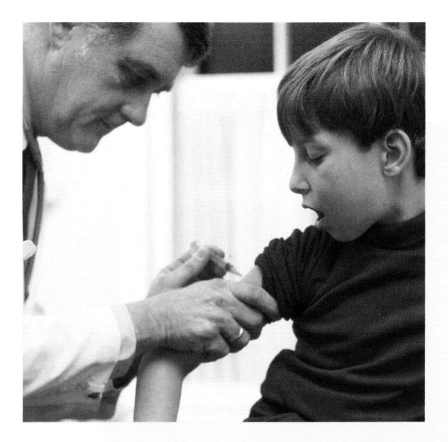

How Do Communities Prevent and Control Disease?

Some communicable diseases can spread quickly, causing large numbers of people to become ill. Other communicable diseases are dangerous, but not because many people become ill. They are dangerous because the few who are ill die or have severe problems. Health department workers watch for the spread of a communicable disease. They track how a disease spreads so they can stop it. Workers may give vaccines to large numbers of people to give them immunity to certain diseases. Workers may encourage parents to have their children get vaccines. Many common childhood diseases can be prevented by vaccines. These diseases include measles, mumps, diphtheria, tetanus, and polio.

■ *Community health departments often provide people with vaccines at little or no cost.*

341

■ Health workers catch stray animals to protect communities from disease.

public clinic (PUHB lihk • KLIHN ihk), a place where people who do not have a family physician can receive medical services.

Community health departments often have an animal control group. Workers in this group find stray animals. They also search for animals that have not had the vaccine against rabies. Rabies is a dangerous disease that people can get from animal bites. Health workers catch animals reported to have bitten or scratched people. The workers may take the animals to an animal shelter.

Other health department workers control insects and other pests that might be a threat to a community's good health. They may help neighborhoods sponsor trash pickup days. Removing trash can get rid of the places where insects, rats, and mice could live.

What Medical Care Do Communities Give?

Many community health departments run public health care clinics. A **public clinic** is a place where people who do not have a family physician can receive medical services.

■ Public clinics, left, and hospitals, right, provide special medical services that people cannot get at home.

Public clinics may give medical tests and may give out prescription medicines. They also give vaccines, dental care, vision testing, and hearing care. Workers at clinics may teach people how to care for themselves and their families. Many clinic services are free or cost very little.

FUTURE SITE OF WOODROW WILSON HOSPITAL

A growing community may need new hospitals.

Most communities have at least one hospital. A **hospital** is a place where people in a community can receive medical care they cannot get at a physician's office or at a clinic. Hospitals offer a wide range of health services. Hospital workers treat illnesses or injuries, help deliver babies, and perform surgery and emergency medical services. The workers may also hold classes about diseases or teach health skills such as being a good parent or managing stress.

hospital (HAHS piht uhl), a place where people in a community can receive medical care they cannot get at a physician's office or at a clinic.

Why Do Communities Keep Health Records?

All community health agencies record important facts. A community's **vital records** are facts about births, deaths, marriages, and divorces. A community health department uses these facts to keep track of the community's health needs. For example, birth records show how fast a community is growing. These records help health workers predict how many people of each age will be in the community in the future. Vital records help community planners decide when new schools, hospitals, or clinics need to be built.

Vital records provide important health information.

vital records (VYT uhl • REHK uhrdz), facts that a health department collects and uses to keep track of community health needs.

343

How Do Communities Protect the Environment?

An important concern of a health department is the community's environment. A community's **environment** is everything in and around the community. Some health department workers check public places, such as restaurants and schools, to be sure they are clean. The workers also enforce rules about the safe disposal of garbage.

In many health departments, a group of workers tests drinking water to make sure it is clean and free of harmful microbes and chemicals. It also tests water in public swimming pools, ponds, and lakes to make sure it is pure. The health department may check rivers and lakes for dangerous chemicals or microbes that have come from factories.

Local health department workers may check for the level of air pollution in the community, especially near factories that give off gases. Workers may check air samples in buildings. They may check offices and schools if many people who work there are having breathing problems or showing signs of allergies.

environment (ihn VY ruhn muhnt), everything in and around the community.

■ Health workers in many communities regularly test the quality of water and air.

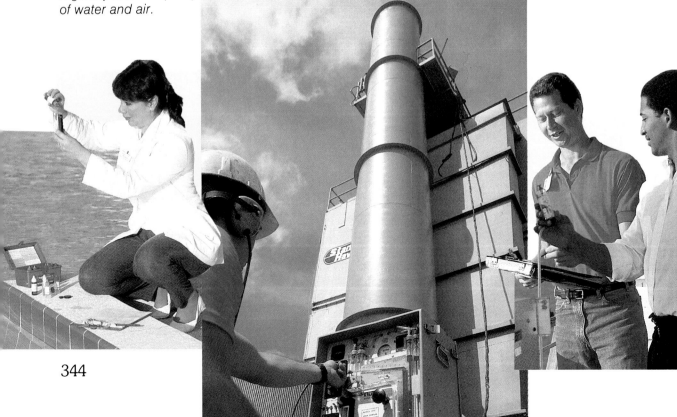

344

What Special Services Do Communities Provide?

The health department of a large community may provide services for people with certain health needs. For example, it may test people for certain diseases, such as tuberculosis or sexually transmitted diseases. It may run community centers or offer home care to provide health services for older people or people who are disabled. One program delivers hot meals to people who cannot shop or cook on their own.

Many health departments have programs that help people with emotional problems. Some health agencies help families or young people with problems. Other agencies help people who have problems with alcohol, tobacco, or illegal drugs. Agencies like these often have certain telephone services called **hotlines.** A person can call a hotline at any time. Trained health workers or **volunteers,** people working without pay, try to help the callers. Many times, just being able to talk to someone can help.

■ Services such as hotlines and food delivery meet special needs for community members.

hotlines, special telephone services offered by certain agencies.

volunteers (vahl uhn TIHRZ), people who work for an agency without pay.

345

Some agencies provide services at low cost to people with little or no money. Many community health department services are free. People who live in small communities with few health department services can often receive more services from their county or state health department. Check your telephone book to find information about the health services in your community.

 **REVIEW**
SECTION 1

REMEMBER?

1. How does a community help people meet their health care needs?
2. How does a health department work to protect the community's environment?
3. Who benefits from community health services?

THINK!

4. What needs to happen to health services if a community grows rapidly?
5. Where could someone with a health problem look first to find help in a community?

Making Wellness Choices

Jan is playing in a wooded area behind her home when she notices a stray dog. The dog moves close to her. It is wet and looks as if it has not eaten in several days. Jan is not sure, but she thinks this dog may be the same one that bit a neighbor last week. The dog looks as if it cannot do anything on its own. But the dog could be a danger to Jan. The dog could also be a danger to other people in the neighborhood.

 What should Jan do? Explain your wellness choice.

346

2 Private Health Agencies

Along with public health departments, your community may have many private health agencies. However, these agencies also work to meet community health needs. They are not given tax money. They are supported directly with money given by people and businesses.

A private health agency often centers its efforts on a certain disease, disorder, or health problem. It teaches people about the health problem. It may also give money to help scientists understand and prevent the problem. Many of the workers at private health agencies are volunteers. Young people volunteer for many of the projects.

What Do Voluntary Health Agencies Do?

Have you ever walked in a March of Dimes walkathon? Or have you ever taken part in a Jump Rope for Heart event? If you have, you were helping to raise money for a voluntary health agency. Both the March of Dimes and the American Heart Association are voluntary health agencies. Like most such agencies, they are private. Money you help raise for them may go for research on ways to treat and prevent certain health problems.

■ *Young people can volunteer to work in many hospitals.*

FIGHT POLIO!

prevention

treatment

Join the MARCH OF DIMES

The National Foundation for Infantile Paralysis

Support the March of Dimes

March of Dimes
Preventing Birth Defects

March of Dimes
Prevent Birth Defects!

■ Young people can help raise money for various health organizations. The March of Dimes was founded to raise money for curing polio, top. The organization is now working to find a cure for birth defects, bottom.

Some voluntary health agencies, such as the American Cancer Society and the American Diabetes Association, deal with only one kind of health problem. Others, such as the American Red Cross, offer many kinds of health care and education.

Sometimes agencies change the purpose of their work. The March of Dimes was set up to help scientists understand what causes polio. When a vaccine for polio was found, the agency began working to help prevent many kinds of birth disorders.

Most voluntary health agencies have offices in large communities. You can write or call an agency if you want to learn more about its work. To find the address and telephone number of a local office, look in your telephone book under the name of the agency. You can also look in the yellow pages under "Associations" to get names.

Here are a number of voluntary health agencies. Which of them have offices in your community?

- American Cancer Society
- American Diabetes Association
- American Heart Association
- American Lung Association
- American Red Cross
- March of Dimes Birth Defects Foundation

What Do World Health Agencies Do?

Some health agencies work to help people all over the world. Through their efforts, people in other countries are given vaccines and medical care. The people are also taught ways to stay healthy.

The World Health Organization (WHO) is part of the United Nations. The United Nations is a group of countries, including the United States, that work together to solve world problems. The goal of WHO is to solve world health problems, such as communicable diseases and hunger.

■ The World Health Organization is part of the United Nations. It works to solve health problems worldwide.

The International Red Cross collects donated blood and helps victims of natural disasters around the world.

The International Red Cross is another example of a world health agency. There are 123 countries in this organization. The work of the International Red Cross is like that of the American Red Cross. In particular, the International Red Cross works to help victims of natural disasters. It helps victims of floods, hurricanes, tornadoes, and earthquakes. The International Red Cross gives victims food, clothing, medical care, and housing.

What Do Professional Health Organizations Do?

Some private health groups are made up of people who are professional health workers. The members of the American Medical Association (AMA), for example, are physicians. The American Dental Association (ADA) is made up of dentists. Members of the American School Health Association (ASHA) are school nurses, physicians, and health teachers. They all are people concerned with the health of school-age children.

350

Organizations like these help a community with its health needs in certain ways. These organizations help make sure their members know about new information in the health field. The American Dental Association, for example, tells all of its dentists about new ways to do their jobs better. Health workers need to know about new ways to treat and prevent health problems. Then they are better able to help you and your family with your health needs.

Some health workers in your community may be members of some of the following professional organizations. You can ask these workers which organizations they belong to.

- American Academy of Pediatrics
- American Dental Association
- American Medical Association
- American Nurses' Association
- American Pharmaceutical Association
- American School Health Association

 **REVIEW**
SECTION 2

REMEMBER?

1. What do voluntary health agencies do for people in a community?
2. What is the goal of the World Health Organization?
3. What is one responsibility of a professional health organization, such as the American Medical Association?

THINK!

4. To which voluntary health agency could you go for help to learn more about safety and first aid?
5. What kinds of health workers would join the American Pharmaceutical Association?

The Role of the International Red Cross in World Health and Safety

To most Americans, the Red Cross is an organization that helps people during major disasters, such as earthquakes, floods, and tornadoes. The American Red Cross has been providing this kind of help for more than 100 years.

The American Red Cross is only one part of the International Red Cross. Almost every country in the world has a Red Cross society. These are called the Red Cross, the Red Crescent, or the Red Lion and Sun societies.

The International Red Cross is not supported by any national government. It gets most of its money from donations. Many of the donations come from people who have been helped by a Red Cross society.

The Red Cross was founded to help people who were victims of a war in Europe in 1859. When the war was over, Red Cross members began helping people who had suffered because of other kinds of disasters.

One part of the International Red Cross, which is called the International Committee of the Red Cross (ICRC), works with the armed services of a country. It helps protect people who have been wounded in battle. It also examines prisoner-of-war camps to see that the prisoners are being treated fairly and are receiving proper medical care. Most countries have signed a treaty agreeing to let the ICRC inspect the

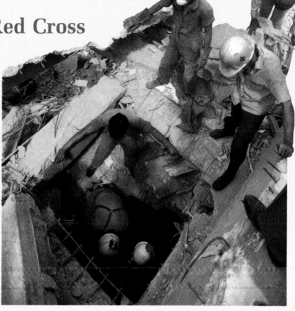

■ *Red Cross workers help during disasters.*

camps. Long after a war has ended, the ICRC continues to work to find people who are missing.

The International Red Cross is best known for helping people who are victims of natural disasters. It helps people who have lost their shelters and have no food. The Red Cross, the Red Crescent, and the Red Lion and Sun societies also develop health and safety programs. Many of these societies have youth divisions that help young people throughout the world learn and practice health and safety skills.

Thinking Beyond

1. What kinds of services might the Red Cross perform in your area?
2. Why is it important to have groups, such as the Red Cross, that are concerned about world health and safety?

The Community's Environment

One day Yuri walked through his community. He looked at all the things around him. He noticed the hard roads and the cool air. He saw hills and fields beyond the houses. He saw birds in the trees and people along the sidewalks. Yuri was noticing his community's environment.

■ *Automobile exhaust can harm the environment.*

Your community's environment is made up of all the living and nonliving things in the community. The people are part of the environment. So is the food people eat and the air they breathe. All these parts of the environment are resources. A **resource** is something people use.

resource (REE sohrs), something people use, such as food or air.

353

Tuning a car and using unleaded gasoline help reduce air pollution from automobiles.

pollution (puh LOO shuhn), harmful matter in the environment.

A clean environment helps people stay healthy and enjoy life. Sometimes harmful matter, or **pollution,** gets into the environment. Pollution can harm your community's resources. Sometimes the harmful matter cannot be seen. In Yuri's community, for example, exhaust from cars sometimes pollutes the air. Gases from the cars make the air smell bad. The gases can also irritate people's eyes and lungs. Water, land, and other resources in the environment can all be polluted in many ways.

People in a community share the responsibility for protecting resources. Together, community members must look for the best ways to prevent pollution and the health problems it causes.

How Can You Protect Your Air?

You and members of your community can work together to help keep air pollution from harming the environment. You can also act on your own or with your family.

Much air pollution comes from cars and trucks. These vehicles put waste gases, or exhaust, into the air. If your family has one or more cars, it has a responsibility to maintain them. An automobile needs regularly scheduled care. The care should include keeping the exhaust system working well and using the proper kind of fuel. These actions can help lower air pollution. You and your family can also help keep air pollution low by using cars less. Whenever you can, ride your bicycle or walk instead of asking for a ride in a car. If you and your friends are going to the same place, you can all ride in one car instead of separate cars.

Buses also put exhaust gases into the air. But a bus can carry 30 or more people. One bus makes less exhaust than 30 cars. When you ride a bus or other public transportation instead of riding in a car, you help cut down on air pollution.

Pollution in the form of gases comes out of factories. Your community may have laws that limit how much smoke and harmful matter factories can put into the air.

In most large cities, smog pollutes the air at times. **Smog** is a mixture of smoke, exhaust, and fog. Sometimes the smog over a city can be so thick that it becomes dangerous to people's health. The city health department may then put out a *smog alert* to warn people about the health dangers. During a smog alert, people are asked not to drive their cars unless they must. They are warned not to stay outdoors longer than necessary for work or travel. People with lung and heart diseases are told to stay indoors.

smog (SMAHG), a form of air pollution that is a mixture of smoke, exhaust, and fog.

Smog occurs in many large cities. It is dangerous to people's health.

Wastewater treatment plants remove pollutants from water.

purification plant (pyur uh fuh KAY shuhn • PLANT), a place that removes disease microbes and wastes from water to make it safe to drink.

wastewater treatment plants (WAYST wawt uhr • TREET muhnt • PLANTS), places where water that leaves homes and buildings is cleaned before flowing into lakes and rivers.

How Can You Protect Your Water?

The water you drink comes from lakes, streams, wells, and rivers. Communities put public water through a purification plant before it reaches your home. This water **purification plant** removes disease microbes and wastes, making the water safe to drink. Families who use wells need to test water regularly for safety.

Water treatment is also needed for water that leaves homes and buildings. For this, communities build **wastewater treatment plants.** A wastewater treatment plant has several parts. First, the waste is stored in a pond or big tank for a month or more. It is kept very still. Dirt and bits of matter slowly settle to the bottom. Then, the clear water at the top is poured off. It is passed through layers of sand and rocks to screen out some microbes and other matter remaining in the water. Finally, in many treatment plants, a chemical called *chlorine* is added to the water. Chlorine kills any microbes that are left. At last, the water is clean and ready to flow into lakes and rivers.

Your community can pass and enforce laws that protect the water people drink or use for fun. The laws may try to prevent factories from polluting lakes and rivers with chemicals or heat.

Some factories dump hot water into nearby rivers or other bodies of water. The factory water may be clean. But it may be hot enough to raise the temperature of the body of water. This is called *thermal pollution.* Even a small rise in the water temperature can kill some fish and upset the balance of animal and plant life in a river.

You and your family have control over using certain harmful substances that can pollute water. Some soaps have chemicals called *phosphates* that can harm plants and animals that live in lakes. You can help reduce water pollution by using low-phosphate soaps.

MYTH
AND
FACT

Myth: Running water is safer than still water for drinking.

Fact: Water running over rocks in a stream may look clean. However, looks can be misleading. Never drink water from streams or ponds. You could become seriously ill.

Heated water can be a form of pollution, causing the death of fish.

How Can You Protect Your Land?

Your community can work to prevent solid-waste pollution by finding healthful ways to dispose of solid waste. Instead of leaving trash in open dumps, the community can have landfills. In a **landfill,** solid waste is buried. Later, parks, playgrounds, parking lots, or buildings can be built on the landfill.

landfill, a place where solid wastes are buried.

■ *The recycling of cans, glass, and paper saves many natural resources.*

recycling (ree SY klihng), using something again or finding a new use for something.

■ *Cleaning up spills with a reusable sponge, instead of a paper towel, can conserve paper.*

conserve (kuhn SURV), to help keep resources from being used up.

Your community can also set up centers for recycling certain kinds of trash. **Recycling** means using something again or finding a new use for it. For example, used aluminum cans and glass bottles can be melted and made into new cans and bottles. Paper can be shredded and made into new paper. When these kinds of trash are recycled, they do not cause pollution in the environment. You and your family can help lower solid-waste pollution by recycling bottles, cans, and paper.

You can also help by making less waste. The average person produces about 1 pound (.5 kilogram) of trash each day. This trash is food packages, wrappers, and other wastes. You can cut down on trash by using containers and materials that can be used again. Buy drinks in bottles or cans that can be returned to the store for a refund. Use paper shopping bags more than once, or use a cloth bag to carry groceries. Keep the plastic containers that some foods come in, and use them to store other foods.

The world has limited supplies of some resources. By using things more than once, you help conserve the resources from which they are made. To **conserve** resources is to keep them from being used up. When you recycle cans, for example, you not only reduce solid-waste pollution but also conserve metals.

How Can You Prevent Noise Pollution?

Loud, harsh noise harms the environment just as other kinds of pollution do. Anything that makes a long, loud noise can cause noise pollution. Outdoor noise pollution can be caused by low-flying airplanes, loud cars with damaged mufflers, heavy traffic, and noisy machines at construction sites or near homes. People who set their televisions or radios at a high volume cause indoor noise pollution.

Use ear protection around loud machines. Using hand tools cuts down on noise pollution.

Your community can pass and enforce laws that tell people to cut down on noise. These laws may tell people not to honk car horns except in emergencies or not to make disturbing noise late at night. Your community might also not allow an airport or factories to be built near people's homes. You can help prevent noise pollution by obeying your community's laws and respecting other people's need to be free from loud noises.

REAL-LIFE
SKILL

Setting Volume at a Healthful Level

Keep the volume on televisions, radios, and stereos in your home at a comfortable and safe level. Gather all family members in the same room. Turn the volume to a level that all family members agree is safe and comfortable.

You and your family can also cut down on noise in your home and outside. In your home, keep televisions, radios, and stereos at a volume that lets people hear each other without yelling. If you carry a radio or tape player outside, keep the volume low to protect your own hearing. Lower volume lets you hear sounds of danger to avoid accidents.

For work in your home and yard, your family might buy machines that are quiet. For example, a manual lawn mower makes less noise than a power mower. Using a manual mower also helps keep the environment healthful in other ways. A manual mower does not use fuel or pollute the air with exhaust. Pushing it even gives you some exercise that helps keep you healthy.

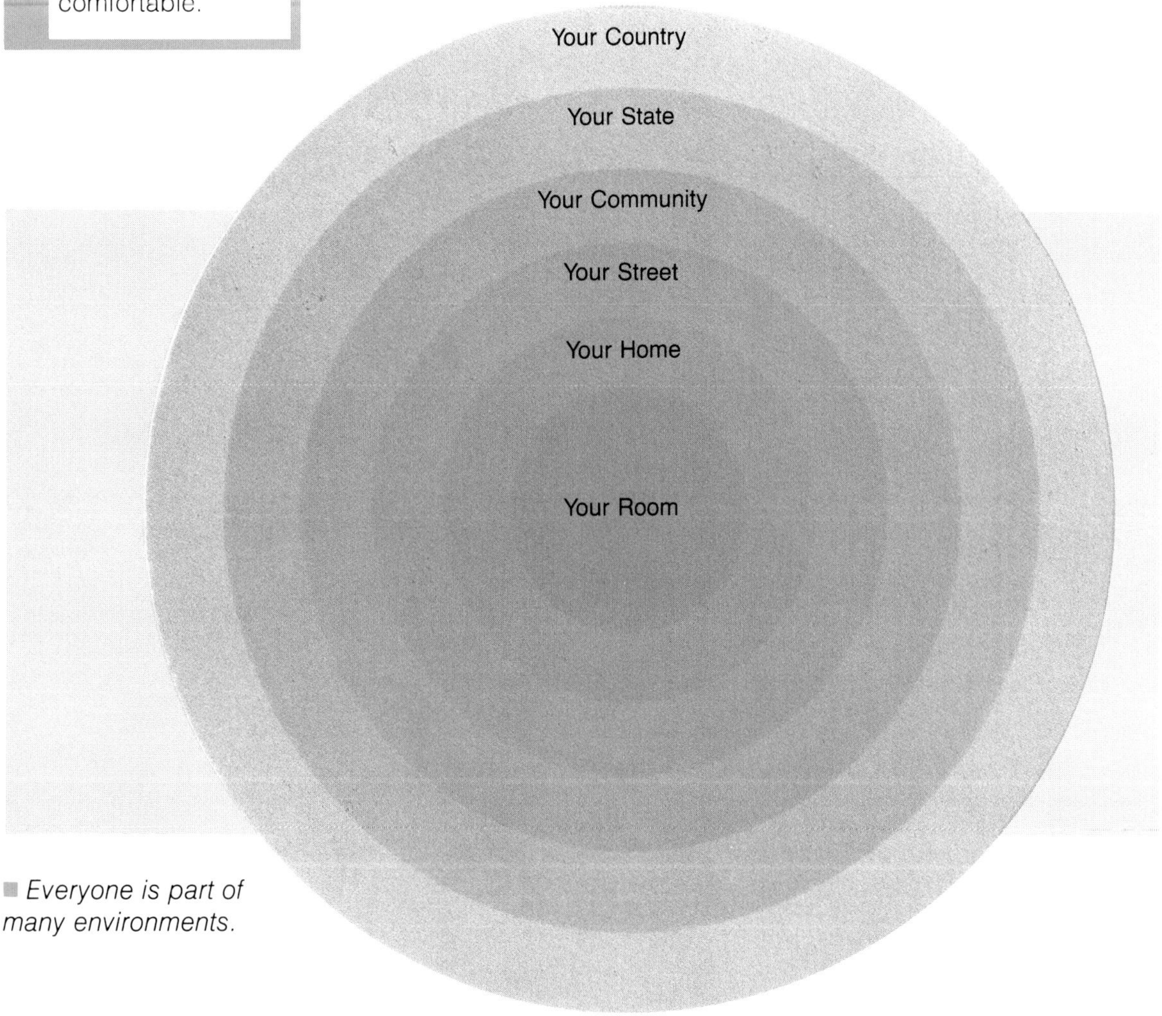

Your Country
Your State
Your Community
Your Street
Your Home
Your Room

■ *Everyone is part of many environments.*

1. What are three things you and your family can do to reduce air pollution?
2. What can you do to protect the land?
3. What can you do at home to reduce noise pollution?

4. Why is thermal pollution a kind of pollution?
5. How does protecting the environment's resources prevent problems for people in a community?

Thinking About Your Health

Pollution Harms Your Body

Different kinds of pollution in your environment harm you in different ways. The different kinds may affect different systems in your body. Air pollution harms your respiratory system. Water pollution and food that is bad harm your digestive system. Noise pollution can harm all of your body systems. Noise pollution harms you by adding stress and tension to your body.

Study the sources of pollution listed here. In your health notebook or on a separate sheet of paper, do the following: (1) Write the source of the pollution. (2) Next to the source of the pollution, identify the kind of pollution it is. (3) Next to the kind of pollution, identify the body system most at risk from this pollution. (4) Next to the risk, describe how you can keep yourself or someone else from being harmed by this pollution.

- trash fires
- fumes from a faulty gas heater
- solid waste
- loud music from a radio
- dust
- paint chips that have fallen from a wall or windowsill
- a canteen of water from a pond in the woods

361

People in Health

An Interview with a Health Educator

Laura Sorce teaches people in her community how to be healthy. She is a health educator in Hinsdale, Illinois.

What do health educators do?

Health educators teach people about health. They work in many different places in a community. They work in hospitals and health clinics. They also work for government and private agencies, in business and industry, at schools, at health museums, and in health education centers. A health educator helps people learn to be as healthy as they can be. They teach people to care about their physical and emotional well-being. They also teach people about the environment.

What are some of the things health educators do in the different places where they work?

In hospitals and clinics, health educators may help patients understand medical procedures. In business and industry, health educators may set up fitness programs for workers. Through health organizations such as the Red Cross, health educators may help people give up smoking or improve their eating habits.

Where do you work?

I work at the Robert Crown Center for Health Education. The Center is a place where people learn about health by attending classes and viewing exhibits. There are programs and classes for people of all ages, from preschoolers to senior citizens. Most of the visitors are students. Around 130,000 students visit the Center each year.

What do you do there?

I teach preschoolers through sixth-graders about health. I teach five different health areas. They include environmental education, drug-abuse prevention, nutrition, general health, and growth and development.

■ Ms. Sorce teaches people in her community how to be healthy.

Ms. Sorce teaches young people about forming the habit of eating nutritious foods.

How do you teach about health?

In every class I conduct, I operate models and displays. The models and displays differ from one classroom to another. Some have lights and motion. Some are computers. One of the most popular models is a transparent talking woman. She is called Lady Valeda. Parts of her body light up, and she explains them. Another display is a computer that looks like a coin-operated food machine. Different foods are selected. Then the computer shows the nutritional value of each food. This display is designed to teach children how to select their foods wisely.

What are the main things you want children to know?

I try to help children appreciate the wonders of the human body. I teach them that by caring for themselves, they are protecting this wonderful gift of the body.

What do you like most about your job?

The best part of my job is the enthusiasm that students have for learning about their bodies and learning how to keep healthy. Sometimes girls and boys write to thank me. It is wonderful to hear from the students after they visit the center.

Learn more about people who teach other people in their communities about health. Interview a health educator. Or write for information to the Robert Crown Center for Health Education, 21 Salt Creek Lane, Hinsdale, IL 60521.

CHAPTER
REVIEW

Main Ideas

- Communities have health workers who are trained to help people prevent the spread of communicable diseases.
- Most communities have places where people can get free or low-cost care for health problems.
- Many communities have health agencies that help raise money for treating and preventing health problems.
- You and your community can work together to help prevent pollution.

Key Words

Write the numbers 1 to 16 in your health notebook or on a separate sheet of paper. After each number, copy the sentence and fill in the missing term. Page numbers in ( ) tell you where to look in the chapter if you need help.

agency (340)
health department (340)
public clinic (342)
hospital (343)
vital records (343)
environment (344)
hotlines (345)
volunteers (345)
resource (353)
pollution (354)
smog (355)
purification plant (356)
wastewater treatment plants (356)
landfill (357)
recycling (358)
conserve (358)

1. The ___?___ is everything around you.

2. Something people use is a ___?___ .

3. Harmful matter called ___?___ can destroy your community's resources.

4. ___?___ is a mixture of smoke, exhaust, and fog.

5. A ___?___ removes disease microbes and wastes from water.

6. ___?___ clean sewage and remove harmful matter from it.

7. In a ___?___ , solid wastes are buried.

8. Using something again or finding a new use for it is called ___?___ .

9. To ___?___ resources is to keep them from being used up.

10. An ___?___ is a place that carries on business or services for other people.

11. A ___?___ is made up of health workers concerned with meeting health needs in the community.

12. In a community, a ___?___ offers many medical services for little or no cost.

13. A ___?___ is a place where people in a community can receive medical care they cannot get at home or at a clinic.

14. A community's ___?___ are facts about births, deaths, marriages, and divorces.

15. Some community health agencies have special telephone services called ___?___ .

16. People who work without pay are called ___?___ .

364

Remembering What You Learned

Page numbers in ( ) tell you where to look in the chapter if you need help.

1. What are two ways community health workers help prevent the spread of disease? (341–342)

2. What is the difference between a public clinic and a hospital? (342–343)

3. How are vital records helpful? (343)

4. What are three services that a health department provides? (345–346)

5. What are two ways in which money raised by a voluntary health agency may be used? (347)

6. How can you learn more about what a voluntary health agency in your community does? (348–349)

7. What are two tasks of professional health organizations? (350–351)

8. What is the purpose of a smog alert? (355)

9. What can you and your family do to avoid polluting water sources? (356–357)

10. How much solid waste does the average person produce each day? (358)

11. What are two ways in which you can reduce the amount of solid waste you produce each day? (358)

12. How can you help reduce noise pollution in your community? (359–360)

Thinking About What You Learned

1. Why are hotlines important?

2. Why is it necessary for professional health organizations to keep their members up to date on what is happening in their health fields?

3. What are some ways in which walking or riding your bicycle might benefit you and your community?

4. What could you do if you saw a person or a factory polluting the environment?

Writing About What You Learned

1. Interview two adults who have lived in your community for many years. Ask them about the changes that have taken place. In what ways has the environment become worse or better? Describe how change has affected your community.

2. Write a law that you think would help people in your school, neighborhood, or community prevent or reduce one kind of pollution. After you write your law, check it with three classmates and an adult to see if everyone understands it in the same way.

Applying What You Learned

SOCIAL STUDIES

Tell how littering affects the appearance of a community. Why do some people continue to litter even though there are laws against it?

Modified True or False

Write the numbers 1 to 15 in your health notebook or on a separate sheet of paper. After each number, write *true* or *false* to describe the sentence. If the sentence is false, also write a term that replaces the underlined term and makes the sentence true.

1. <u>Volunteers</u> work without pay.
2. A public health department is paid for by <u>contributions</u>.
3. People who have alcohol problems can get help by calling <u>hotlines</u>.
4. The American Cancer Society is a <u>public health department</u>.
5. A dentist may be a member of the <u>American Dental Association</u>.
6. The air you breathe is a <u>resource</u>.
7. <u>Smog</u> is a form of air pollution.
8. If you need special medical care, you should go to a <u>public clinic</u>.
9. Recycling <u>conserves</u> resources.
10. Water is cleaned at a <u>landfill</u>.
11. Health department workers watch for <u>noncommunicable</u> diseases.
12. Your birth certificate is part of your community's <u>vital records</u>.
13. Most voluntary health agencies get money from <u>donations</u>.
14. The <u>International Red Cross</u> tries to solve problems of world hunger.
15. Your drinking water is made safe at a <u>wastewater treatment plant</u>.

Short Answer

Write the numbers 16 to 23 on your paper. Write a complete sentence to answer each question.

16. How are public clinics different from hospitals?
17. Why is a landfill better for a community than an open dump?
18. What are three health needs a health department fills?
19. How is a purification plant different from a wastewater treatment plant?
20. What are two benefits of recycling aluminum cans?
21. How do hotlines help people with problems?
22. Why does a community keep vital records?
23. What are the benefits of being a volunteer?

Essay

Write the numbers 24 and 25 on your paper. Write paragraphs with complete sentences to answer each question.

24. What are the everyday needs of your community? Describe how you can help meet those needs.
25. Describe why voluntary health agencies are so important to everyone. Include in your essay the services these agencies can bring to a community.

ACTIVITIES FOR HOME OR SCHOOL

Projects to Do

1. You and your class can learn about the services offered by your community health department. Call or write different units of the department for information about their services. Your health department may send you booklets or a schedule of programs, perhaps about how to conserve water, how to take care of your vision, or how to control communicable diseases.

2. What hotlines are available in your community? Find out from your local health department or some other health agency. Put up a list of local hotline numbers in your classroom.

3. Groups from your class can check sections of your school and school grounds for litter and other pollution problems. Then the groups can report their findings to the whole class. Invite the principal to attend if possible. Suggest ways to prevent pollution and remove litter. You might suggest a student cleanup day. Make announcements asking students in other classes to help prevent litter inside the building, including in the rest rooms, as well as on the grounds.

Information to Find

1. Ask your librarian or school nurse for booklets by private health agencies, such as the American Heart Association or the American Dental Association. Look up answers to health questions you might have.

2. Find out about solar heating systems. They are designed to conserve certain resources. Ask someone from the local utility company or electric company to describe how solar heating systems work. Or ask your school librarian for reference books.

Using solar energy can save other energy resources.

Books to Read

Here are some books you can look for in your school library or the public library to find more information about protecting your environment from pollution.

Santrey, Laurence. *Conservation and Pollution.* Troll Associates.

Woods, Geraldine, and Harold Woods. *Pollution.* Franklin Watts.

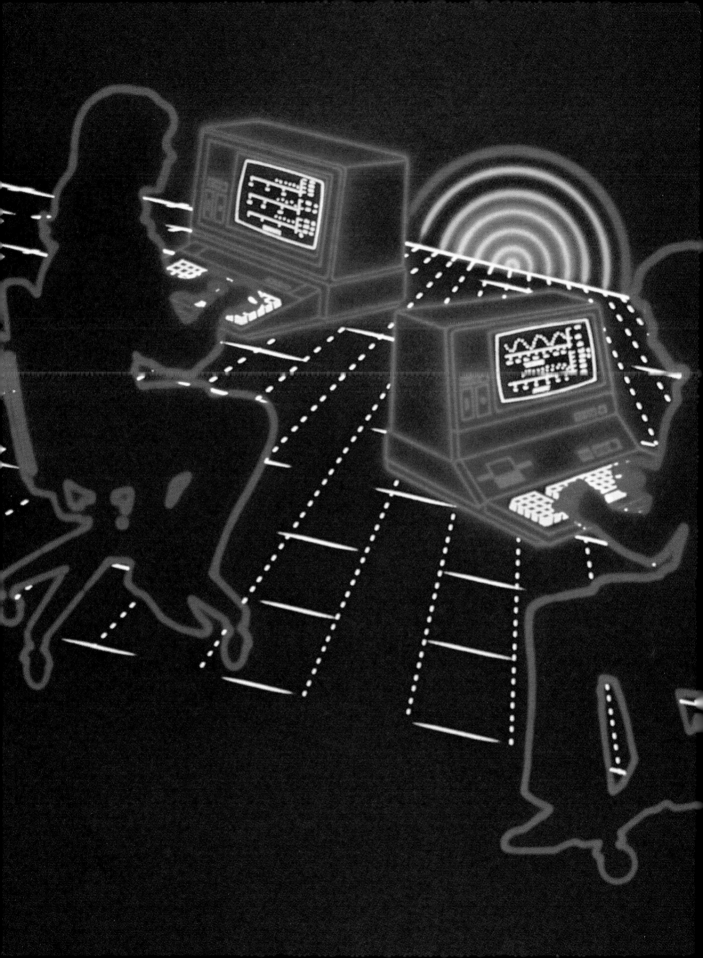